THE FINAL DAYS OF JESUS

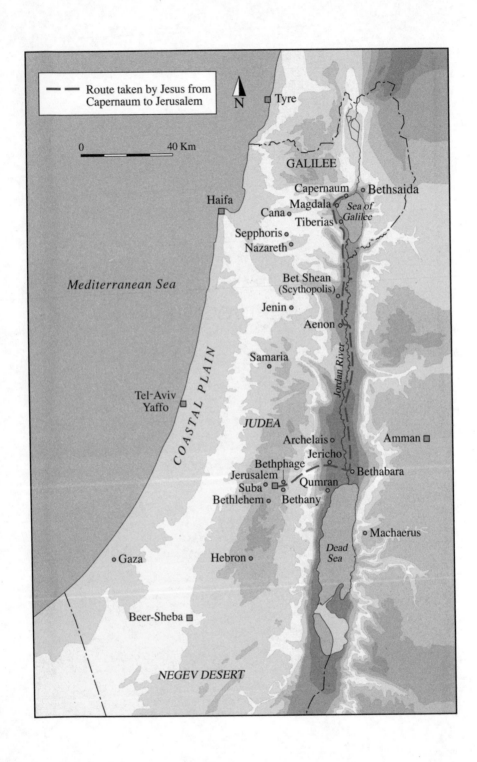

Jerusalem in the First Century CE

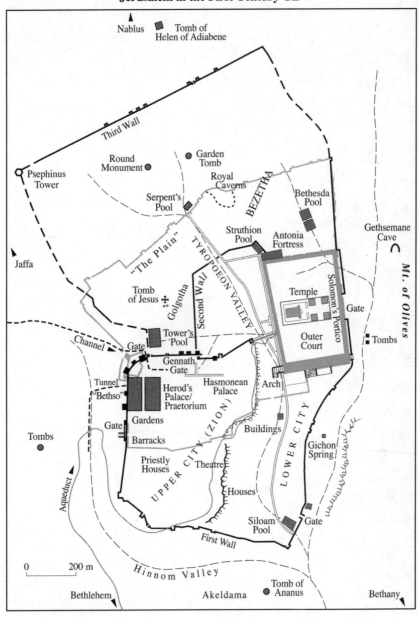

The
FINAL DAYS
of
JESUS

The Archaeological Evidence

SHIMON GIBSON

HarperOne
An Imprint of HarperCollinsPublishers

HarperOne

HarperCollins Web site: http://www.harpercollins.com

HarperCollins®, 📖®, and HarperOne™ are
trademarks of HarperCollins Publishers

FIRST EDITION
Designed by Level C

Library of Congress Cataloging-in-Publication Data

Gibson, Shimon.
The final days of Jesus : the archaeological evidence / Shimon Gibson. — 1st ed.
p. cm.
Includes bibliographical references (p.) and indexes.
ISBN 978–0–06–145848–4
1. Jesus Christ—Biography—Passion Week. 2. Jesus Christ—Historicity.
3. Bible. N.T. Gospels—Antiquities. 4. Jerusalem—Antiquities. I. Title.
BT414.G53 2009
226'.093—dc22   2008051765

09 10 11 12 13 RRD(H) 10 9 8 7 6 5 4 3 2 1

CONTENTS

To the memory of my mother,
Fiona Gibson

INTRODUCTION

Who was Jesus, and what can archaeology tell us about him? I am sure many people want to know this. The theologians and historians have had their go—many thousands of books attest to this—but what can archaeology contribute in the quest to find out more about the historical Jesus? Does archaeology just provide illustrative material for the context/background of the Gospel accounts, a kind of "garnish" for the focused historical perspective? Or can it provide us with unique, valuable information that can change substantially the way we perceive Jesus and his final days in Jerusalem as set forth in the Gospel accounts?

I believe archaeology is an undervalued and untapped source of rich data on the historical Jesus, and I hope to show this in the pages of this book. Archaeology should be allowed its own voice alongside the information and ideas that emerge from the historical exegesis of the Gospels. They both have their problems: Archaeological remains may be too fragmentary or interpreted incorrectly; textual sources may be too garbled from transmission or replete with errors by copyists. Archaeology, therefore, should be used appropriately—neither to support and prop up the account of Jesus in Jerusalem nor to deny and tear down the historicity of that account. It should be an independent means of "testing" the validity of the Gospel accounts, to compare and contrast them with historical studies. Archaeology can provide structured explanations and interpretations of specific events, such as the trial of Jesus, and these subsequently need to be tested and woven into the historical perspective.

Archaeological sites are multi-layered, as are the textual accounts— both require dissection and critical examination to elucidate the many "truths" of the past. This is admittedly a difficult and complex task. Understanding the topography of Jerusalem and the layout of the city is essential. Also, having a good grasp of Jewish material remains of the first century is vital. Artifacts with inscriptions can be very help- ful: A fragment of a block of stone from Caesarea bearing the name and exact title of Pontius Pilate is a major find and a boon for scholar- ship. A tomb with the name of Caiaphas on one of its ossuaries is yet another major archaeological discovery highlighting the Gospel story. Other inscriptions, such as the "James" ossuary, are of dubious value because they come from the collections of antiquities dealers and not directly from scientific excavations, but this should not dampen the usefulness of archaeology in elucidating the Gospel narrative.

The need to know more about the places in which Jesus spent his last critical days began a long time ago. This is clearly reflected in the constant flow of Christian pilgrims to the Holy Land and particularly to Jerusalem, which began in the fourth century and continues to the present day. Most worshippers desire to see with their own eyes the main sites associated with the Gospel stories: the traditional site of the room of the Last Supper on Mount Zion; the gnarled olive trees of Gethsemane on the Mount of Olives; the pavement of Gabbatha at the place where Jesus was tried by Pontius Pilate; the Via Dolorosa along which Jesus carried his cross; the Rock of Calvary where Jesus was brought for crucifixion; and the Edicule in the Church of the Holy Sepulchre covering the vestiges of the Tomb of Jesus.

Inevitably, the same questions are asked by visiting pilgrims and travelers: How reliable are these traditional spots? How certain can we be that the authentic tomb of Jesus is indeed located at the Church of the Holy Sepulchre? In the nineteenth century, alternative locations for some of the secondary holy sites in Jerusalem were given by local guides and by resident clergy, resulting in a lot of confusion and some suspicion amongst those visiting the city. The discomfort pilgrims and travelers felt in having to make educated guesses is apparent in some of their travel accounts.

In the early twentieth century, travelers were confronted with an alternative tomb of Jesus at the "Garden Tomb" on the north side of the city, which caused further confusion. Today, Christian pilgrims are much more demanding and discerning and require "scientific" verification for explanations given by tourist guides in respect to the "traditional" Gospel sites. However, this does not mean they always get what they want.

From where have people derived information about the final days of Jesus? Visual reconstructions occasionally appear on the stage and the big screen. I am thinking particularly of Andrew Lloyd Webber and Tim Rice's excellent musical "Jesus Christ Superstar." For cinematic renderings, there is the wonderful black-and-white movie by Pier Paolo Pasolini and the other newer movie, "The Last Temptation of Christ," which managed to create quite a furor when it was released. More recently, I came out of Mel Gibson's movie about Jesus's final days, "The Passion of Christ," feeling like I'd been drenched in gratuitous Hollywood blood. The movie was not being shown in Jerusalem because local distributors deemed the subject "uninteresting" for the general Israeli public; instead I watched a bootleg version, subtitled both in Arabic and English, in the rather quaint sitting room of the British School of Archaeology in East Jerusalem.

Thousands of scholarly studies have been written about Jesus the prophet and healer; his early mission around the Sea of Galilee; his ideas, sayings, and eschatological messages; and his experiences with John the Baptist at the Jordan River. Scholars agree that none of the Gospels is an eyewitness account of the events it describes, since each was written almost forty to sixty years after the death of Jesus. And so, at best, the Synoptic Gospels (Mark, Matthew, and Luke) may be regarded as conveying oral tradition that was to some extent embroidered and embellished as part of the literary process. The Fourth Gospel (John) undoubtedly made use of a lot of historical data that were not available to the other three Gospel writers. The best way to get to some degree of truth about what actually happened, it has been argued, is through the careful historical and literary analysis of the Gospels and their possible sources. However, archaeology has quite a lot to offer, more so than has previously been realized.

In this book I concentrate on Jesus's final days during the Passover week in Jerusalem in 30 CE. Beginning with the road Jesus took to Jerusalem and his sojourn in Bethany, I examine Jesus's activities within the city, particularly at the Jewish Temple and in the adjacent Pools of Bethesda and Siloam. The scene of the trial is investigated and fresh archaeological discoveries are revealed for the first time. Knowing what the place of the trial looked like allows one to visualize the proceedings in a way not previously possible. Questions relating to the exact place of Jesus's crucifixion and burial are also dealt with and new archaeological discoveries are presented. A burial shroud from the first century, uncovered in Jerusalem, is compared to the famous Turin Shroud. Many new ideas and explanations have resulted from my personal quest to follow in the footsteps of the historical Jesus in Jerusalem. The reader may be astonished by some of these results.

"So you're a bit of an Indiana Jones?" the inquisitive shopkeeper asked me upon discovering I'm a professional archaeologist. He looked me up and down to see if I fit the bill, and didn't seem impressed. True, I'm nothing like that fictional movie character, at least not when it comes to fleeing from a mammoth stone ball hurtling down a narrow underground tunnel somewhere deep in a jungle, but I've had my fair share of excitement and danger while working in the Middle East. Archaeology is a lot of fun, but it is also meticulous detective work with a lot of dull recording, and there are many hours spent in dusty libraries. But you also get the exciting moment of discovery when suddenly out of the ground you lay your hands on a rare and unique artifact: an inscription, the head of a statue, or a hoard of coins. There is also the feeling of high expectation when you open the door to an underground chamber and become the first to pass through its portals for thousands of years. Such moments bring a sublime feeling of exhilaration, with blood pounding in your head as you think about what you might find ahead. There is also danger. I have crawled through partly collapsed tunnels deep underground, some very narrow with very little room for maneuvering around, knowing that the oxygen might run out and the ceiling might suddenly cave in. Wild animals and insects also present a problem—I remember being chased by an angry wild boar and on another occasion by a swarm of stinging hornets, but usually it is just snakes and scorpions. There is further danger when working in areas where the military have left behind unexploded shells and other deadly devices, literally keeping you on your toes. But archaeology mostly consists of long seasons of backbreaking digging, meticulous recording procedures, sessions of post-excavation analysis, and days spent in research libraries fitting the pieces of evidence together.

In my mind, Jerusalem is one of the most exciting archaeological sites in the world, with an amazing array of ancient remains underground. Some have already been uncovered; some await discovery. It is one of the most excavated places in Israel, even though large portions of the ancient city, hidden under modern houses and buildings, are inaccessible for digging purposes. I am fortunate to have spent some of my professional years digging into the depths of this amazing city, seeking out the vestiges of its past and fitting together history with archaeology. I have dug next to the palace of Herod the Great, where the trial of Jesus took place, and in the Church of the Holy Sepulchre, not far from the Tomb of Jesus. I have also made detailed archaeological studies of the underground cavities beneath the Temple Mount and a new survey of the Pool of Bethesda. I am now digging in the area of the Upper City, close to where Byzantine tradition places the House of Caiaphas. They say that each spade sunk into the ground is bound to reveal rich information about Jerusalem's past, and in my experience this is true. There are still major lacunae and uncertainties in our knowledge regarding the development of ancient Jerusalem, but, as we shall see, recent scientific archaeological excavations have been able to provide solutions to quite a few thorny historical difficulties. The problem is, the more we know, the more clearly we see the need to know more, and the questions we derive from the new archaeological data begin to multiply. And so the quest for exacting more knowledge from the ground goes on. In the past decades, many archaeological discoveries have fundamentally changed the way we perceive the appearance of the city where Jesus spent his final days.

The general raison d'etre for this book was my wish to unravel once and for all the mystery surrounding the final days of Jesus in Jerusalem: why he went there; how he came to be arrested, tried, and crucified; and where his place of burial was located. This book is the first to examine the final days of Jesus using the *full* array of archaeological finds dug up in Jerusalem. Some of my conclusions regarding Jesus and Jerusalem may be controversial, but readers should remember the dictum established by the master of detection, Sherlock Holmes: "When you have eliminated the impossible, whatever remains, however improbable, must be the truth." If the reader reaches the final page of this book and goes away feeling that it has indeed made a small contribution in illuminating the story of Jesus's final days in Jerusalem, then I will have succeeded in what I initially set out to do.

THE ROAD TO JERUSALEM

"Jerusalem, Jerusalem, the city that kills the prophets and stones those who are sent to it! How often have I desired to gather your children together as a hen gathers her brood under her wings, and you were not willing!"

(*Luke 13:34*)

No visitor to modern Jerusalem can ignore that it is the place where Jesus spent his final days and was ultimately crucified. Jesus's impact on the city of Jerusalem was major, perhaps more so than that of any other individual in history. Ever since the fourth century, when Christianity was recognized as the official religion in the Holy Land, millions of Christian pilgrims have poured into Jerusalem seeking out the places associated by tradition with Jesus's Passion week.

Almost 2,000 years later the formidable presence of Jesus still lingers over the Old City, whether at the Garden of Gethsemane and the Mount of Olives, at the Stations of the Cross along the Via Dolorosa, or at the various shrines within the Church of the Holy Sepulchre. Walking the city streets are Christian priests and monks of different denominations: Dominican, Franciscan, Greek Orthodox, Armenian, Ethiopian, and others. Souvenir shops have wall-to-wall icons and olivewood carvings depicting the Nativity and Calvary and are stocked with crucifixes, large baskets heaped with incense and candles, and various mementoes such as guidebooks and postcards of the Holy

Sites. Groups of Christian worshippers pass along the Via Dolorosa during Easter week carrying full-scale replica wooden crosses, singing and praying and with tears rolling down their cheeks. Jesus is on everyone's lips.

Jerusalem was and still is a city imbued with holiness and a sense of extreme tension, with ongoing battles between the liberal and free, the strict and authoritative. It is a place you thrive in or drown in; you can spout philosophy there or wander in lunacy. There is magic in its stones. Jerusalem is one of those special cities that many put on the list of places they most want to visit during their lifetime.

In Gospel accounts, Jesus first visited the city as a child with his parents during one of the major Jewish festivities held there. Jesus climbed the steps leading into the Temple precinct, establishing his footsteps firmly in the history of the city; some would say that from that moment his fate was sealed. At the time of Jesus it was a place dominated by the Temple of God, and this looming and majestic building was visible anywhere in the city. It was truly a City of the Temple. As a sensitive child fascinated with learning, Jesus would undoubtedly have been fully aware of the significance of Jerusalem as a place connected with some of the major events in Israelite history. It was here King David and King Solomon reigned; it was to this place that the Ark of the Covenant was brought; eventually the Temple of God was built on Mount Moriah; and it was in these city streets that the Israelite Prophets berated their people. As an adult, Jesus continued returning to Jerusalem to participate in the main Jewish festivities and to teach and heal, perhaps starting to gain a reputation as a man of "signs and wonders." Jerusalem became almost a forbidden magnet for Jesus: It was a place, we may surmise, he very much wanted to be in because of his Jewish upbringing and his need to be close to the Temple of God, but the city also drew out his anger and compassion, and eventually brought him into conflict with the Jewish and Roman authorities.

Finally, during Passover week in the year 30, Jesus's fate was sealed and he died on a wooden cross opposite one of the gates of the city. The crucifixion of Jesus was a traumatic event that eventually opened the door to the birth of Christianity. Archaeology, as we shall see, has been able to fill in the gaps regarding the appearance of Jesus's Jerusalem, the places where Jesus preached and healed, the whereabouts of his trial, the manner in which he was crucified, and the spot where he was ultimately buried.

But first, we need to pull back to an earlier time in Jesus's life, to establish something about his Galilean background and clarify the dates of his birth and death in order to place him within the correct historical context. We will then consider the archaeological facts regarding the road Jesus took on his final trip to Jerusalem and the places he probably visited or passed en route.

Jesus, son of Mary and Joseph, was known in Hebrew as Yeshua Ben Yoseph (John 1:45: "Philip found Nathanael and said to him, 'We have found him about whom Moses in the Law and also the prophets wrote, Jesus son of Joseph from Nazareth'"). What many know from the Gospels is that Jesus spent his childhood and much of his formative life in Nazareth, a somewhat modest, small village nestling in the hills of Lower Galilee, and it was from there he set forth on his mission to Jerusalem.[1] But there is much yet unknown about Nazareth from the time of Jesus, except that it appears to have been an agricultural village, surrounded with terraced orchards and vineyards. Animal husbandry would have been practiced as well. A few burial caves of the period, wine presses, and a stone-vessel industry are known from the vicinity of the village. Nazareth was by no means isolated and remote; it existed near the large and thriving town of Sepphoris, the restored capital of the tetrarchy of Herod Antipas, though its name is not mentioned in the Gospels.[2] Judging by the relative sizes of rural villages in Palestine at that time, Nazareth must have been quite small, perhaps with only a couple of hundred people living there. The bottom line is that everyone living in the village would have known each other.

In addition, Jesus's family was not poor as some have thought it to have been. As an artisan (carpenter/stone mason) Joseph had professional skills that would have put him and his family within the top echelon of village society, on a par with small landowners.[3] Joseph's profession is clearly stated in Matthew in regard to Jesus: "Is not this the carpenter's son? Is not his mother called Mary? And are not his brothers James and Joseph and Simon and Judas?" (13:55). Whether or not Jesus learned the trade is unclear, but the imagery of the artisan pops up in Jesus's sayings, such as "Why do you see the splinter in your neighbor's eye, but do not notice the plank in your own eye?" (Matthew 7:3–5). Jesus also liked to quote Psalm 118: "The stone that the builder rejected has become the cornerstone" (Luke 20:17). Joseph clearly possessed the financial means to cover the costs of traveling to Jerusalem to ensure that Jesus was presented in the Temple ("When the time came for their purification according to the Law of Moses, they brought him up to Jerusalem to present him to the Lord") and even to celebrating Passover there on an annual basis (Luke 2:41: "Now every year his parents went to Jerusalem for the festival of the Passover"). The cost of traveling in those days was exorbitant and could not have been undertaken by everyone. Not only was there a loss of earnings for the period the family was away from home, but food had to be bought along the way, and inns and road tolls had to be paid for. Jerusalem was an expensive city to stay in and accommodations were dear, especially at the time of festivities. Hence, the family of Jesus cannot have been poor.

What about the origins of the family of Jesus? Were they Judean or Galilean?[4] According to Matthew and Mark, Jesus is said to have come from Nazareth. But John is doubtful that anything good can come out of Nazareth. John refers to those raising questions about Jesus's origins: "But some asked, 'Surely the Messiah does not come from Galilee, does he? Has not the scripture said that the Messiah is descended from David and comes from Bethlehem, the village where David lived?'" (7:41–42). Bethlehem was situated not in the Galilee but in Judea and was regarded as the ancestral town of King David. Matthew makes a point of emphasizing the link between Jesus and David in his genealogy at the beginning of his Gospel. Matthew goes on to say that the family of Jesus at one point "withdrew" into Galilee at the time of Herod Archelaus, whereas Luke (2:4) says they were resident in Nazareth and only traveled to Bethlehem in order to enroll in a census.

Hence, there are two possibilities: First, that Jesus was born in Nazareth and came from a Galilean family of long standing. The idea is that the connection to Bethlehem was forced by certain Gospel writers to establish a firm genealogical link between Jesus and King David. The second possibility is that the family, or at least those from Joseph's side, originally came from the Judean Hills south of Jerusalem, but eventually relocated to the Galilee at some stage after Jesus was born.[5]

Since the people of Nazareth were subsequently unfriendly toward the adult Jesus, treating him like an outsider, not as a member of a well-established local family, this points to Jesus's family being originally of Judean stock. Indeed, at one point Jesus was cast out of Nazareth in an undignified and positively murderous fashion: "and they [the inhabitants] rose up, and cast him forth out of the city, and led him unto the brow of the hill whereon their city was built, that they might throw him down headlong . . ." (Luke 4:28–29). This sounds like they intended to harm Jesus, perhaps even to kill him by stoning, had they managed to push him over the cliff. It is not surprising that in later rabbinical writings we read that a cliff, which had to be at least twice the height of a man, was a designated execution place where criminals were thrown over and stoned to death.[6]

In Jesus's time, archaeology shows Nazareth to have been a very small place; a violent disagreement of this kind would have had a disruptive effect on the entire village. Since Jesus managed to escape from Nazareth to Capernaum, we must assume his family were also banished or left of their own accord. Perhaps this explains why in Mark we hear of the fishing village Capernaum subsequently being referred to as "home": "When he [Jesus] returned to Capernaum after some days, it was reported that he was at home." Capernaum, on the shore of the Sea of Galilee, was undoubtedly Jesus's main base of operations as a rabbi, teacher, and healer. Jesus spent most of his life in the Galilee, initially at Nazareth and then for a few years more in Capernaum, until he was more than 30 years of age (Luke 3:23).[7]

What do we know about the chronology of Jesus's life? This is a subject that has been and continues to be a major bone of contention among scholars. My own view is that the crucifixion probably took place in the year 30 CE, when Jesus was 36 years of age, and two years after the beheading of John the Baptist by Herod Antipas.[8] But how does this date square with the chronological data in the Gospel narratives?

There is common agreement that Jesus was born toward the end of the reign of Herod the Great (37–4 BCE) and that this Herod is the same one referred to in Matthew and Luke: "In the time of King Herod, after Jesus was born in Bethlehem of Judea, wise men from the East came to Jerusalem, asking, 'Where is the child who has been born king of the Jews?'" (Matthew 2:1–2). The story Matthew provides of the Slaughter of the Innocents (babies up to the age of 2 years old) cannot be confirmed from any historical source, but it would be in keeping with Herod's known cruelty and dementia, as reported by the Jewish historian Josephus Flavius. Herod's health began deteriorating rapidly after 7 BCE.[9] The bottom line is that Jesus would have been born during the two years preceding Herod's death, i.e. between 6 and 4 BCE.

Luke's story (2:1–5) of Joseph and Mary traveling to Bethlehem to register in the census undertaken by the Roman governor in Syria,

P. Sulpicius Quirinius, is muddled and incorrect, and so must be disqualified as an historical event.[10] First, Quirinius only arrived in Syria in 6 CE, ten years after the death of Herod the Great, and so the census could only have been undertaken in 6 CE or a year later. Second, there is no historical attestation for a census having been ordered by decree of Caesar Augustus.

Matthew, however, suggests that Mary, Joseph, and the "young child" Jesus returned to Palestine from Egypt while Herod Archelaus was still ruling his kingdom, which included the regions of Judea, Samaria, and Idumea. If we take into consideration the fact that Archelaus was deposed in 6 CE and Jesus was still only a "young child" at that time (i.e., he was twelve or younger), then 6 BCE would therefore be a reasonable date for the birth of Jesus.

What seems certain is that the crucifixion took place during Pontius Pilate's governorship of Judea, between 26–36 CE, and while Caiaphas was serving as the Jewish High Priest in Jerusalem, between 18–36 CE.[11] Assuming that Jesus's birth was in 6 BCE, the crucifixion would have taken place in 30 CE (two years after the beheading of John the Baptist) and Jesus would have been thirty-six years of age at the time of his death.[12] One has to admit, however, that there can be no absolute certainty about the 6 BCE to 30 CE date for the life of Jesus. Indeed, the scholar E. P. Sanders has stated that until new chronological data becomes available, it is perhaps best "if we accept the accuracy of the sources in a more general way. This allows not only one of them, but even all of them to be fuzzy or wrong on some details."[13]

As a thirty-six-year-old, Jesus would have been regarded by his contemporaries as a man in his prime when he set out on his final journey to Jerusalem, because life expectancy was much lower; few lived past forty. According to Mark: "He left that place [Capernaum] and went to the region of Judea and beyond the Jordan. And crowds again gathered around him" (1:10). The Gospel accounts are confused and somewhat contradictory.[14] Indeed, Jesus's last journey from Galilee to Jerusalem is not even referred to in the Gospel of John, at least only obliquely concerning Jesus's appearance in the lower Jordan Valley.[15]

Jesus set out south from Capernaum with his disciples, family members, and followers. Luke says they made their way *between* the borders of Galilee and Samaria, which must mean they entered into the independent territory of Scythopolis (Beth Shean). The rich agricultural lands of Scythopolis were not passed to Herod's sons upon his death, but were in the possession of the province of Syria.[16] From there, Jesus might have considered taking one of three possible routes to reach Jerusalem: a road ascending the northern hills of Samaria to Jenin, where it runs south along the backbone of the hill country as far as Nablus, and then on to Jerusalem. A more direct route would have run south from Scythopolis along the western edges of the Jordan Valley toward Jericho, passing Phasaelis and Archelais. Another road running along the eastern edges of the Jordan Valley, reached via a ford over the Jordan River not far from Scythopolis (the ed-Damieh bridge), extended through the Ghor and ran south all the way to Bethabara, which was situated more or less opposite Jericho. The significance of the path taken by Jesus is important for understanding the background to Jesus's appearance in Jerusalem. Had he taken the first route, Jesus might have exposed his followers to danger. By taking the second route, Jesus would have encountered needless conflict with Judean authorities even before reaching Jerusalem.

However, the third route "beyond the Jordan" led him into familiar territory, since he joined a band of baptizers here under the leadership of John the Baptist a couple of years earlier. Also, as a resident of Lower Galilee in the territory of Perea (the territory of Herod Antipas), it probably would have been easier for Jesus to travel through these additional territories of Perea "beyond the Jordan"' (which included a substantial part of central Transjordan) without too much hindrance from the authorities. The same would not have been true had he decided to travel through Judea.

The second route through the highlands of Samaria was deemed dangerous; Samaritans were known to accost caravans of Jewish travelers. The Jewish historian Josephus relates how while traversing the plain of Samaria "a large company of Jews on their way up [to Jerusalem] for the festival" was attacked and a few of its members were murdered. Although Sebaste—the Samaria of the Old Testament—was a pagan city, the Samaritan presence in the countryside was strong. That Jesus himself made visits to the Samaria region is clear from Luke and John, but according to Matthew Jesus forbade his disciples from going there. Indeed, at a watering hole close to Sebaste (Jacob's Well), a local woman pointedly questioned Jesus about his activities there, "for the Jews have no dealings with Samaritans" (John 4:9).[17]

Finally, Jesus was reportedly being followed around by a multitude of people, which would have made his appearance along the western edges of the Jordan Valley, deemed Judean territory and under the control of the Roman Procurator, dangerous and foolhardy. After all, Jesus was not just a pilgrim in a caravan on its way to the Passover festivities in Jerusalem, but the leader of disciples and additional followers—a fact the authorities might have regarded as threatening. The town of Archelais, which was built astride the road, 12 Roman miles north of Jericho, would have been difficult for Jesus to pass through unnoticed. Archelais was founded by one of Herod the Great's sons, Herod Archelaus, who named it after himself to serve as a center for his vast date groves. It has been identified at Khirbet Beiyudat and I visited the site recently to make an appraisal. Only a small part of the site has been excavated, but the remains uncovered from the first century CE are impressive, including residential quarters, ritual bathing pools, and a lot of pottery and stone vessels.[18] Today the surrounding area looks quite bleak and arid, but in ancient times this would have been a thriving town situated within a flourishing green oasis.

For these reasons, the route indicated by Mark and Matthew "beyond the Jordan," i.e., along the eastern edges of the Jordan Valley and within the territory of Perea, makes much more sense as the road Jesus took to Jerusalem.

The journey from Capernaum to Jerusalem would have taken most of a week, depending on the time Jesus and his entourage spent at each stopping point.[19] The main roads of that period were simple, between 2 to 6 meters wide, with tamped-down hard surfaces and stones cleared to their edges.[20] There were no paved roads at that time. Caravans consisted of people on foot with walking sticks, carrying food and provisions on their backs. The elderly and young probably rode donkeys or mules. The Jordan Valley is a hellish place to walk through in summer, when the heat becomes oppressive. However, the region is mild during the winter and spring months, permitting sleeping in the open at prescribed halting spots. They may have stopped at small villages and water springs along the way. The American scholar Chester Charlton McCown wrote that "the balmy air and the relative infrequency of storms, which at that season may be very severe in the mountains, would seem to qualify the Jordan route as by all odds the one best suited to the movements of considerable bodies of peasant pilgrims to and from the Passover feast."[21]

Jesus's route would have taken him next to places of baptism previously frequented by his mentor John the Baptist, namely Aenon and Bethabara. I think Jesus's appearance in the Jordan Valley was strategic: There, he could practice his healing and consolidate his position as the perceived successor of John the Baptist. Jesus was probably unsuccessful in his endeavor to get major support from the Baptist movement. He most certainly would have visited Salem, near the Spring of Aenon, not far south of Scythopolis, perhaps even staying there for a short while before moving on. Aenon is where John the Baptist spent time baptizing before his death in 28 CE: "And John too was baptising at Aenon, near Salem, because there was much water there, and [people] came and were baptised" (John 3:23). According to Eusebius, writing in the early third century, "the place is still shown today, eight miles south of Scythopolis [Beth Shean], near Salem and the Jordan." The traveler Egeria (384 CE) wrote that on descending to the Jordan River from the main road on the west, she passed through a wide plain and approached a big village called Sedima, with a church on a hillock, and close by "a good clean spring of water which flowed in a single stream. There was a kind of pool in front of the spring at which it appears holy John Baptist administered baptism."[22] Salem also appears in a similar location on the sixth-century Madaba mosaic map of the Holy Land.

Salem is identified with Tell er-Ridrha (known today as Tell Shalem) and Aenon with the nearby spring ('Ain Ibrahim) situated at the foot of the hill to the northeast, but previous archaeological surveys were unable to show the existence of pottery or other remnants from the site dating from the time of John the Baptist and Jesus.[23] A trip I made to the site last year, however, was quite enlightening: A large fragment of a cooking pot and fragments of red gloss *terra sigillata* bowls from the first century CE were picked up from the site's surface, showing that the spring indeed existed at the time Jesus passed by. So it is likely that the adjacent village was one of the stopping places for him and his followers.[24] Unfortunately, the area of the spring and its pool cannot be excavated since it has been converted into a modern fishpond belonging to nearby Kibbutz Tirat Zvi. There are also one or two unexploded landmines in the area of the spring and village, judging by military signposts.

Another place Jesus probably reached during his final journey is Bethabara, situated in the lower Jordan Valley to the north of the Dead Sea, although this place is not mentioned by Mark, Matthew, or Luke. John, however, does say that Jesus went "beyond the Jordan into the place where John was at the first baptizing; and there he abode" (10:40), and we have to assume this is a reference to Bethabara. Jesus's presence there was undoubtedly important in his attempt to consolidate his position as John the Baptist's successor: "And many came unto him [Jesus], and they said, John indeed did no sign: but all things whatsoever John spoke of this man were true. And many believed in him there" (John 10:41–42).

Bethabara ("house of crossing") was a village situated next to a ford across the Jordan River, to the north of the Dead Sea, with a road leading west from Transjordan to Jericho. The importance of this location as a place of transition cannot have escaped Jesus. It was from here Joshua crossed into the Promised Land with the Israelites, where Elijah divided the waters of the Jordan River and went up to heaven in a blazing chariot, and where John the Baptist began his ministry and baptized Jesus.[25] New archaeological excavations and surveys on the east bank of the Jordan River have brought to light fragmentary remains dating from the first century CE, but unequivocal signs of the village of Bethabara from the time of Jesus have yet to be found.[26]

Having passed over the Bethabara ford at the Jordan River, Jesus traveled across the Jericho Plain to reach the road ascending west through the hills toward the villages of Bethany and Bethphage and the city of Jerusalem.[27] Jericho was a major halting spot for caravans of pilgrims arriving from the north and east. Traveling along the road, Jesus reached the oasis of Jericho but probably didn't stay there for very long: "They came to Jericho. As he and his disciples and a large crowd were leaving Jericho, Bartimaeus son of Timaeus, a blind beggar, was sitting by the roadside" (Mark 10:46). Mark describes the arrival of Jesus at Jericho so awkwardly that we wonder whether incidents occurred there that Mark or his source might have thought irrelevant and so were excised. Alternatively, this might have been a stylistic matter due to the translation of the original source material in Mark from Aramaic into Greek.[28]

According to Matthew there were *two* blind men near the town:

"As they were leaving Jericho, a large crowd followed him. There were two blind men sitting by the roadside. When they heard that Jesus was passing by, they shouted, 'Lord, have mercy on us, Son of David!' The crowd sternly ordered them to be quiet; but they shouted even more loudly, 'Have mercy on us, Lord, Son of David!' Jesus stood still and called them, saying, 'What do you want me to do for you?' They said to him, 'Lord, let our eyes be opened.' Moved with compassion, Jesus touched their eyes. Immediately they regained their sight and followed him" (20:29–34).

An entirely different story is related by Luke:

"He entered Jericho and was passing through it. A man was there named Zacchaeus; he was a chief tax-collector and was rich. He was trying to see who Jesus was, but on account of the crowd he could not, because he was short in stature. So he ran ahead and climbed a sycamore tree to see him, because he was going to pass that way. When Jesus came to the place, he looked up and said to him, 'Zacchaeus, hurry and come down; for I must stay at your house today'" (19:1–10).

If Luke is right and Jesus stayed for a while in Jericho, it would be nice to know what the houses of Jericho looked like at that time. Unfortunately, nothing much archaeologically is known about the residential parts of the town of Jericho, except that it was quite large, with an important spring (the spring of Elisha, or in Arabic 'Ain es-Sultan), and a cemetery.[29] A large community of priests who served in the Jerusalem Temple lived in the town. The oasis of Jericho was renowned for its date-palm plantations and for producing balsam, which had numerous medicinal uses. Herod the Great built a large complex of sumptuous winter palaces south of the town, at a site now known in Arabic as Tulul Abu el-'Alayiq.[30] I know the ruins well, having clambered around them on numerous occasions. The palaces were excavated from the 1970s, revealing pavilions, residential and service areas, bathhouses, swimming pools, and gardens. In one of the swimming pools Herod had the innocent teenager Aristobulus from the Hasmonean family drowned.

Having made the steep climb up the winding road through the hills, Jesus finally approached Jerusalem from the east, a day's journey from Jericho. Looming in front of him was the large mountainous massif known as the Mount of Olives, with the villages of Bethphage and Bethany (see more about these places in the next chapter); hidden behind it was the city of Jerusalem and the Temple of God.

Why would Jesus have wanted to go to Jerusalem in the first place? Having established himself successfully as an itinerant teacher and healer at the Sea of Galilee, with a dedicated band of disciples and a devoted following, Jesus managed to avoid conflict with the local authorities by distancing himself from the large cities of Sepphoris and Tiberias. On face value, there was no apparent need for Jesus to go to Jerusalem. It is possible that Jesus simply desired to make a religious pilgrimage to the city for the purpose of the Passover festivity, following the custom set by his father. Alternatively, he may have felt the need to go there to intentionally stir things up through his teaching. It is not surprising that sign and prophetic movements, referred to by the first century historian Josephus, originated in Judea or were active there, but not in the Galilee, although malcontents undoubtedly existed everywhere.[31]

A critical analysis of the Gospels (especially Mark) has shown that the account of Jesus's movements and his final journey were apparently edited so that they might be consistent with Jesus's apparent premonition, while still in Galilee, about a journey to Jerusalem, and a likely struggle and death that would ensue when encountering the city authorities. Whether Jesus had a clear working strategy for the time he was to spend in Jerusalem is unknown, but it seems to me that Jesus went there to consolidate his position as a "baptizer" and to expand upon his healing activities. What is clear is that having arrived in Jerusalem, at least six days before the Passover holiday began (if one accepts the testimony of John 12:1), Jesus had sufficient time to mingle intentionally with the crowds of Jewish pilgrims for the festivities, to persuade them of his beliefs and ideas, and to try to get them to join his following.[32] Indeed, Jesus's well-known previous association with John the Baptist, who had been beheaded owing to Antipas' fear of an insurrection, would have made the religious and military authorities of Jerusalem suspicious of Jesus's overall motives in visiting the city at the height of the Passover holiday. We do not know when the authorities first became aware of Jesus's presence, but it was probably when crowds began gathering around him to observe his cleansing and healing work.

Without doubt, Jesus's arrival in Jerusalem was planned, and he clearly wanted to use the Passover period to visit the Temple and other locations in the city, to spread his message among the numerous visiting pilgrims. However, Jesus's final intentions in Jerusalem remain mysterious and unclear. Did he plan to clash with the local Jewish and Roman authorities, or did things simply get out of hand?

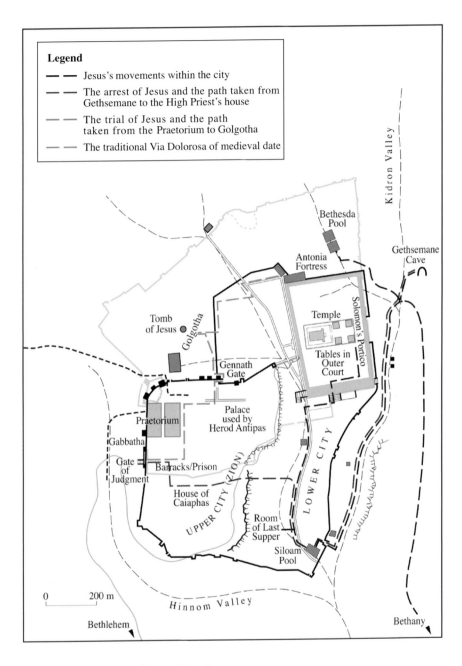

Kidron Valley

Bethesda Pool

Antonia Fortress

Gethsemane Cave

Temple

Solomon's Portico

Tomb of Jesus

Golgotha

Tables in Outer Court

Gennath Gate

Palace used by Herod Antipas

Praetorium

LOWER CITY

Gabbatha

Gate of Judgment

Barracks/Prison

House of Caiaphas

UPPER CITY (ZION)

Room of Last Supper

Siloam Pool

0 200 m

Hinnom Valley

Bethlehem

Bethany

Jerusalem at the time of Jesus (30 CE).

General view of Capernaum, with wall foundations of houses built of basalt and with the façade of the synagogue to the left.

General view of the Temple Mount and the Old City of Jerusalem.

The Holy Land model of first-century Jerusalem showing the southern Temple Mount façade from the direction of the Siloam Pool.

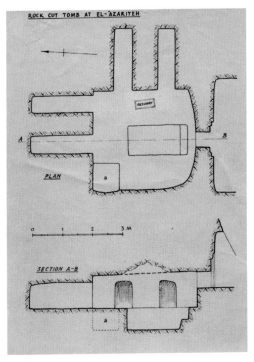

Archival plan of a tomb of the first century CE at Bethany.

The Theodotus Inscription.

The massive dressed stones in the Western Wall of the Temple Mount.

A stone plaque from Barcelona depicting a sacrifice scene at the Temple.

A paved and stepped street leading from the Siloam Pool toward the Temple Mount.

Inscription in Greek: "No alien may enter within the barrier and wall around the Temple. Whoever is caught [violating this] is alone responsible for the death [penalty] which follows."

The rock-cut part of a multistoried house of the first century CE uncovered near the Siloam Pool.

A Roman mosaic floor from Sepphoris depicting a banqueting scene.

A stepped ritual bathing pool next to the Temple Mount.

A ritual bathing pool beneath the traditional house of the nativity of John the Baptist in Ain Karim.

The southeastern corner of the Siloam Pool.

RAISING A DEAD MAN

"Then they brought the colt to Jesus and threw their cloaks on it; and he sat on it. Many people spread their cloaks on the road, and others spread leafy branches that they had cut in the fields. Then those who went ahead and those who followed were shouting,
'Hosanna!
Blessed is the one who comes in the name of the Lord!
Blessed is the coming kingdom of our ancestor David!
Hosanna in the highest heaven!'"

(*Mark 11:7–10*)

Jesus and his entourage managed to reach Jerusalem safely from the direction of Jericho, without any harassment or hindrance from the Roman authorities who were controlling the road; probably they did this by blending into the even flow of crowds of Jewish pilgrims joyfully making their way to the city for the forthcoming Passover events. But on reaching the village of Bethany, on the eastern outskirts of the city, everything apparently changed: The crowds suddenly knew who Jesus was and were almost in a state of ecstasy, exclaiming and singing with a lot of fanfare.

In my search for the historical Jesus I have often wondered what exactly happened on that spring day in the year thirty at the village of Bethany on the outskirts of Jerusalem. Was there a sudden realization among the crowds that their messianic expectations might now be fulfilled? Would people have had in their minds the words of the prophet Zechariah concerning the triumphal entrance of a king riding on a colt into Zion? Would news of Jesus's triumphal arrival not have spread like wildfire through the city as he and his disciples descended the slope of the Mount of Olives to enter into Jerusalem? Would Jesus's reception not have been monitored by the Roman authorities and would not the excitement have made them wary? Or was it after all just a modest affair and not as colorful as the Gospel accounts would suggest, organized by the disciples simply to celebrate the arrival of their beloved leader and rabbi (Hebrew, "my master") at Bethany?

I believe it more likely that Jesus and his followers adopted a quieter approach to entering the city, otherwise their actions could have been interpreted by the Romans as seditious and Jesus might easily have been arrested even before entering the city. There is nothing to suggest that Jesus did not make his way, as the Gospels describe, astride a colt, with a few people spreading their garments and tree branches in front of his path, and crying out praises: "blessed is the one who comes in the name of the Lord." But all in all it would have been a modest, low-key affair. From the point of view of the Roman soldiers keeping an eye on the Bethany road, the actions of Jesus and his group would have been indistinguishable from the excitable behavior and joyous exclamations of many other newly arrived Jewish pilgrims when first approaching Jerusalem from afar.

Scholars have spent a lot of time debating the historicity of the Gospel accounts connected to Bethany: the arrival of Jesus, the anointing of Jesus, and the raising of Lazarus.[33] But what about the village of Bethany itself: Where was it situated and what would it have looked like at the time of Jesus?

The three Gospels, Mark, Matthew and Luke, are in agreement that Bethany was in the near vicinity of another village named Bethphage, close to the Mount of Olives, and that both villages were situated not far from the road Jesus took to Jerusalem from Jericho.

These were small villages, probably no larger than Jesus's hometown of Nazareth, and he would have felt quite comfortable staying there. There are eleven references to Bethany in the Gospels, and three to Bethphage.[34] Bethany was one of a group of villages dotted around Jerusalem in the first century CE and delimiting the extent of its rural hinterland on all sides. Bethphage was seen specifically to mark the eastern limits of the city in rabbinical sources.[35] This group of villages included Shu'fat and Gabaath Saul (Gibeah of Saul) to the north of the city, Motza (Emmaus) and En Kerem (Beth Haccerem) to the west, Ramat Rahel to the south, Hizma (Azmaveth) and Isawiye to the northeast, and Et-Tur (Bethphage) and el-Azariyeh (Bethany) to the southeast. Scattered between these villages are numerous ancient remains of farms, cisterns and ritual bathing pools (the Jewish *miqwa'ot*), terraces and fields, and burial caves. This land was the bread basket of Jerusalem, supplying the inhabitants of the city with olive oil and wine, various fruits and nuts, and vegetables grown in the irrigated plots below springs of water.

Bethany is clearly to be identified with the modern Palestinian village of el-Azariyeh since it is situated about 3 kilometers to the southeast of Jerusalem—which roughly fits the distance of 15 stadia mentioned in John—or a forty-minute ride on horseback.[36] The modern name el-Azariyeh is a corruption of the Greek *Lazarion* ("the place of Lazarus"), but in Old Testament times Bethany may have been known as (Beth) Ananiah. The last time I visited the village and its ruins in the 1990s was in the company of Musa, the son of the local Muslim cemetery attendant. I was struck by the absolute poverty of his existence; his house was virtually empty except for a tap and basin and some bedding in the corner. At the time of Jesus the houses of ancient Bethany would have been sturdy and well built, with good air circulation and large external courtyards, with mangers for beasts of burden in the lower rooms, and with upper living rooms, some of which had simple geometric designs on the interior walls.

Numerous archaeological remains have been uncovered in the area of the present-day village of Bethany and around the area of the traditional rock-hewn Tomb of Lazarus.[37] As an archaeologist I have investigated many rock-cut tombs from the time of Jesus, but the interior of the Lazarus tomb has been modified to such an extent in later medieval periods that nothing of its original appearance can be deduced. A Christian church was erected there in the Byzantine period and there are also substantial remains at the spot dating from Crusader times. For our purposes, there can be no doubt that Bethany was a flourishing rural village at the time of Jesus, and numerous agricultural installations, ritual bathing pools (*miqwa'ot*), and cisterns from the first century CE have been uncovered in excavations. In later centuries many Christian pilgrims visited the village seeking out the house of Martha and Mary—where Jesus was reputed to have stayed during Passion week—and the Tomb of Lazarus. In one of the ritual bathing pools uncovered by archaeologists at Bethany there were red-painted drawings of crosses, and incised graffiti of various kinds and inscriptions on the walls, evidently made by Byzantine-period pilgrims visiting the village.[38]

Bethphage (which means "house of green figs," from the Hebrew *paggim*) is identified with the village of Et-Tur on the east side of the southern summit of the Mount of Olives. Various archaeological remains have been investigated there, including, recently, the remains of an oil press within a building. Like Bethany, the village from the time of Jesus was probably quite small. It was to this place that Jesus sent two of his disciples to collect a she-ass and colt that were needed for his triumphal entry into Jerusalem: "When they were approaching Jerusalem, at Bethphage and Bethany, near the Mount of Olives, he sent two of his disciples and said to them, 'Go into the village ahead of you, and immediately as you enter it, you will find tied there a colt that has never been ridden; untie it and bring it'" (Mark 11:1–2; cf. the variant accounts in Matthew 21:1–2; Luke 19:29–30). In the

Byzantine period many pilgrims visited the village and a church was built there as well; numerous remains from the Crusader period have also been identified. Unfortunately, the new "barrier-wall," which is under construction to separate Israel from Palestinian territories, will eventually cut off this village from its fields.

The village of Bethany apparently served as headquarters—perhaps like a second home—for Jesus and his disciples during their visits to Jerusalem. The Gospels of Mark, Matthew, and Luke refer only to the one visit made by Jesus to Jerusalem during his final week, but John indicates he frequently came to Jerusalem to attend festivals, visiting a number of locations including the Temple and the adjacent pools. But did Jesus lodge at Bethany in his final week in Jerusalem because of the scarcity of accommodations in Jerusalem, congested as it was with pilgrims for the Passover, or was it because he was afraid to be in the proximity of the Roman authorities?

It seems to me that Jesus's deep friendship with Lazarus and his sisters Mary and Martha was probably the main reason he lodged at their house in Bethany rather than anywhere else. Indeed, Jesus's daily movements in and out of the city would more likely have alerted the authorities—since he would have had to pass frequently through the guarded gates of the city—than had he remained in permanent lodgings in the city for the duration of the holiday. The names Mary (Miriam) and Martha (Marta) were very common female names in the first century. Bone boxes (ossuaries) inscribed with the name Martha are known from a tomb at the so-called "Mount of Offense" not far from Bethany, and many ossuaries inscribed with the name of Mary have been found in other tombs around Jerusalem.[39] In addition to the siblings Lazarus, Mary, and Martha, we also hear of another resident of Bethany: Simon the Leper, who may have been a Pharisee, and who was perhaps related (as a husband or father?) to Martha or to Mary.[40]

There are two episodes in the Gospels that are of significance for understanding the relationship between Jesus and the Bethany family.

The first relates to the anointing of Jesus with oil, and the second with the raising of Lazarus. We shall examine each one of these stories separately and see if archaeology can shed light on them.

The contradictions in the details of the anointing episode in the various Gospels have generated a lot of discussion among scholars.[41] According to John, Mary anointed Jesus's feet with oil and then wiped them with her hair. Mark and Matthew, however, say that it was Jesus's head that was actually anointed, with expensive oil contained in an *alabastron*, and that this was done by an unnamed woman (but presumably a member of the household) while Jesus was attending an evening meal at the house of Simon the Leper. The Greek word used to denote this external physical anointing is *aleipho*. The *alabastron* was a typical kind of bottle at that time used to contain perfumes or choice oils, and many examples have been found in archaeological excavations. In Luke, however, the anointing appears earlier on in the Gospel story and seemingly refers to a different location while Jesus was still in the Galilee. The story, I believe, actually refers to an occasion during one of Jesus's earlier visits to Jerusalem—if one accepts John's references to earlier visits—and in relating the story Luke may not have been overly concerned with the exact geographical location. The house is acknowledged to be that of Simon the Pharisee, who invited Jesus to dine with him. A woman, identified only as "a sinner" but evidently a member of Simon's household, has an *alabastron* containing oil, and "standing behind at his feet, weeping, she began to wet his feet with her tears, and wiped them with the hair of her head, and kissed his feet, and anointed them with the ointment." Later, Jesus says to Simon: "I entered into thy house, thou gave me no water for my feet: but she has wetted my feet with her tears, and wiped them with her hair. . . My head with oil thou did not anoint: but she has anointed my feet with ointment. . ." (Luke 7:44–46).

The anointing of feet with oil/ointment has generally been regarded by scholars as a practice that was out of place in ancient Palestine and therefore evidently wrong.[42] The argument is that if any part of Jesus was anointed then it should have been his head (as in Mark and Matthew) so as to confirm his messianic status. Indeed, the verb *m-sh-h* in Hebrew, which is used in biblical accounts to denote the act of anointing, is the source of the word "messiah," which literally means the "anointed one." In the Old Testament human beings were anointed to enhance their royal or prophetic status (e.g., the anointing of King Saul), as well as sacred objects. Not only are there ample ancient texts referring to the anointing of feet with oil in the context of the Greek and Roman worlds, but also in Deuteronomy a covenant was struck by the dipping of a foot in oil.[43] The anointing of other parts of the body with oil was also commonly referred to in the biblical sources and in many cases it was connected to ritualistic and purification activities, and at times of fasting and mourning. The dead were also anointed: It was part of a purification procedure that consisted of the washing of a body with water, the anointing of the body with oil, and the wrapping of the body in a shroud.

What is compelling is that at the time of Jesus and in the following century the practice of anointing with oil for purification purposes appears to have been prevalent in domestic settings as well. In the archaeological excavation of Jewish houses from the first century CE in Jerusalem, small stone tubs were found outside the stepped ritual bathing pools (*miqwa'ot*). Scholars have correctly assumed that these tubs were used for the washing of the hands or feet of the person entering the pool to be purified, and indeed in early rabbinical writings (the Mishna) we hear about some washing of the extremities of the body before entering the ritual bath (m. Miqwa'ot 9:2). We must not discount the possibility, however, that on leaving the ritual bath the person's feet and hands were anointed with oil as part of the purification procedure, and perhaps even in the same small tubs. In one of the tractates in the rabbinical literature it is stated that on the Sabbath a man "should not put oil on his foot while it is in a sandal."[44]

Figure 1: Reconstruction drawing showing the anointing procedure undertaken in the first century CE *at the Suba Cave west of Jerusalem.*

Recently, an archaeological discovery was made that sheds new light on the anointing of feet with oil at the time of Jesus. The discovery was made in a cave I excavated at Suba, to the west of Jerusalem, not far from the traditional hometown of John the Baptist at En Kerem.[45] What is exciting is that a stone installation was found that was used for the cultic anointing of feet with oil in the earliest levels of this cave dating to between the late first century BCE and the early first century CE, i.e., to the time of Jesus.[46] The upper surface of the stone was carved with an indentation in the shape of a right foot and leading to it was a channel extending from a small round depression that would have held a jug containing olive oil. The fact that only right feet were anointed on this stone must indicate it was part of some cultic ritual; otherwise there should also have been a corresponding stone with a sunken imprint of the left foot. The stone installation was found embedded in a floor on the edge of a water pool in which water purification rites—similar to those practiced by John the Baptist—were carried out.

The archaeological evidence suggests that the cave was used for group rituals performed in the cave *before* and *after* water immersion procedures. People would have gathered in the front of the cave; the ceremony was performed with individuals standing within stone circles and using ceramic jugs, perhaps to pour water over each other before ceremonially smashing them. Subsequently, those gathered there immersed themselves in the water at the back of the cave. On emerging from the water their feet were anointed with oil. Presumably the anointing of the right foot marked the transition of an individual from an "ordinary" state of being to that of a "purified" state of being. In my reconstruction of the event, I believe it was another person rather than the initiatory himself who would have administered the washing and anointing of the foot with oil from a jug. The ceremony of baptism performed by John the Baptist at the Jordan River bears similarities that may not be coincidental. First, people gathered on the banks of the river for prayers and to receive a remission of sins, and then they entered the water of the river to cleanse the flesh by immersion. On emerging from the water, initiates may have been anointed with oil, but the Gospels are silent about this.

The identity of the people who used the cave at Suba is uncertain: They were undoubtedly Jews, but the rites of water purification they undertook in the cave differed from those practiced by their contemporaries, suggesting perhaps that this cave was used by some peripheral sect in Judaism that laid emphasis on water purification, or that, alternatively, it was used by the actual followers of John the Baptist. If this is the case, it is perhaps not surprising that a couple of hundred years later in the Byzantine period the cave at Suba was converted

into a memorial for John the Baptist—following the Christian identification of this region as the "Wilderness" of John—with drawings
incised on the cave walls bearing images of John the Baptist and his
symbols.

Turning back to the account of the anointing of the feet of Jesus
at Bethany, I would submit that Mary's actions were not at all surprising. As we shall see in regard to the washing of the feet of the
disciples at the Last Supper, had Mary simply washed Jesus's feet,
this would be regarded as a typical Near Eastern act of hospitality
toward a guest and as a token of the humility of the host, but nothing more. However, the use of expensive perfumed oil indicates the
procedure was actually one of ritual purification and that Mary's tears
symbolically represent a preliminary washing of the feet with water
that would have been done before any oil was applied. This, I think,
is very clear from the description of these events as given by Luke.

We may surmise that travelers entering into any given house
during the first century CE, whether in Jerusalem or in any one of
the outlying villages, might have been expected to undergo one of a
number of forms of ritual purification. Jesus as a guest in the house
of Mary and Martha would have been expected to follow the rules
of purification common at that time. This would have included the
washing and anointing of feet (to rid the feet of impurities derived
from the road), full immersion in a stepped pool (*miqweh*) in the basement of a house (to cleanse the entire body of impurities and emissions), and the washing of hands (*netilat yadaim*) prior to meals (to
cleanse hands that would touch food).[47] It is interesting to note that
when John the Baptist, in speaking of the Messiah, says that he is one
"whose sandals I am not fit to take off" (Matthew 3:11; cf. Mark 1:7;
Luke 3:16; John 1:27; Acts 13:25), this may be a reflection not just of
John's humility but also a stated preamble to a subsequent process of
ritual purification of feet that would have been obvious to all Jews at
the time. Hence, the anointing of Jesus's feet was a scene that would

not have been out of place in first-century Jerusalem. The fact that the oil was perfumed and therefore expensive must indicate that Jesus's friends Mary and Martha were definitely not poor.

We now turn to the fascinating and somewhat grisly story of the raising of Lazarus at Bethany. The account of his raising appears only in the Gospel of John. But Luke does have a story of Jesus raising another dead man in a village called Nain, situated to the southeast of Nazareth, in the Galilee. The dead man in this story was brought out of the gate of Nain on a funerary bier, his mother weeping next to it, when Jesus called upon him "he that was dead sat up, and began to speak" (7:11–15). Archaeological work in the area of the village, now known as Nein, has brought to light remains dating from the first century CE, including a number of burial caves.[48]

The reference to a funeral bier in the story is quite interesting. In one of the rabbinical sources (the Babylonian Talmud) it is mentioned that in earlier times (i.e., in the first century) the practice was to carry a rich person to his burial place on a fancy litter (*dargash*), whereas a poor person would be carried on a plain bier (*kliva*) made of wooden boards or of tree branches tied together:

"We learn here what our Rabbis taught [elsewhere]: They [may] do all that the dead requires, they cut his hair and wash a garment for him and make him a box of boards that had been sawn on the day before the Festival. Rabban Simeon b. Gamaliel says, they [may] even bring trees and he saws them [into] boards in his house, behind closed doors" (Talmud Babylonian, Mo'ed Katan, 8b).[49]

The raising of Lazarus is a very different story compared to the Nain incident. First, it takes place after he has been buried for four days. Second, Lazarus is a friend of Jesus and not a stranger, as in the case of Nain. Martha, we are told, on hearing that Jesus is on the road to Bethany from Bethabara, goes out to meet with him while Mary stays in the house. Later Mary goes to the tomb of Lazarus, which is described as follows: "now it was a cave and a stone lay against it" (John 11:38). Martha fears that the body of Lazarus may have begun to decay, and Jesus orders that the stone blocking the entrance to the cave be removed. The fact that Lazarus' body was not rotting after having been in the tomb for four days suggests he must have been in a trance or state of catalepsy. Jesus shouts out Lazarus' name, perhaps hoping to rouse him from his comatose trance. Lazarus eventually emerges "bound hand and foot with strips of cloth, and his face . . . bound about with a cloth . . ." (John 11:44). This description brings to mind scenes from grisly old Egyptian mummy movies, quite horrifying and shocking, but amusing at the same time.

The description of Lazarus emerging from his tomb makes it clear that the cloth covering his head (*soudarion*) was a separate feature from the actual shroud made of strips of cloth (*keiria*) that was wrapped around his body. This separation is also clear from rabbinical writings: "Formerly they were wont to uncover the face of the rich and cover the face of the poor, because their faces turned livid in years of drought and the poor felt shamed; they therefore instituted that everybody's face should be covered, out of deference for the poor" (Talmud Babylonian, Mo'ed Katan, 27a). Elsewhere we hear that the jaw of the deceased was tied up before his head was covered: "All the requirements of the dead may be done; he may be anointed with oil and washed, provided that no limb of his is moved. The pillow may be removed from under him, and he may be placed on sand [i.e. the ground], in order that he may be able to be kept [flat]. The jaw may be tied up . . ." (Talmud Babylonian, Shabbat, 151 a–b).[50]

On the basis of what is known about tombs of this date in the surroundings of Jerusalem, we have a pretty good idea about the setting of the tomb of Lazarus and what its rock-hewn interior might have looked like. All tombs of that period were family tombs. Hence, Lazarus' tomb would also have been the intended final resting place for the entire family, with spaces for his father Simon and his siblings Mary and Martha, unless one of them happened to marry out of the family.

An interesting tomb from this period was excavated at Bethany in 1941 by the Hebrew University archaeologist Eleazar Sukenik; we can use its plan as a model for imagining what the tomb of Lazarus most probably looked like.[51] A small opening in a narrow courtyard gave access to a more-or-less square chamber, with a standing-pit at its center to allow family members to stand erect within the tomb, and with benches on three sides on which the bodies of the deceased would have been placed. A stone ossuary decorated with rosettes was found on one of the benches. Four tunnel-like *kokhim* were cut horizontally into the side walls of the chamber, in which bodies were most probably placed, though they may have been used to store additional stone ossuaries. Such ossuaries were used to collect the bones of the deceased once their bodies had decomposed. A pit cut into the top of a bench in one corner of the chamber was also used for the secondary gathering (known as *ossilegium*) of bones of family members from earlier generations.

To fully understand Jesus's actions in regard to Lazarus, one must understand how death was perceived by first-century Jews. Unless a person died through mutilation or execution, Jews were hard-pressed to know if their family member had actually died or was still in some sleep-like repose (a form of "slumber") between *Sheol* (the Jewish equivalent of the underworld Hades) and the waking world. This is why the dead were more likely to be placed on benches in burial caves than in trench-dug graves in the ground. Those that were placed in trench-graves—usually poor peasants and shepherds, not townspeople—were only buried, however, after their bodies had first lain for at least three days within a mortuary chamber in a cemetery.

This is also why separate shroud wrappings were used for the body and for the face—to allow a person awakening from a trance or comatose condition to "blow" the napkin-like covering away from the head. They could then shout and alert mourners that they were still alive. In rabbinical sources we hear of a man buried in a cave who when visited by relatives after three days was found still to be alive, and remarkably went on to live for another twenty-five years.[52] But generally, the final acceptance of death by the family would occur a year or so afterward when the body of the deceased had finally succumbed to decomposition and when the bones were ready to be collected into an ossuary.

In Jesus's time, people shared a deep fear of being buried alive and therefore made very specific arrangements to ensure that this could never happen. Bells and small cymbals sometimes appear in tombs, but only from the Byzantine period onwards (in more recent times this led to the saying "saved by the bell").[53] Indeed, the visits made to the tomb of Lazarus by Mary, on the one hand, and to the tomb of Jesus by a number of women, on the other, was definitely not a matter of chance. They were there to check on the situation of the deceased after three days or more. There are instances even today of people waking up in morgues after they had been pronounced dead and with death certificates having been issued. I recall being told the horrific story by the widow of a person who was badly injured during the King David Hotel blast in Jerusalem in 1946 and who was accidentally thought to have been dead for over a week. He dramatically (but unsuccessfully) tried to extricate himself from his coffin with his bare hands. The phenomenon of people being declared dead and then miraculously reviving in morgues is known as the "Lazarus Syndrome."[54] Edgar Allan Poe wrote about this in his story *The Premature Burial* adding: "The boundaries which divide Life from Death are at best shadowy and vague. Who shall say where the one ends, and where the other begins."

Owing to the state of medicine in the first century it is conceivable that the phenomenon of people waking up in tombs inevitably led to stories of people being raised from the dead. Jesus, with his healing skills and knowledge of comatose conditions, might have been able to facilitate this phenomenon for his own purposes and thus draw people to him. This may explain why Jesus describes to his disciples Lazarus' condition simply as: "our friend Lazarus has fallen asleep; but I go, that I may awaken him out of sleep" (John 11:11), perhaps suspecting that Lazarus suffered from some form of disease such as epilepsy.[55]

Prior to the raising of Lazarus, Martha berates Jesus for not being present when her brother died, and then says, "I know he [Lazarus] shall rise again in the resurrection at the last day" (John 11:24), which was the common Jewish belief at that time. The idea was that the dead entered a shadowy subterranean landscape (*Sheol*, the equivalent of the underworld Hades) to receive reward or retribution, either as an elect or righteous person passing into Paradise or as a sinner to Gehenna, and there they awaited resurrection at the end of time, initiated by the Messiah.[56] But Jesus replies and offers immediate eternal salvation: "I am the resurrection, and the life; he that believes in me, though he die, yet shall he live; and whosoever lives and believes in me shall never die" (John 11:25–26).[57]

During his stay at Bethany Jesus was on very friendly terms with Simon the Pharisee, and ate food at his house. We are also told that Simon was a leper. One of the terrible afflictions of that time was leprosy, and one may infer from the frequent mention of lepers in the Gospel accounts that Jesus attempted to help many of them.[58] But what do we actually know about the disease of leprosy in first century Jerusalem? Was the leprosy treated by Jesus some form of skin rash or was it the horrific ailment known today as Hansen's disease?

Jesus had already earned a reputation for himself in the Galilee and elsewhere as a healer and as a man of "signs and wonders."[59] While John the Baptist was still alive, Jesus reportedly cured many "diseases, plagues and evil spirits" (Luke 7:21). Interestingly, John seemed worried about what he was hearing about Jesus, perhaps because he regarded him ostensibly as one of his flock of baptizers, and so sent two of his followers to Jerusalem to find out what was happening.

One has to remember that John did not at any time perform miracles or healings of *any kind*, and his baptism ceremonies were ritualistic procedures that were accompanied only by prayers and invocations.

In response to the inquiries of John's followers, Jesus boasted: "Go and tell John the things which you have seen and heard: the blind have received their sight, the lame walk, the lepers are cleansed, and the deaf hear, [and] the dead are raised up . . ." (Luke 7:22).[60] The Gospel accounts underline the fact that in Galilee the sick came to Jesus from great distances suffering from various diseases and afflictions, including, it seems, the insane, the epileptic, and the paralyzed.[61] Olive oil was used for anointing many of the sick and its medicinal properties are well known. Jesus also sent his disciples out to heal (and purify) but they were not paid and were presumably reimbursed by the villagers with food and shelter.[62] Between eighteen to twenty miracle stories appear in the Synoptic Gospels and so it is not surprising that when Jesus was eventually brought to trial he was regarded by some accusers as a wonder-worker rather than a blasphemer or insurrectionist.

Unlike other diseases that Jesus dealt with by *healing*, leprosy was dealt with by *cleansing* (presumably indicated by the Hebrew word *tohara*, meaning "purification"). There are two episodes relating to Jesus healing lepers in the Gospels. The first appears in Mark and deals with a leper who asks Jesus to be cleansed of his affliction.[63] When Jesus succeeds, he asks the leper not to broadcast anything about it publicly, but the leper does so anyway. In Luke's version, a report about the success of the cure simply "goes out" (Luke 5:15) and Jesus is subsequently chased by a multitude of people who wish to be healed of their diseases.

The second episode is in Luke and relates to a time when Jesus was traveling close to the borders between Samaria and Galilee, perhaps on the outskirts of the lands of Scythopolis. He enters a certain un-named village and encounters ten male lepers (one of them a Samaritan). The fact that they were at a distance and needed to shout to get Jesus's attention probably indicates segregation was maintained by the community in which they lived. They were regarded not only as defiled but also as a source of defilement for their neighbors. Leprosy is listed in the rabbinical Jewish writings as one of the worst in the degrees of uncleanness, exceeded only by the uncleanness of bones or of a corpse.[64] Jesus reportedly sent the lepers to the priests to be cleansed (perhaps in a ritual bath or in a spring), and subsequently one of them (the Samaritan) returned to give thanks.

There are two kinds of leprosy mentioned in the Old and New Testaments, the first is known in Hebrew as *tsara'at* and it denotes various skin afflictions. The second is the leprosy caused by the bacterium *Mycobacterium leprae* and known today as Hansen's disease.[65] From the biblical texts it emerges that leprosy was regarded as a punishment from God for sins supposedly made by the sufferer. Many different types of *nega'im* (afflictions) are referred to in the Old Testament: scabs, bumps, spots, rashes, sores, boils, and scales.[66] In the second Book of Kings one hears of Na'aman the Leper and it appears he suffered from some kind of skin disease (*psoriasis*) with rashes and eruptions of flaky skin. In the sense of Leviticus, Na'aman's body had become invaded by the unclean (13:12). It was not believed the diseased flesh required curing and it was thought the condition could only be dealt with ceremonially in the cleansing waters of the Jordan River. Hence, Na'aman was sent by the prophet Elisha: "Go and wash (*rehaz*) in Jordan seven times and thy flesh shall come again to thee, and thou shalt be clean" (II Kings 5:10, 11, 14). Finally, "he [Na'aman] went down, and dipped (*taval*) himself seven times in the Jordan, according to the saying of the man of God [Elisha], and his flesh came again like unto the flesh of a little child, and he was clean."

Accurate evidence for the real leprous condition is known from India and China from at least the middle of the first millennium BCE, and an Asian origin for this disease therefore seems fairly certain. In the Near East proper, leprosy (Hansen's disease) was not generally thought to predate the Hellenistic period and the troops of Alexander the Great (327–326 BCE) were thought to be the ones responsible for bringing this deadly disease back from the Far East (specifically India). A new theory suggests that Hansen's disease first appeared in the region not with Alexander but sometime earlier (circa 400 BCE or later), with diseased young slaves conveyed from India to Egypt on cargo ships.[67] Clear evidence of the leprous condition of a skeleton from the fourth–third century BCE has been unearthed in the Celtic cemetery at Bologna in Italy, suggesting that Hansen's disease was prevalent in other countries around the Mediterranean.[68] In Egypt, evidence of Hansen's disease was found in skeletal remains uncovered in the Dakhleh Oasis from the second century BCE, and in the Holy Land physical evidence of leprosy has been found dating from the Byzantine period.[69] The disease was eventually spread unknowingly by merchants and travelers over great distances, throughout the Near East and in Europe, where it prevailed in medieval times as one of the major afflictions dreaded by all, rich and poor.

In 1874, a Norwegian physician named Gerhard Henrik Armauer Hansen was the first to identify the *Mycobacterium leprae* bacillus as causing leprosy. There are in fact two forms of this leprosy: the first, a limited tuberculoid form that produces a few small skin lesions and enlarged nerves; and the second, a more extensive lepromatous form that consists of multiple hard nodules and skin folds that appear on the face and particularly around the nose and eyes. Until the use of modern drugs, those suffering from the disease were banished from the societies in which they lived, or at least segregated, and their expected life span once the disease had manifested itself was expected to be no more than nine years. Poor nutrition often led to the weakening of the immune system, enabling opportunistic infections such as tuberculosis to settle in.[70] Those suffering from this disease in nineteenth-century Jerusalem lived in hovels situated just inside the Old

City and to the east of the Zion Gate, and they appear in a number of photographs from that period.

New evidence on Hansen's disease emerged unexpectedly at the Akeldama Cemetery in the Hinnom Valley, close to the southern foot of Mount Zion in Jerusalem, when signs of leprosy were detected in a shrouded skeleton found in a tomb dating from the time of Jesus. The rock-hewn tomb came to light in 2000 during a tour that I arranged for students from the University of North Carolina at Charlotte to the well-known ancient cemetery of Akeldama and the Hinnom Valley.

We stumbled across the tomb entrance entirely by accident. The tomb had recently been robbed, and freshly burrowed earth and scattered fragments of ossuaries were visible next to it. The full story of the discovery will be given later on in this book, but what really astounded me when we eventually crawled into the tomb, apart from the scene of devastation with smashed ossuaries and scattered bones left behind by the modern tomb robbers, was the excellent preservation of a burial shroud covering the skeletal remains and a reddish-brown clump of hair of an adult man in one of the loculi (*kokhim*) in a lower chamber. This was an unexpected discovery. A sample of the shroud was immediately sent to the States for radiocarbon dating, which confirmed that it dated to the first century CE, and the scientific study of the remains began. The multidisciplinary scientific team investigating the shrouded man concluded that he had been co-infected with tuberculosis and leprosy.[71] The skeleton of the shrouded man was not so well preserved, but a metatarsal bone was identified with very clear evidence of pathological change ascribable to leprosy. The evidence for leprosy from the Shroud Tomb is the oldest archaeological evidence for Hansen's disease found in the Holy Land, but, more importantly, it underlines for the first time that in all probability *some* of the lepers Jesus encountered suffered from true leprosy and not just from *psoriasis* or other skin ailments.

Jesus, having established himself comfortably in the house of Mary and Martha at Bethany, spent the entire Passover week traveling to Jerusalem visiting the Temple where he taught, talking to people and exchanging views, and to the Pools of Bethesda and Siloam where he healed and cared for the diseased, among them lepers and the disabled. At face value, none of these activities could be regarded as seditious, however extreme his teachings might have been. So what was it that led Jesus on a direct collision course with the local Jewish and Roman authorities? In order to fully understand the "how" and "why" of this unusual situation, I will first present a comprehensive picture of what the city looked like when Jesus visited it in the year 30 CE. After all, archaeological excavations in the last three decades have brought to light a wealth of new information about the city, much of it vitally important for the details of Jesus's final days.

THREE

FESTIVITIES AT
THE HOUSE OF GOD

*"The Passover of the Jews was near, and Jesus went up to Jerusalem.
In the Temple he found people selling cattle, sheep, and doves, and the
money-changers seated at their tables. Making a whip of cords, he drove
all of them out of the Temple, both the sheep and the cattle. He also
poured out the coins of the money-changers and overturned their tables.
He told those who were selling the doves, 'Take these things out of here!
Stop making my Father's House a market-place!'"*

(*John 2:13–16*)

A s Jesus descended the steep slope of the Mount of Olives toward
the city, he must have been impressed by the beauty of the city
that spread out before him. Jerusalem, like many important cities
in ancient Palestine, was surrounded on all sides by strong and high
battlements and well-defended gates. It was a city strung across a
number of hills, its residential quarters linked by a web of winding
streets and alleyways, and on the slopes of the hills were ascending
tiers of flat-roofed dwellings. There were many hundreds of these,
with a few public buildings and prominent residences showing up
here and there. At the top of one of these hills was a very large royal
palace, the residence of the Roman governor, which dominated the
Upper City from the west. But the jewel in the crown was undoubtedly the Jewish Temple, which dazzled those who entered the city

from afar. Situated on a massive rectangular platform on the east side of the city, it was truly one of the wonders of the ancient Near Eastern world. The building gleamed all over with gold and polished stones. Glinting in the sun, it served as a happy beacon to weary Jewish pilgrims nearing the city at the end of a long journey.

When Jesus first set foot in Jerusalem, the city was a place of great antiquity with a history going back a couple of thousand years. Originally only a small town next to a bubbling spring of water at the beginning of the second millennium BCE, the city eventually expanded and receded in size at different periods of time over the next millennium or so, finally reaching its largest area, spread over two hills, at the time of King Hezekiah in the late eighth century BCE. Unfortunately, this expanded city fell to the Babylonian sword in 586/587 BCE, the holy Jewish Temple went up in flames, and the sacred Ark of the Covenant was lost forever. Hence, the Jerusalem seen by Jesus was not the one from Old Testament times, but the one rebuilt almost from scratch by the Jewish rulers of the Hasmonean dynasty in the late second century BCE. It was later richly embellished with monumental buildings by Herod the Great after he entered the city in triumph as King of the Jews in 37 BCE. It was Herod who rebuilt the Jewish Temple, making it gleam with gold and turning it into a wonder for everyone reaching Jerusalem.

The general appearance of Jerusalem has changed quite considerably since the time of Jesus circa 30 CE, and some of its important parts are buried deep beneath the level of the present-day houses of the Old City of Jerusalem and are impossible to access even by excavation. Topographically, the city was built on a number of sprawling hills, principally the South-Eastern Hill and the Western Hill. The heart of the city goes back at least a couple of thousand years before the time of Jesus and it was situated on the South-Eastern Hill, the area later known as the "City of David," since it was here King David built his palace and the fortress of Zion. David's Tomb was also supposed to have been within the city, but it is more likely to have been outside on the slope facing the city from the west (i.e., somewhere on the slope of the traditional Mount Zion of today). The South-Eastern Hill was known in Jesus's day as the "Lower City." Mount Moriah was linked by a natural saddle to the City of David from the north, and it was on its summit that Solomon built the Temple to God. In Jesus's day Mount Moriah had disappeared almost entirely beneath the massive platform of the Herodian Temple Mount.

The Western Hill comprises the area of traditional Mount Zion, with the present-day Armenian and Jewish Quarters to its north and east respectively. At the time of Jesus the Western Hill was known as the "Upper City" and it was distinguished by the Royal Palace (known also as the *Praetorium*) on its summit and by three prominent fortified towers at its northern end (named Hippicus, Phasael, and Mariamme). On the northwestern and northeastern sides of the city are the smaller hills of Golgotha and Bezetha. Cleaving its way through the center of the city from north to south is the deep Tyropoeon ("Cheese-maker's") Valley, which at its southern end separated the Upper City from the Lower City. A gentle valley, the Transversal Valley, separated the Upper City from the hill of Golgotha to its north. Surrounding the city to the west, south, and east are two major ravines, the Hinnom and Kidron Valleys, both of which join up near the southeastern flank of the city, close to the place known as "Tophet" where in Old Testament times small children were cruelly sacrificed.

Every city has a weak chink in its armor, an "Achilles' Heel" in its defenses, and in Jerusalem this was its northern flank. Everywhere else, the city possessed excellent natural defenses, but on the north side where there was no valley or formidable natural barrier, only gentle sloping and rocky ground, armies could easily attack and bring the walls tumbling down with their sappers and military machines. Hence, throughout history there were repeated attacks from this side of the city. It was here Pompey and his Roman soldiers attacked the city in 63 BCE; more than one hundred years later, Titus, at the head of Roman legions, broke through the northern fortifications during a lengthy siege of the city that eventually ended in its destruction in 70 CE.[72]

The city at the time of Jesus was defended by two strong fortification walls, with heavy rectangular towers and gates built at intervals. Our principal source of historical information about the defenses of first-century Jerusalem is in the writings of Josephus, namely his books *Jewish Wars* and *Jewish Antiquities*, which were written between 93–94 CE. The older of these defense walls is known as the "First Wall," and was originally built around 140 BCE by the Hasmoneans, Simon and Jonathan. It was an impressive wall, 3 to 5 meters in width and built of alternating courses of hewn stones to a height of about 13 meters. This fortification wall protected much of the city, including its "Lower" and "Upper" parts. The northwest angle of the First Wall was occupied by Herod's palace (also known as the *Praetorium,* where Jesus was tried), whereas the southeast corner was taken up by the large Pool of Siloam.

The "Second Wall" was built to incorporate an area outside the city, namely the southern part of the area that Josephus referred to as the "plain," which is in the upper part of the Tyropoeon Valley, and also part of the new quarter of Bezetha, which was situated to the northwest of the Temple Mount. Unfortunately, not one segment of the Second Wall has been uncovered in archaeological excavations, and all we know about it is from Josephus' writings. This wall is believed to have excluded the quarried area of the hill of Golgotha—the place of Jesus's crucifixion—to its west, as well as the Amygdalon ("Towers") Pool, which was a large rectangular water reservoir, and its adjacent gardens. The Bethesda Pool was probably also outside the wall. The exact date when the Second Wall was built is unclear, but many scholars believe that Herod the Great was responsible for its construction perhaps early on in his reign (in the 30s BCE). It would make sense

(Luke 2:41–50). They clearly went into the Temple precincts. Hence, Jerusalem was definitely not a faraway and unknown city when Jesus arrived there for his final days. He knew the city quite well and had been there often, not just as a child but also as an adult. Jerusalem was also important to Jesus because it was in a village named Beth Hacerem, in the western hinterland of the city, that John the Baptist was born and spent much of his life.[75] Hence, to be in Jerusalem was one way of proclaiming to the crowds that John the Baptist was his mentor and that he was there with John's blessing (Mark 11:28–32).

On the day Jesus arrived in Jerusalem from Bethany during his final week, the first thing he did was to visit the Temple Mount, as did many other pilgrims for the Passover holiday. Indeed, Mark puts it quite bluntly: "then he [Jesus] entered Jerusalem and went into the Temple; and when he had looked around at everything, as it was already late, he went out to Bethany with the twelve [disciples]" (11:11). Crowds of Jewish pilgrims frequented Jerusalem at least three times a year, on Passover, the Feast of Tabernacles, and Pentecost, as required by Jewish custom (Exodus 23:14; Deuteronomy 16:1–16). Josephus mentions that many groups of pilgrims came from the rural areas and during one of the festivals "the whole neighborhood of the Temple and the entire city were crowded with country-folk" (*War* I.253). We also know of visitors who arrived in Jerusalem from long distances and from distant countries (such as Gaul and Mesopotamia).[76] Josephus adds in regard to the Passover festival that "they [the Jews] celebrated with gladness, and it is their custom to slaughter a greater number of sacrifices at this festival than at any other, and an innumerable multitude of people come down from the country and even from abroad to worship God" (*Antiq.* XVII.213–214). Many of the pilgrims stayed in tent encampments outside the city in the area to the north and east of Golgotha (close to the present-day Damascus Gate), but undoubtedly there were also inns inside the city for those who were better off financially. Indeed, in the "Theodotus Inscription" dating from the first century, which was found in Jerusalem, we hear of an assembly hall (synagogue) in the Lower City and of "the guest room, the chambers, and the water fittings, as an inn for those in need from foreign parts . . ." The problem that the city authorities had was how to provide food for the multitude of pilgrims living in tents. In addition to this, there was also a great demand for beasts for sacrifice. The Passover lamb, which could only be lawfully slain in Jerusalem, is referred to by Josephus, who speaks of hundreds of thousands of Passover sacrifices, but some scholars think this may be an exaggeration.[77]

A question arises as to when exactly Jesus arrived in Jerusalem. According to the Fourth Gospel Jesus came to Bethany "six days before Passover" (John 12:1), whereas Mark says Jesus was in Bethany two days before Passover. This apparent contradiction may be resolved if one attributes the story of the Priest's plot as it appears in Mark (14:1–2) as occurring on *one* of the days of the holy week and not on the first day of Jesus's arrival.[78] John's account of Jesus's arrival makes more sense since there was a practice at the time among Jewish pilgrims going to Jerusalem for Passover to prepare themselves with purification in water before the actual holiday: "Now the Passover of the Jews was at hand: and many went up to Jerusalem to purify themselves" (John 11:55). As we shall see, these purification procedures most likely took place in the Siloam and Bethesda Pools, situated respectively on the south and north sides of the Temple precincts.

The Temple was originally situated on a massive elevated esplanade, now known as the Temple Mount (or in Arabic as the "Haram al-Sharif"). It was truly one of the wonders of the ancient world, and its size was remarkable.[79] For comparison purposes, the Temple platform was more than twice the size of the ancient Athenian Acropolis. Solomon's Temple was rebuilt and restored on a number of occasions before being utterly destroyed by the Babylonians in 586/587 BCE, but the most serious rebuilding was undertaken by Herod the Great more than five centuries or so later, over a period of slightly less than two years, and it was completed in 18 BCE.[80] It is sad to say but there are absolutely no archaeological vestiges that have survived of the Temple built by Herod or by his predecessors, except perhaps for a deep rock-cut scarp investigated in 1872 immediately northwest of the Dome of the Rock, beneath a medieval structure known as the Masjid al-Nabiy. In my opinion this little-known scarp probably marks the position of the western wall of the Temple building.[81]

The construction work that was done on the Temple precincts— on the Royal Stoa and on the surrounding porticoes, on the Inner and Outer Courts, and on the portals and passages leading into the esplanade—were initiated by Herod the Great in the late first century BCE, but continued long after his death in 4 BCE. According to John (2:20) the construction of the Temple took forty-six years, but this reference is not to the sanctuary itself (completed in 18 BCE) but to the Temple Mount proper. It would appear that some of the building operations were still going on near to the time of the Roman destruction of the city in 70 CE. This is clear from certain unfinished pavements in a street adjacent to the northern end of the western wall of the Temple Mount that have been uncovered in archaeological excavations.[82] The outer walls of the Temple Mount were constructed of massive hewn stones, some more than one hundred tons in weight, and the admiration that Jesus's disciples had for this work is expressed by Mark: "Teacher, behold, what manner of stones and what manner of buildings!" (13:1; cf. Luke 21:5).[83] The construction of the Temple Mount is undeniably an engineering feat that has never been surpassed in Jerusalem.

With the ransacking of the Temple in 70 CE, the treasures that were kept within—a golden candelabrum, silver trumpets, a showbread table, and many other precious objects—were taken back to Rome as spoil by the conqueror Titus. An interesting depiction of the Jewish candelabrum (*menorah*) with an animal sacrificial scene taking place in front of the Temple exists on a unique marble plaque from

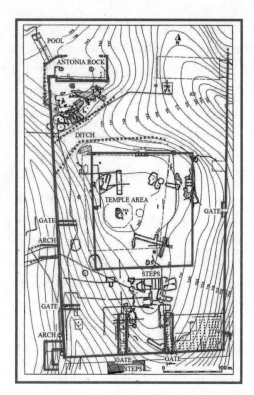

Figure 2: Plan of the Temple Mount area based on archaeo-logical remains.

the late Roman period, which I came across quite by chance while visiting Barcelona.[84] What is important is that it shows the candelabrum mounted on a plinth (decorated here with an ox-head) and not on tripod legs as in later depictions.[85] Various theories have been put forward regarding the later vicissitudes of the Temple treasures.[86]

The Temple Mount is like the Holy Grail for many Jewish archaeologists who would like to conduct scientific excavations there, but the precincts of the Haram al-Sharif are out of bounds since this is a Muslim holy site and religious sensitivities have to be preserved. The only digging operations done there in recent years were made by the Muslim authorities in order to allow access for worshippers to the lower mosque in the area of Solomon's Stables. This work was not done with proper archaeological supervision, which is a pity. The Temple Mount was the focus for much western exploration in the nineteenth century, particularly with the work undertaken by the intrepid Charles Wilson and Charles Warren. Wilson mapped the Temple Mount area in 1865 with the assistance of soldiers from the Royal Engineers, and recorded many of its underground chambers, cisterns, and conduits.[87] Subsequently, Warren conducted hair-raising and dangerous excavations in shafts and tunnels along the Temple Mount walls from 1867 to 1870, with the assistance of Henry Birtles. They encountered many difficulties and objections to their work from the Turkish authorities and some of the local inhabitants. They had interesting adventures and sometimes narrowly avoided losing their lives. These explorers undertook the work on behalf of the Palestine Exploration Fund, a society that was established in England in 1865 under the patronage of Queen Victoria. Charles Warren, whose archaeological achievements at the Temple Mount are legendary, later became infamous as the Commissioner of Police in London leading the (unsuccessful) hunt in 1881 for the notorious "Jack the Ripper" responsible for the gruesome murder of countless women in Whitechapel in London.[88]

What do we know about Jesus's movements in the city? The Gospels actually tell us very little. However, archaeology can fill in some of the gaps. Coming from Bethany, Jesus would have entered the city at the gate near the Siloam Pool, and then would have ascended the main street leading to the southern wall of the Temple Mount. This broad stepped street, paved with enormous rectangular flagstones, has recently been uncovered in archaeological work just north of the Siloam Pool. It was here Jesus had a choice: He could go directly into the Outer Court (*hieron*) by climbing the steps leading to one of the southern gates in the Temple Mount. These gates led to subterranean passages ascending north beneath the Royal Stoa in the direction of the Holy Temple. Alternatively, Jesus might have climbed the magnificent flight of steps with landings, perched on top of a series of vaults, and at the gate just above "Robinson's Arch" would have entered into the magnificent columned building known as the Royal Stoa. Josephus wrote that a person standing in the area of the Royal Stoa looking down "would become dizzy, and his vision would become unable to reach the end of so measureless a depth" (*Antiq.* XV.410–413). It is noteworthy that in archaeological excavations just below the southwest corner of the Temple Mount a broken monumental Hebrew inscription was found, reading "[Belonging] to the place [literally, house] of trumpeting." Scholars assume its ending would have been "to herald the Sabbath" and that the inscription was a built feature, perhaps even a seat, marking the pinnacle of the Temple Mount. Josephus actually refers to the spot: ". . . it was the custom for one of the priests to stand and to give notice, by sound of trumpet, in the afternoon of the approach, and on the following evening of the close, of every seventh day, announcing to the people the respective hours for ceasing work and for resuming their labors" (*War* IV.582–583).[89]

Judging by the testimony of the Gospels, Jesus arrived daily in Jerusalem from Bethany and spent some of the days leading up to his arrest, trial, and crucifixion teaching in the area of the Temple.[90] The reference to the "Temple" in the Gospels clearly does not refer to the sanctuary itself, but to the Outer Court and to other peripheral areas around the Temple Mount, which were even open to Gentiles. It was in the Outer Court that Jesus came across the money changers and people selling animals (cattle and sheep) for the Temple sacrifices, and with a whip of cords drove out the merchants, overturned the tables of the money changers, and told those who were selling doves to leave the area (John 2:13–16). Confirmation regarding the existence of money changers and stalls selling sacrificial animals appear in rabbinical writings (m. Shekalim 1:3); they were probably set up in the area within Herod's extension works, particularly on the southern side of the Temple Mount, where the Jewish purification laws apparently did not fully apply, or at least were not as strict.[91]

While Jesus is portrayed as creating momentary mayhem in the Temple area, Mark relates that after this incident he immediately carried on with his teaching in the Outer Court, which Jesus described as a "den of thieves" (11:17). This suggests that his actions were not as violent as they have sometimes been perceived, otherwise Jesus would immediately have been arrested by the Temple police and ousted unceremoniously from the Temple Mount. Temple police or attendants kept order within the Temple Mount, and this was essential, especially during the festivities with crowds of people milling around. Gentiles were also allowed on the Temple Mount but only in the Outer Court. Two Greek inscriptions (one complete and one fragmentary) are known that were originally placed on a screen separating the Inner and Outer Courts of the Temple Mount, forbidding Gentiles from entering into the Inner Court. According to Josephus, four degrees of purity were mandated for the Temple area with clearly defined separations: the first being the Outer Court, which was open to Gentiles, except for women who were menstruating; the second the Inner Court to which men and women were allowed access if they had first undergone purification; the third a court in which only purified men were allowed; and, finally, the fourth where only priests could go in their holy vestments (*Apion* II.103–104). The sanctuary could only be accessed by the High Priest himself.[92] According to John, Jesus also walked in one part of the Temple area known as "Solomon's Porch" (10:22–23). This porch is most probably to be identified as the name of the portico that ran along the eastern side of the Temple Mount, and it is at this location that the "Beautiful Gate" should also be identified (Acts 3:2).

The limited and incidental information about places in Jerusalem provided in the Gospels does not contradict what is known from archaeological excavations; in fact they fit in fairly well. One such example is the story of the Last Supper as given by Mark, which was followed by Matthew and Luke in almost every detail:

"On the first day of Unleavened Bread, when the Passover lamb is sacrificed, his disciples said to him, 'Where do you want us to go and make the preparations for you to eat the Passover?' So he sent two of his disciples, saying to them, 'Go into the city, and a man carrying a jar of water will meet you; follow him, and wherever he enters, say to the owner of the house, "The Teacher asks, Where is my guest room where I may eat the Passover with my disciples?" He will show you a large room upstairs, furnished and ready. Make preparations for us there.' So the disciples set out and went to the city, and found everything as he had told them; and they prepared the Passover meal.

When it was evening, he came with the twelve. And when they had taken their places and were eating, Jesus said, 'Truly I tell you, one of you will betray me, one who is eating with me.' They began to be distressed and to say to him one after another, 'Surely, not I?' He said to them, 'It is one of the twelve, one who is dipping bread into the bowl with me. For the Son of Man goes as it is written of him, but woe to that one by whom the Son of Man is betrayed! It would have been better for that one not to have been born.' While they were eating, he took a loaf of bread, and after blessing it he broke it, gave it to them, and said, 'Take; this is my body.' Then he took a cup, and after giving thanks he gave it to them, and all of them drank from it. He said to them, 'This is my blood of the covenant, which is poured out for many. Truly I tell you, I will never again drink of the fruit of the vine until that day when I drink it new in the kingdom of God.' When they had sung the hymn, they went out to the Mount of Olives" (14:12–26).

Mark, in speaking of the preparations made for the Passover sacrificial meal, has Jesus, who is presumably at Bethany, giving two of his disciples directions so that they might find the place where the meal is to take place in Jerusalem. We are told very little about the movement of Jesus's disciples within the city. They are there, but not there—almost invisible. Why is this? Perhaps this was deliberate and purposeful. Perhaps Jesus thought that being surrounded by a band of disciples might be suspicious to city authorities always on the lookout for possible insurrectionists. Alternatively, Jesus might have wanted to attract new followers and being continuously surrounded by disciples might have been a hindrance. John tells us that the rendezvous spot with his disciples was at Gethsemane outside the city (18:2).

Jesus rented a room in the house especially for the occasion of the Passover meal, which must have cost him a bit because free room was always at a premium during the Passover holiday. Jesus went on to say to his disciples, "he [the landlord] will show you a large room upstairs, furnished and ready."

The reference in Mark to "a man carrying a jar of water" suggests the house was at a location close to the Gihon Spring or to the Siloam Pool. This is where people filled their jars with water and carried them back home, otherwise they would have drawn water from cisterns next to their homes. The location near the Siloam Pool makes sense for a number of other reasons. The disciples would have approached the city from the direction of the road from Bethany, entering through a gate at the lower end of the city close to the spring and pool. There were one or perhaps even two gates at the southeast corner of the city, and one of these was excavated by the British archaeologist Kathleen Kenyon in the 1960s.[93] In recent excavations, a large portion of the stepped Siloam Pool was uncovered, and on its northern side is a magnificent broad, paved, and stepped street ascending from the pool along the lower Tyropoeon Valley toward the Temple Mount. We can easily imagine this street as the meeting place of the disciples with the man with the jar of water.

Another useful piece of information is Mark's account of the Passover meal taking place in an "upper room." On face value, this should not be surprising because two-storey houses dating from this period have been excavated in Jerusalem and especially in the Upper City, and some of them are palatial. Close to the Siloam Pool and on the lower eastern slope of the Upper City, a series of rock-cuttings were excavated, representing the "negative" of the back of a three- or even four-storey house dating from the first century CE.[94] A room rented in a house such as this might have been used for the Last Supper of Jesus.

The Lower City was thought to have been populated by the poorer sections of Jerusalem's society, and so it made sense to scholars, based on their understanding of the Gospel accounts, that this was where Jesus would have felt most at home. This general view is reflected in the "Holyland" model of first-century Jerusalem, prepared by Hebrew University Professor Michael Avi-Yonah, with the Lower City covered with small cramped houses with flat roofs, and with the Upper City having fancy dwellings with red-tiled roofs. Recent archaeological work, however, has overturned the theory that the Lower City was the exclusive domain of the poor. First, none of the domestic dwellings unearthed in Jerusalem, whether in the Upper or Lower parts of the city, had tiled roofs, except perhaps for a few public buildings here and there. Not one roof tile from the first century CE has been found in Jerusalem excavations. Second, a number of extremely well-built and palatial domestic buildings have been uncovered in the area of the Lower City. One of these was tentatively identified by its excavator as the Palace of Queen Helene of Adiabene, though it could conceivably have been the Palace of Agrippa or Berenice, since both of these Josephus tells us were situated not too far away from the Temple Mount. These buildings may also hint at the possible location of the undiscovered old Palace of the Hasmoneans (*War* II.427–429; cf. *Antiq.* XX.189 ff).[95] The popular notion that the Lower City was the haunt of Jesus precisely because this was where the poor lived is incorrect. Strange as it may seem, the "poor" in Jerusalem were probably quite well off and were able to benefit economically from the special status and prestige of the "City of the Temple." As a city attracting massive

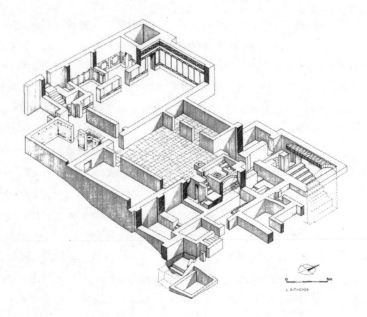

*Figure 3: Reconstruction drawing of a large Herodian mansion in the
Upper City of Jerusalem.*

Jewish pilgrimages three times a year and with permanent ongoing building works on the Temple precincts and elsewhere, it seems
unlikely there were many unemployed among its inhabitants. Hence,
a "poor" family in Jerusalem probably possessed the same social and
economic advantages as a "rich" family living in one of the outlying
villages of Jerusalem or in other places in Judea.

But where was the exact spot of the Last Supper? I would suggest
that it was in close proximity to the Siloam Pool. Today, the traditional site of the Last Supper is shown to visitors and tourists within a
complex of medieval structures on the summit of present-day Mount
Zion, some distance from the Siloam Pool.[96] The current traditional
room itself is undoubtedly of Crusader date. However, there is nothing to this medieval tradition and so the search must go on.

Unlike the three other Gospels, John provides a different version of
the farewell meal on Passover Eve, with interesting information about

purification practices with water that may have been specific to Jesus and his followers.

> "Now before the festival of the Passover, Jesus knew that his hour had come to depart from this world and go to the Father. Having loved his own who were in the world, he loved them to the end. The devil had already put it into the heart of Judas son of Simon Iscariot to betray him. And during supper Jesus, knowing that the Father had given all things into his hands, and that he had come from God and was going to God, got up from the table, took off his outer robe, and tied a towel around himself. Then he poured water into a basin and began to wash the disciples' feet and to wipe them with the towel that was tied around him" (13:1–5).

Clearly this would have been an unusual act of humility since the act of purification with water should have been undertaken by one of the disciples. Hence, it is not surprising that the disciple Peter questions what Jesus is doing. Peter went on to suggest that if Jesus was already washing feet, perhaps their heads and hands should be washed as well.

The description in John of the washing of the disciples' feet fits in well with the multiplicity of ritual water-purification procedures in Jerusalem in the first century CE, though foot-washing undertaken by the host or house-owner was thought to have been performed *before,* not after, the meal. In archaeological excavations conducted in the Jewish Quarter of Jerusalem, ritual bathing pools (*miqwa'ot*) were uncovered in the basements of houses dating from the first century CE, with small foot-baths next to the entrances. Those entering into the *miqweh* were required to first wash their feet. In antiquity, the foot was regarded as a symbol of humility and of willing servitude. This was because the foot was the part of the body closest to the ground and so could easily come into contact with impurities. There was also the practice of the ritual cleansing of hands in water prior to the partaking of a meal, or before prayers.[97] This may not have been mentioned by John simply because it was common practice, whereas the ritual purification of the disciples' feet after the meal was deemed unusual. However, it may also be that Jesus did not believe in the constant washing of hands and showed more flexibility on the subject, since Mark states the following: "And when they [the Pharisees and Scribes in Jerusalem] saw some of his [Jesus's] disciples eat bread with defiled, that is to say, with unwashed hands, they found fault" (7:2–3, 5). The Jewish practice of the time was clearly the purification of the entire body, with the cleansing of hands prior to meals. In Luke we read: "And when the Pharisee saw it, he marveled that he [Jesus] had not first washed before dinner" (11:38). Either this was a reference to the total immersion in a ritual pool, or to hand-washing.

What emerges is that Jesus and his followers did not abstain from water purification procedures, but may have practiced rituals slightly different from those known to their fellow Jews. Judging by the reference in John (13:10), we may assume that Jesus and his disciples immersed in a ritual pool prior to the meal, and although they were sometimes averse to washing hands, they may have done this as well, or perhaps they regarded their total immersion sufficient. In rabbinical writings we hear of the use of stone vessels for the purpose of the ritual cleansing of hands, and it is not surprising that in John we are told that six stone jars at Cana were used "for the Jewish rites of purification" (2:6).[98] It would appear that large lathe-turned jars of this type, known as *qalal*, were used together with small hand-carved mugs for ritual hand-washing purposes. A variety of smaller lathe-turned and hand-carved stone vessels, such as bowls and platters, are known, and workshops in which they were made have been uncovered at several locations in the hinterland of the city.[99] An enormous quantity of stone vessels have been recovered in Jerusalem, indicating that the city's inhabitants were fastidious in ensuring ritual purity during the early first century CE and even more so a few decades after Jesus's death, when between 50 and 70 CE "purity burst forth in Israel."[100]

The passage in John might have implied that at the meal's end, the observance was to purify the head, hands, and feet of the person partaking of the meal (13:1–5). Whether this was general practice among Jews at that time or something more specific to Jesus's followers is unclear. I would think that this was something unique to Jesus's group, which explains the objections made by the Pharisees and Scribes in Jerusalem. We might speculate that these rituals were adapted by Jesus's followers from those previously used by John the Baptist.

In those days the sacrificial Passover meal had to be eaten within the walls of the city.[101] We assume the Last Supper was indeed the Eve of Passover meal, but the chronology of the final days is uncertain because of ambiguities in the Gospels. Mark has the twelve disciples gathering in the evening, sitting with Jesus and eating. Matthew implies that they ate meat in addition to the unleavened bread and wine. People at that time ate separate courses of food on small saucer dishes rather than on large plates as we do today. John speaks of the disciples "reclining next to the table." This was probably in a room known as a *triclinium*, the participants spread out in a semi-reclined state with cushions on couches or low beds. These would have been arranged in a typical Π-shaped form as we know from Roman artistic depictions.[102] At the end of the meal, Jesus and his disciples sang a hymn together and then left for the Mount of Olives and Gethsemane.

To get to Gethsemane, Jesus and his disciples had to exit the city; they probably did this via the same gate they had entered near the Siloam Pool. Walking north parallel to the bed of the Kidron Valley, passing rock-hewn tomb monuments on the right, one of which is the so called Tomb of Absalom, they would have reached the lower parts of the Mount of Olives. Mark goes on to describe what happened next:

"They went to a place called Gethsemane; and he said to his disciples, 'Sit here while I pray.' He took with him Peter and James and John, and began to be distressed and agitated. And he said to them, 'I am deeply grieved, even to death; remain here, and keep awake.' And going a little farther, he threw himself on the ground and prayed that, if it were possible, the hour might pass from him. He said, 'Abba, Father, for you all things are possible; remove this cup from me; yet, not what I want, but what you want.' He came and found them sleeping; and he said to Peter, 'Simon, are you asleep? Could you not keep awake one hour? Keep awake and pray that you may not come into the time of trial; the spirit indeed is willing, but the flesh is weak.' And again he went away and prayed, saying the same words. And once more he came and found them sleeping, for their eyes were very heavy; and they did not know what to say to him. He came a third time and said to them, 'Are you still sleeping and taking your rest? Enough! The hour has come; the Son of Man is betrayed into the hands of sinners. Get up, let us be going. See, my betrayer is at hand.'" (14:32–42).

Why did Jesus go out to Gethsemane on the Mount of Olives following the Last Supper? We know on previous evenings Jesus stayed at his lodgings at Bethany, though Gethsemane was a daytime rendezvous for his disciples. So what was the purpose of this outing? One possibility is that due to the difficulties of sleeping in the city because of the festivities and the lateness of the hour, Jesus and his disciples elected to take temporary accommodations on the slope of the Mount of Olives instead of returning to Bethany, an hour's walk away. What it clear is that the room rented out for the Last Supper was not suitable for sleeping purposes. According to Mark and Matthew, Jesus arrived at the place known as Gethsemane where his disciples promptly fell asleep. Matthew and Luke make it clear that Jesus had visited Geth-semane and the Mount of Olives before, but they do not indicate an exact location (Matthew 24:3; Luke 21:37; 22:39). John is much more specific about the geography of the place, describing it as being on the other side of the Kidron Valley (i.e., east of the city), "where there was a garden [*kēpos*] into which he entered, himself and his disciples. Now Judas also, who betrayed him, knew the place, for Jesus often resorted thither with his disciples" (18:1–2). The term, which is used here for a garden, can also be used for an agricultural plot and there were un-doubtedly terraced groves on the slopes of the Mount of Olives. The Greek word Gethsemane derives from the Aramaic or Hebrew word for "oil press," suggesting that there was an oil press in the area. Near Jerusalem, a number of oil presses have been found within caves, nota-bly at Ras Abu-Ma'aruf, not far from Tel el-Ful, and so it is plausible that Jesus and his disciples might have taken shelter in a cave. At the traditional site of Gethsemane on the lower slope of the Mount of Olives a large cave is pointed out as the spot of Jesus's arrest.[103]

It would appear that the idea of staying the night at Gethsemane was actually something prearranged by Jesus and his disciples and this destination was undoubtedly known to Judas. When Judas ar-rived at the spot in the company of soldiers and Temple police, Jesus was arrested and taken away along the Kidron Valley and back into the city. Mark (14:51) relates the strange incident at Gethsemane of a young man wearing "a linen cloth cast about him, over his naked body" who fled from the scene when an attempt was made to arrest him. Who this person was and what part he had to play in the Geth-semane story is unknown. All of Jesus's disciples fled for their lives, probably along the upper reaches of the Mount of Olives and in the direction of Bethany.

What happens next is mysterious. Jesus was led through the city, but instead of being taken to await trial in the prison of the Jewish

SIGNS AND WONDERS AT BETHESDA AND SILOAM

"The disciples of John {the Baptist} reported all these things to him. So John summoned two of his disciples and sent them to the Lord to ask, 'Are you the one who is to come, or are we to wait for another?' When the men had come to him, they said, 'John the Baptist has sent us to you to ask, "Are you the one who is to come, or are we to wait for another?"' Jesus had just then cured many people of diseases, plagues, and evil spirits, and had given sight to many who were blind.

And he answered them, 'Go and tell John what you have seen and heard: the blind receive their sight, the lame walk, the lepers are cleansed, the deaf hear, the dead are raised, the poor have good news brought to them. And blessed is anyone who takes no offense at me.'"

(*Luke 7:18–23*)

The story of the arrest and trial of Jesus has been examined by numerous scholars, and many are puzzled by the events as they appear in the Gospel accounts. Why did Jesus pose such a threat to the city authorities? Why did Jesus have to be killed and who, ultimately, was responsible for making that fateful decision? Were the Jewish or Roman authorities to blame? Since Jesus made a disturbance by overturning tables in the Outer Court of the Temple, why was he not arrested on the spot by the Temple Police? And why did the authorities wait until the beginning of Passover to arrest Jesus at Gethsemane? Was this because he was suspected of being the leader of a popular movement of resistance and the Romans and/or Temple Police feared that arresting him in a public place might lead to rioting? Since Jesus's activities were seemingly thought to be seditious by the Roman authorities, why was Jesus first taken to the High Priest's house after his arrest and not straight to the prison at the *Praetorium*? Why did Jesus undergo two separate trials, first before select members of the Sanhedrin Court and finally in front of Pontius Pilate? Why was Jesus brought before Herod Antipas for questioning, when he evidently lacked jurisdiction on legal matters in Judaea? And why did Pilate even consider relinquishing his control to Herod on the matter of Jesus's guilt?[104] Finally, how were the Gospel writers' sources privy to what was going on behind closed doors during the Thursday night session with members of the Sanhedrin, and early on the Friday morning at the trial with Pontius Pilate?

The Gospels are the main source of information we have for the final week in the life of Jesus. They suggest the arrest was made at Gethsemane on counts of blasphemy, sedition, or a combination of the two, and that it was instigated by the Temple authorities and followed through by the Roman authorities, albeit somewhat reluctantly. Another consideration that might affect the way Jesus's arrest and trial was portrayed in the Gospels is the date of their composition. Scholars are in agreement that the earliest of the Gospels only began to be formulated a couple of decades following Jesus's death, in the devastating aftermath of the Jewish revolt against the Romans (from 66 CE), which resulted in the fall of Jerusalem and the destruction of the Temple (in 70 CE). One result of this was the somewhat acrimonious parting of ways between mainstream Judaism and the incipient "Jesus" movement. This may explain the antagonism evident in the Gospels toward the collective "Jews," of which there were religious authorities, civic authorities, and nameless "crowds."[105]

This might also help explain puzzling elements in the accounts: the lengthy deliberations at the house of the High Priest on the guilt of Jesus but without any certain resolution, and Pilate's rather weak and out-of-character performance during the trial, with the curious incident of Pilate washing his hands (which was not a Roman custom but a distortion of the Jewish purification rite of *netilat yadaim*). It clearly suited the purposes of the Gospel writers to make Pilate a sympathetic person recognizing Jesus's innocence all along, but one whose hand was deliberately forced by the Jerusalem religious authorities, on the one hand, and by the will of the antagonistic crowd milling around outside the *Praetorium*, on the other. In Matthew there is the following passage: "Pilate said to them [the crowds], 'Then what should I do with Jesus who is called the Messiah?' All of them said, 'Let him be crucified!' Then he asked, 'Why, what evil has he done?' But they shouted all the more, 'Let him be crucified!' So when Pilate saw that he could do nothing, but rather that a riot was beginning, he took some water and washed his hands before the crowd, saying, 'I am innocent of this man's blood; see to it yourselves.' Then the people as a whole answered, 'His blood be on us and on our children!'" (27:22–25). The negative image of the role of Jews as portrayed in this trial account would ultimately have a disastrous long-term effect with the development of anti-Semitism in the Middle Ages, and it led in part to the Inquisition, pogroms, and eventually to the Holocaust.

We could argue that Jesus's peaceful motives were misunderstood by the city authorities and thus he was framed and accused of blasphemy or sedition, both punishable by death. But what evidence do we have for this? Jesus's triumphal entrance into Jerusalem might have been construed by the Romans as dangerous fist-waving by a man in charge of a seditious mob of "out-of-towners," and that he was trying to set himself above the law as "King of the Jews" in direct opposition to their Imperial rule. I have already suggested that Jesus's entrance into Jerusalem was actually a modest affair; otherwise he on mankind might lead to some form of sedition [or revolt]. For it looked as if they would be guided by John in everything that they did. Herod decided therefore that it would be much better to strike first and be rid of him before his work led to an uprising, than to wait for an upheaval, get involved in a difficult situation and see his mistake" (XVII, 116–119).

The same probably happened to Jesus. His entrance into Jerusalem went largely unnoticed by the Romans and his activities close to the Temple were easily monitored and controlled by the Temple guards. But once Jesus began stirring up crowds of discontented and marginalized people in other parts of the city and doing "signs and wonders you will not believe" (John 4:48), it was then that he became a serious threat and could not be ignored.[106] At first, without hindrance from the city authorities, Jesus was able to work steadily as a healer and miracle-maker and to gather around him supporters in the same way he had done in the Galilee: "Jesus had just then cured many people of diseases, plagues, and evil spirits, and had given sight to many who were blind" (Luke 7:21). It was perhaps at this point that the Jewish and Roman city authorities were made aware of the connection between Jesus and the executed John and began to feel threatened by the large crowds milling around him. "Strike first and be rid of him," as Josephus put it, may have been their chosen policy to deal with the Jesus problem.

But what were the places in Jerusalem where Jesus might have drawn people to him, where he performed his healing activities? Other than at the Temple Mount, the only other open spaces inside the city where crowds could gather were at the amphitheater and theater—surely unsuitable since they were places of entertainment—and the Siloam and Bethesda Pools, which scholars for many years thought served primarily as water reservoirs. Were these suitable locations and could they have been used for water purification? What can archaeology tell us about these two pools?

In the first century the Jewish population in Palestine had a very distinctive practice of purification within water installations known as *miqwa'ot* (singular, *miqweh*; Hebrew for a "collection" or "gathering" [of water]). Large numbers of stepped-and-plastered *miqwa'ot* have been found in excavations in Jerusalem, in outlying villages, as well as at various rural locations. Most of the installations in Jerusalem were in basements of private dwellings and therefore served the specific domestic needs of the city inhabitants. Numerous examples are known from different parts of the city. A few slightly larger *miqwa'ot* are known in the immediate area of the Temple Mount, but it is hard to see how these installations might have met the needs of tens of thousands of Jewish pilgrims from outside the city attending the festivities at the Temple three times a year. The logistics of getting a multitude of people in and out of these relatively small installations would have been impossible. Where did they all go to purify themselves upon reaching Jerusalem and before ascending to the courts of the Temple? Could it have been at the Bethesda and Siloam Pools situated on either side of the Temple Mount?

In an article published in 2005 I suggested that the Bethesda and Siloam Pools were not designed, as many thought, as reservoirs to conserve large quantities of rainwater for the city, but were actually purposefully built to accommodate all the ritual purification needs of Jewish pilgrims flocking to Jerusalem for the festivals.[107] Death and affliction greatly concerned the inhabitants of first-century Jerusalem trying desperately to maintain the overall ritual purity of their sacred city, and the annual influx of huge numbers of pilgrims bearing impurities scared them. At the same time, they could not prevent pilgrims from entering the city for the festivities, and many were frail and elderly, or diseased and seeking cures. Many of the diseased wanted to reach the proximity of the Jewish Temple, though none would have been allowed access to the holy areas. Only those deemed absolutely "pure" were allowed to officiate close to the Temple, and to that end crowds of pilgrims underwent mass purification ceremonies at the Bethesda and Siloam Pools before being allowed to enter the courts of the Temple Mount. Pilgrims also had to undergo a pre-scribed waiting period until sundown or to the next morning, before they could enter the inner Temple area. Those precluded from admis-sion to the Temple owing to disabilities and bodily defects could seek solace at these pools. It is not surprising that Jesus went there to heal and intentionally mingle with those who were considered diseased and unclean and to draw people to him, and it seems reasonable this must be the background for the healing accounts in the Gospel of John (5:1–13; 9:7, 11).

Before turning to the archaeology of the Bethesda and Siloam Pools, let us first go over the general phenomenon of Jewish water purifica-tion procedures in the stepped-and-plastered installations known as *miqwa'ot*. Jesus and his followers would have regularly used such installations for daily purification, even if some of their purification practices differed from those of their contemporaries. The basis for our information about what was or was not permitted in regard to *miqwa'ot* appears in rabbinic sources: the Mishnah and Tosefta.[108] We must take into consideration, however, that this information is likely to have been idealized by the later rabbis, at least in part, and that the reality of purification practices in the first century may have been much more flexible than one would suppose from these sources. The Mishna indi-cates there were at least six grades of *miqwa'ot*, listed from the worst to the best: (1) ponds; (2) ponds during the rainy season; (3) immersion pools; (4) wells with natural groundwater; (5) salty water from the sea and hot springs; and (6) natural flowing "living" waters from springs and rivers.[109] Clearly, the ubiquitous stepped-and-plastered installation known to scholars from archaeological excavations since the 1960s and now commonly referred to as the *miqweh* (listed under No. 3, above), was not the best nor the worst of the six grades of *miqwa'ot*. It is de-scribed as follows: "more excellent is a pool of water containing forty *seah*; for in them men may immerse themselves and immerse other things [e.g. vessels]" (m. Miqwa'ot 1:7).

Stringent Jewish regulations (*halakhot*) are referenced in regard to certain constructional details and how the installations were to be used. A *miqweh* had to be supplied with "pure" water derived from natural sources (rivers, springs, or rain) throughout the year and even during the long dry season, and it had to contain a minimum of forty *seah* of water—the equivalent of less than one cubic meter of water—so that a person might be properly immersed (if not standing, then lying down). Once the natural flow of water into a *miqweh* had been stopped, it became "drawn" water (*mayim sheuvim*). Water could not be added mechanically, but there was a possibility of increasing the volume by allowing drawn water to enter from an adjacent container, so long as the original amount of water did not decrease to below the minimum requirement of water. Hence, an additional body of water, known since medieval times as the *otsar* (the "treasury"), could be connected to the *miqweh*, and linked by pipe or channel. There was, of course, the problem of the water becoming dirty or stagnant (though not impure), but the *miqweh* was not used for daily ablutions for the purpose of keeping clean. Indeed, people appear to have washed themselves (or parts of their bodies, notably the feet and hands) before entering the ritual bath. Basins for cleansing feet and legs have been found in front of *miqwa'ot* in first-century dwellings in Jerusalem.[110]

The *miqweh* was required, according to rabbinical sources, to be sunken into the ground, either through construction or by the process of hewing into the rock, and into it natural water would flow derived from a spring or from surface rainwater in the winter seasons. The walls and floors of the *miqweh* chambers were plastered (frequently made of slaked quicklime mixed with crushed charcoal); ceilings were either natural rock or barrel-vaulted with masonry. These installations are distinguished by flights of steps leading down into them and extending across the entire breadth of the chamber; such ubiquitous steps, however, were not referred to in the sources. The riser of the lowest step tended to be deeper than the rest of the steps, presumably to facilitate the immersion procedures when the level of water had dropped to a minimum. Some of these steps had a low raised (and plastered) partition, which is thought to have separated the descending impure person (on the right) from the pure person leaving the *miqweh* (on the left). Similarly, there were *miqwa'ot* with double entrances; these may indicate that the activities carried out inside them resembled those undertaken in installations with the partitioned steps.

This arrangement of steps or double entrances is known particularly from Jerusalem, but also from sites in the region, as well in the Hebron Hills and at the Dead Sea Scrolls' site of Qumran. The installations from Jerusalem and the Hebron Hills with the single partitions fit the double lane theory, that it was constructed to facilitate the separation of the impure from the pure, but at Qumran installations were found with three or more of these partitions, which is odd. According to one suggestion, maintaining the utmost in purity *inside* the *miqweh*, reflected by the addition of features such as the partitions, would have been a concern mainly for priests, but little support for this hypothesis has come from the archaeological evidence itself.[111] Indeed, the partitions are at best symbolic rather than functional, and in some of the installations at Qumran they were not even practical, providing in one installation a stepped lane that was only 15 cm wide. The *miqweh* was also used for the purifying of contaminated vessels.[112] It is not surprising, therefore, that in the excavation of *miqwa'ot* at Jericho and Jerusalem, some were found to contain quantities of ceramic vessels.

The date of the first appearance of stepped-and-plastered *miqwa'ot* is a matter still debated by scholars, but the general consensus of opinion is that this occurred in the Late Hellenistic (Hasmonean) period, at some point during the end of the second century BCE or very early in the first century CE.[113] One thing is certain: Only a handful of *miqwa'ot* are known from the time of the Hasmoneans, whereas large numbers of *miqwa'ot* are known dating from the time of Herod the Great (late first century BCE) and up to the destruction of Jerusalem (70 CE). There can be no doubt that the *floruit,* or high point, in the use of *miqwa'ot* was in the first century CE.

The average size of the *miqweh* suggests that ritual bathing was ordinarily practiced individually—no more than one person would enter the installation at a time—and the location of *miqwa'ot* within the basements of private dwellings suggests purification was done regularly and whenever deemed necessary. The purpose of the immersion was to ritually cleanse the flesh of the contaminated person in pure water, but it may also have been undertaken within households before eating or as an aid to spirituality before reading the Torah or praying. It was neither used for the cleansing of the soul nor for the redemption of sins (as with the purification procedures of John the Baptist), nor any other rituals (except for the conversion of proselytes following their acceptance of the Torah and circumcision).[114]

We assume that disrobing took place before the immersion and that new garments were put on immediately afterward. Ritual bathing could be conducted in the comfort of a person's dwelling, but there were also more public *miqwa'ot* such as those used by peasants and other workers (such as quarrymen, potters, and lime burners) who would cleanse themselves at various locations in the countryside. A few *miqwa'ot* are known in the immediate vicinity of tombs (such as at the Tomb of the Kings in Jerusalem), but they are quite rare, indicating that immediate ritual purification following entrance into tombs was not common. The *miqweh* was not used for general cleaning and ablution purposes: This was done in alternative installations located within the house, or in public bathhouses instead.

Large numbers of *miqwa'ot* have hitherto been investigated from first-century levels in Jerusalem. Almost all of these installations were found within the basements of private dwellings and would not have been used other than by their owners. There are, however, exceptions that cannot have belonged to private individuals. Three *miqwa'ot* are known in the southern part of the Temple Mount: two large ones beneath the area of the principal Muslim modern fountain (*k'as*) and a third small one near the entrance to the present-day Aqsa Mosque.[115] These could only have been used by those who had already ascended to the Outer Court via the gates situated in the southern Temple Mount wall. The third might have been accessed from the area of the Royal Stoa. But even these installations cannot have been used by very many individuals and I would suggest that their small size and their proximity to the Temple must mean they were only used for the select immersion of Temple officials, dignitaries, or other people of special status.

Sources refer to various *miqwa'ot* in the Temple precincts—for example, a subterranean place of immersion near the Temple, which was used by priests, and perhaps also the "trough of Jehu."[116] Additional *miqwa'ot* have also been found outside the Temple Mount walls, but they too are quite small and so were likely to have been used by shopkeepers or by the overseers/police in charge of supervising entrance into the Temple area. They may also have been for those suspected of receiving a last-minute form of contamination and directed to immersion by the officials appointed by the *bet din* to keep an eye on the crowds of visitors and pilgrims. One of these installations is in the form of a rectangular pool, presumably open to the sky, with plastered steps leading down on all four sides, and it was found in the Ophel region immediately south of the Temple Mount.[117]

Small installations of the kind found in Jerusalem have also been investigated in the vicinity of the city, in the Judean and Benjamin Hills, in the area of the Hebron Hills, and in the Shephelah foothills. All these installations are small and would have served the private needs of the local Jewish inhabitants of the towns, villages, and farms of those regions. One may assume that a *miqweh* of this kind existed within the household of Martha and Mary at Bethany. There are, however, a few exceptions to the rule: a number of exceptionally large installations situated particularly close to highways. One scholar, David Amit, has suggested that they may have serviced Jewish pilgrims *en route* to the Jewish Temple in Jerusalem during the festival periods. However, these large installations were most probably used for the immersion of groups of workmen gathering at industrial or agricultural sites, and especially at places where there were large public oil presses or groups of wine presses, since the absolute purity of the resulting oil or grape juice was of the utmost importance. This makes more sense, because a pilgrim could not be expected to maintain purity simply by dipping in such an installation, and in any case during the continued trip to Jerusalem he would most likely come into further contamination. Large stepped *miqwa'ot* do exist at the Qumran settlement of the Dead Sea Scroll sect, but their size is most probably a co-efficient of the arid environment in which the settlement was situated. This would have meant very high evaporation levels, especially during the summer months.[118]

To accommodate the multitude of pilgrims flocking to Jerusalem for the festivals, only large pools could have been used for their immersion, otherwise we would have to envision the unlikely scenario of the Temple precincts being open to contamination and impurity by those wishing to gain admission. The Siloam and Bethesda Pools are excellent examples of pools that could have served as large *miqwa'ot*. Clearly the many small *miqwa'ot* that have hitherto been excavated in Jerusalem would not have sufficed for the needs of tens of thousands of pilgrims streaming to Jerusalem on an annual basis. Indeed, it would appear that most of the small *miqwa'ot* excavated in Jerusalem were used solely for the private immersion of its inhabitants and only very few, notably those at the Temple Mount, may have had some form of public function, but even then for only a very limited number of people. Certain arrangements were made on the streets of Jerusalem to ensure that the masses of pilgrims who immersed themselves in the waters of the large pools of Siloam and Bethesda would not subsequently lose their state of ritual purification *en route* to the Temple precincts for the festivities. In rabbinic sources we read:

> "Other times of the year [during non-festival days] they [that walk] in the middle [of a street] must be deemed unclean, and they [that walk] at the sides may be deemed clean; but during a Feast they [that walk] in the middle [may be deemed] clean and they [that walk] at the sides [must be deemed] unclean; because when they are but few they withdraw to the sides [of a street]" (m. Shekalim 8:1–2).

First-century Jerusalem had a number of large pools of water, mostly reservoirs: Amygdalon (Hezekiah's) Pool situated north of the Upper City; Struthion Pool at the foot of the Antonia Fortress, to the northwest of the Temple Mount; Serpents Pool situated somewhere on the north side of the city; Siloam Pool (at the southern end of the Tyropoeon Valley); and Bethesda Pool (near St. Anne).[119] The Siloam and Bethesda Pools were situated on the south and north sides of the Temple Mount, respectively, so they might provide a service for Jewish pilgrims arriving in Jerusalem from different directions. Of the two, the Siloam Pool was fed largely with "living" water derived via a hewn channel from the Siloam Spring, whereas the Bethesda Pool was fed by collected rainwater stored within a separate (upper) pool. Both pools, as we shall see, were associated with Jesus's healing activities.

The Siloam Pool is already mentioned in the sources as a pool adjacent to the city fortifications in Nehemiah's day. It is referred to as "Solomon's Pool" in Josephus, and in rabbinical writings it was the place where stone cups or mugs were filled with water for purification purposes.[120] In the Gospel of John, we hear it was used as a place for ritual immersion in connection with the miraculous story of the blind man regaining his sight: ". . . And [Jesus] said unto him [the blind man], Go wash in the Pool of Siloam. . . He went his way therefore, and washed, and came seeing." In response to the questioning of querulous neighbors, the blind man repeats his story: "A man that is called Jesus made clay and anointed my eyes, and said unto me, Go to the Pool of Siloam, and wash: and I went and washed, and received sight" (9:7, 11). The Siloam Pool was an ideal location for Jesus to gain recognition for his healing activities.

We should mention in this connection an interesting text from Oxyrhynchus in Egypt—a fragment of an uncanonical gospel—that refers to a *miqweh*-like "Pool of David" close to the Temple area with separate stairs for going in and out, appears to refer to the Siloam Pool. The text has Jesus being challenged by a priest about the state of his purity: "He [Jesus] saith unto him, I am clean; for I washed in the Pool of David [probably named after its proximity to the "City of David"], and having descended down one staircase I ascended by another, and I put on white and clean garments, and then I came and looked upon these holy vessels [in the Temple area]."[121] Elsewhere, it is said that the Pool of David had "running waters," a reference to the flowing "living" waters entering the Siloam Pool from the spring of Siloam. We could assume that the "pool" mentioned in the Oxyrhynchus fragment was a relatively small type of *miqweh* with partitioned steps for those entering and leaving, but I think this unlikely.[122] The evidence points to the Siloam Pool, where some form of segregation would also have been established between those entering the pool for purification and those leaving it. The priest who challenged Jesus may very well have been one of the Temple officials connected with establishing the purity of those entering the Temple Mount precincts.

The concern for purity in Jerusalem and the use of the Siloam and Bethesda Pools is further clarified in rabbinical writings in relation to the subject of *zabim*, that is, men with bodily emissions (semen). The

Rabbis advocated that following an emission of semen the man "conveys uncleanness to what he lies upon or sits upon, and [therefore] he must bathe in running water" (m. Zabim 1:1; cf. m. Miqwa'ot 1:8).

Recent archaeological excavations in 2004 at the junction of the Tyropoeon and Kidron Valleys by Israeli archaeologists Ronny Reich and Eli Shukrun brought to light the Siloam Pool from the time of Jesus. It was apparently trapezoidal in shape (estimated to be 40–60 x 70 meters) with built steps and landings along at least three of its sides; the fourth (west) side is unexcavated. Their findings indicate the pool was most likely built in its present form during the Second Temple period, with two stages of construction of which the earliest is dated to the late first century BCE or first century CE based on the plaster type and other features.[123] The pool was fed with water that was channelled directly from the Siloam spring without any holding basin, but the excavators suggest the pool might also have been fed with runoff rainwater obtained from other directions. Due to the situation of this pool at the lowest point in the city, with the houses of the Upper City extending up in serried fashion toward the west and with the rocky scarp of the Lower City looming to the east, it is clear the archaeologists have yet to discover how bathers might have been able to enter the pool naked without being observed by people from neighboring houses. It is also unclear how the sexes were separated, since mixed nude bathing would not have been allowed. Judging by a few cuts and grooves on the surface of paving stones at the pool it is possible that the interior of the pool was originally divided up into compartments covered by canvas or that the entire pool itself was covered with tarpaulin. Alternatively, all those wishing to immerse themselves into the Siloam Pool might simply have been provided with plain tunics that had previously been purified—before entering into the pool.[124]

The other pool, known as the Bethesda Pool (*piscina probatica*), is situated to the north of the Temple Mount in the grounds of the

Church of St. Anne, which is now under the custodianship of the Catholic White Fathers. The pool was situated outside the Sheep Gate, which was presumably at the north-eastern end of the Second Wall close to the Antonia Fortress, and in the area just beyond the new domestic quarter mentioned by Josephus on the hill of Bezetha. Excavations were undertaken there with breaks from 1865 to 1967, but the results of this work are still largely unpublished.[125]

According to the Gospel of John, the Bethesda Pool (from the Aramaic Beth Hesda, i.e., "house of mercy"), was surrounded by five porticoes and served as a place of purification for a multitude of people. It was the scene where Jesus healed a lame man:

"After this there was a festival of the Jews, and Jesus went up to Jerusalem. Now in Jerusalem by the Sheep Gate there is a pool, called in Hebrew Bethesda, which has five porticoes. In these lay many invalids — blind, lame, and paralyzed. One man was there who had been ill for thirty-eight years. When Jesus saw him lying there and knew that he had been there a long time, he said to him, 'Do you want to be made well?' The sick man answered him, 'Sir, I have no one to put me into the pool when the water is stirred up; and while I am making my way, someone else steps down ahead of me.' Jesus said to him, 'Stand up, take your mat and walk.' At once the man was made well, and he took up his mat and began to walk" (5:1–19).

There are a number of matters arising from this passage that, as we shall see, fit well with the archaeological remains of the pool as they exist today. First, the pool had a twin basin, which explains why there were five columned porticoes: one portico on each of the four sides and one additional portico on the barrier wall in the middle separating the twin basins. Second, the lame man was waiting for someone to take his bed down to the water of the pool, which suggests that one of the basins must have had broad steps with landings at intervals, otherwise invalids would have had difficulty in gaining access. Third, the man wanted to be put in the pool so that he could benefit from the waters that on occasion became "stirred up," indicating that some curative value was placed at that time on this phenomenon. Early Christian sources also refer to the separation of the twin basins, with the one filling up with rainwater and with the second with water "of a ruddy color" according to the early Christian writer Eusebius and "reddish" according to another writer, Eucherius.

I have been investigating the archaeological remains at Bethesda since 1995 and the exciting work has consisted of examining remains of ancient chambers, walls, and subterranean tunnels, mapping the remains, and taking photographs. I reached the conclusion that at the time of Jesus the Bethesda Pool was used specifically for ritual purification, and it could not have been a city reservoir used for gathering drinking water or a swimming pool for entertainment purposes. There are two large basins: the "northern pool" (53 x 40 meters), which served as a reservoir (the *otsar*) for collected rainwater, and the "southern pool" (47 x 52 meters), which was used as the place for purification (the *miqweh*). The two basins would have been surrounded by porticoes on four sides, with an additional portico extending across the barrier wall separating the two basins. The plastered barrier wall separating the two parts of the pool was partly hewn into the rock and partly built of alternating courses of well-dressed header-and-stretcher ashlars with smoothed exteriors, typical of other first-century building ventures in Jerusalem. It was clearly a well-planned building initiative that took place before the construction of the new quarter on the Bezetha Hill and most likely at the time of Herod the Great. The date of the pool is therefore definitely not Iron Age or Hellenistic, as some scholars have suggested.[126]

An impressive flight of hewn and built steps extended down along the entire western side of the "southern" pool (a length of some 53 meters), with sets of steps (in groups of one to six) extending between landings. The steps clearly would have facilitated access down to the very base of the pool, depending on the amount of water available there for bathing, and the landings at different intervals would evidently have been used for the placing of the beds of disabled people, as John implies (5:3).

Both "pools" at Bethesda were evidently built at the same time and were part of the same pre-planned water system. Within the massive barrier-wall separating the two large basins (6 meters thick) was a vertical shaft leading to a horizontal tunnel with a sluice-gate at the bottom, which meant that the water of the *otsar* to the north could easily have come into contact (by a process known as *hashaka*, literally "touching") with the water of the *miqweh* to the south by simply lifting the sluice-gate. Further on, at a lower level of the tunnel, there was a covered trough in which more than 1 cubic meter of valid water (40 *seah*) could have "mingled" with the added water, before then rising and replenishing the waters of the southern pool. When necessary, a sluice gate was opened at the far end of this trough and this, in turn, led to a covered channel that helped drain surplus water away to the south for a considerable distance, perhaps even as far as the Temple Mount. The bubbling and frothing, which must have occurred during the draining of water into the southern pool, may have given rise to the idea of the "stirred up" waters, which was a phenomenon that apparently attracted people to the pool at the time of Jesus. In addition, layers of bright red soil trapped between geological layers, seen within the lower part of this area, may have contributed to the picture provided by early Christian writers regarding the color of the "stirred up" waters.[127]

The Bethesda Pool fits perfectly the Jewish *halakhic* principals as spelled out in rabbinic sources by which "any [pool of water] that is mingled with [water from] an immersion pool is deemed like to the immersion pool itself" (m. Miqwa'ot 6:1); and "they may render immersion pools clean [by mingling the drawn water in] a higher pool [with undrawn water] from a lower pool" (m. Miqwa'ot 6:8). We might relate this type of installation to the dispute between the Pharisees and Sadducees over the matter of the "unbroken stream of liquid" (m. Yadaim 4:7) and suggest that the type of installation with a storage tank next to it was typical of the Pharisees since they were more lenient and accepting in regard to the system of mingling, as opposed to the Sadducees.[128]

What has puzzled scholars, however, is that this type of *miqweh* with an attached storage chamber for water, as described in the rabbinical sources, does not fit the physical appearance of most *miqwa'ot* unearthed during excavations in Jerusalem and its vicinity, at Qumran, in the hills of Hebron and Benjamin and in the Shephelah, as well as those uncovered in the Galilee, notably at Sepphoris, and elsewhere. Perhaps the reason for this is that this kind of installation—as described in the Mishna—was an idealized form of *miqweh*. This meant that it was not as good as one with "living" water supplied from a spring or flowing source of natural water, but still far better than the ubiquitous stepped-and-plastered pools situated beneath private homes in towns and villages or next to agricultural farms; these had to be topped up with drawn water (*mayim she'uvim*) whenever they no longer contained the required one cubic meter of valid water.

The fact that so many *miqwa'ot* are known from greater Jerusalem, from within the city itself as well as from the villages and farms in its hinterland, is a very clear reflection of the preoccupation Jerusalemites had in the first century with the concept of separating and fixing the boundary between the pure and the impure. A general concern about purity was common to all Jews at that time and especially in the city that contained the House of God—the Jewish Temple.[129] There are definitely no grounds for linking the phenomenon of *miqwa'ot* in Jerusalem to any one specific group within Judaism, as some scholars have done. In the eyes of the inhabitants of the city, a clear separation would have been made between the use of *natural* and *built* places for purification. While rabbinical sources extolled the higher sanctity of immersing in natural sources of water, the ease of immersion in a specifically designed installation in the basement of a house made it far more convenient than having to set forth into the countryside in search of a natural water purification source. Natural sources of water were either situated at a distance from the city (e.g., the Jordan River), were difficult to access (e.g., a spring used for irrigation agriculture), or were only available at the right season (e.g., pools in rocky depressions that fill up after the winter rains).

Above all, it would appear that convenience counted as the most important consideration when a *miqweh* came to be built in the first century. A stepped-and-plastered installation in the basement of a house satisfied all who wished to immerse themselves on a regular basis for purification. To that end, the installation had to have had a satisfactory incoming source of pure water, and in most instances rainwater sufficed. Everything else was done to fashion and for personal preference, and I would include such things as foot-baths outside the *miqweh*, double entrances, and lane partitions on the steps. The idea that the construction of *miqwa'ot* was done in strict accordance and adherence to religious rules and stipulations (such as those debated in the "Chamber of Hewn Stone") is highly unlikely and finds no support in the archaeological evidence itself. Hence, the information about *miqwa'ot* in the rabbinical tractates should probably be regarded as representing a certain degree of rabbinical idealism rather than a record of the reality of empirical practice of *miqweh* construction, as it was supposedly passed down through the generations following the destruction of Jerusalem in 70 CE.

The important and obvious conclusion, however, is that the rise in the popularity of this bathing installation during the first century reflects changing attitudes in regard to the perception of everyday purity and possible sources of ritual contamination. In a way, we may regard the later rabbinical writings about *miqwa'ot* as the reflected culmination of a heightened Jewish awareness regarding purity that began to intensify particularly in the early first century CE. An unprecedented number of *miqwa'ot* ultimately came to be built, sometimes with more than one or two installations per household, and not only in the city of Jerusalem, but also in the outlying villages and farms. This development may also be paralleled with the sudden upsurge seen in the manufacturing of stone vessels in the mid–first century CE (from circa 50 CE or perhaps 60 CE) onward.[130] Such vessels were perceived as being able to maintain purity and as such were extremely popular in the "household Judaism" assemblage of that time, with small mugs and large jars (*qalal*) serving a particularly useful task during hand-washing purification procedures.[131] Perhaps we should regard *miqwa'ot* and stone vessels as two sides of the same coin representing the overall "explosion" of purity that took place within Judaism in the first century CE ("purity broke out among the Jews": tosef. Shabbat 1:14), stemming from changing religious sensibilities on the one hand and perhaps serving on the other as a form of passive Jewish resistance against encroaching traits of Roman culture in the critical decade or so preceding the Great Revolt.

For the out-of-town Jewish festival-goers such as Jesus and his followers, full of anticipation for the entrance into the gates of the Temple precincts, ritual immersion within *miqwa'ot* under the private houses of the city was clearly not an option, unless they were personally invited to do so by the inhabitants. The few oversize *miqwa'ot* found in front of the gates to the Temple precincts, as well as beneath the Outer Courts, can only have been used by the festival overseers and Temple officials, and were definitely not large enough to serve the many thousands of pilgrims to the city at the height of the festivals. The sizes and interior arrangements of the Bethesda and Siloam Pools, however, were suitable for exactly such a task and they should therefore be identified as large ritual immersion pools.

A reconstruction drawing of the Siloam Pool by Uwe Beer.

The northwestern corner of the southern basin of the Bethesda Pool.

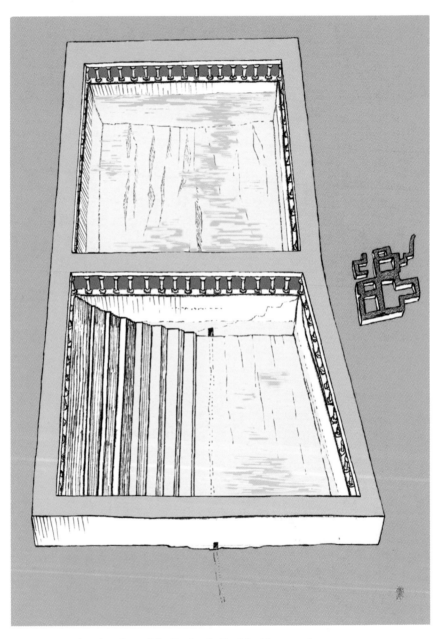

A reconstruction drawing of the Bethesda Pool looking north.

The rock-cut ceiling of a tomb at Akeldama identified as the Tomb of Annas.

A crevice with bright red soil in the lower part of the north barrier wall of the Bethesda pool.

Excavations in progress in the area of the traditional Armenian "House of Caiaphas."

The short end of an ossuary bearing the name "Caiaphas" on it.

Wall painting of the first century CE from the area of the "House of Caiaphas" excavations.

The interior of the "Bethso" tunnel toward the west.

The base of the tower Hippicus built by Herod the Great.

The gate leading to the *Praetorium* at the time of its excavation.

The gate leading to the *Praetorium* the way it looks today.

The crucified Jesus in a reconstruction of that event.

The top of an ossuary from the Giv'at ha-Mivtar tomb showing the human bones inside.

A typical iron nail from the first century CE.

A reconstruction showing how the skeletal foot of the crucified man from the Giv'at ha-Mivtar tomb would have been fixed to the cross, with the original nail and heel bone next to it.

The nail and the heel bone of the crucified man from the Giv'at ha-Mivtar tomb at the time of the discovery.

FIVE

THE HEAVY HAND OF
THE LAW: A TRIAL

*"As soon as it was morning, the chief priests held a consultation with
the elders and scribes and the whole council. They bound Jesus, led him
away, and handed him over to Pilate. Pilate asked him, 'Are you the
King of the Jews?' He answered him, 'You say so.' Then the chief priests
accused him of many things. Pilate asked him again, 'Have you no
answer? See how many charges they bring against you.' But Jesus made
no further reply, so that Pilate was amazed."*

(Mark 15:1–5)

Of the many stories appearing in the Gospels, the one that is
the most familiar is the one about the trial and crucifixion
of Jesus, and many readers feel assured that its historicity must be
beyond question. However, even a cursory look at the narrative from
the time of Jesus's arrest at the Garden of Gethsemane and until his
conviction at the court of Pontius Pilate raises more questions than
there are reasonable answers.[132] The Gospel accounts on the trial are
replete with contradictions and discrepancies, sowing confusion and
some exasperation among scholars trying to figure things out; a few
have even gone as far as labeling the trial narrative as largely fiction.[133]
Numerous arguments and explanations have been put forward to explain the inconsistencies in the trial accounts. In my opinion, a point
of stagnation has been reached in scholarly studies, and archaeology

is still a seriously undervalued source of data. It can contribute quite dramatically to the solving of one of the key problems regarding the trial, namely its exact physical setting. In fact, I can pinpoint the exact spot of the trial for the first time. This new information turns things around and allows us to take a fresh look at some of the other events relating to the trial.

Following his arrest at the Garden of Gethsemane, Jesus was brought by soldiers and the Temple police "to the house of Caiaphas the high priest" (Matthew 26:57). Mark, for some reason, does not mention the name of the High Priest. We are also not told where the house was located, but the assumption is that it was in the Upper City on the west side of the city, not far from the Roman Governor's palace, also known as the *Praetorium*. If the house of Caiaphas and Annas are one and the same, as I propose, then according to Josephus it was situated in the Upper City, close to the palaces of Agrippa and Berenice (*War* II.427). The officiating High Priest at that time was Joseph Caiaphas (18–36 CE) and Jesus was brought to him in 30 CE.[134] Appointed by Valerius Gratus, Caiaphas had a difficult career and was ultimately deposed as High Priest by Vitellius, Governor of Syria, in the same year that Pilate was removed as *Praefectus*. Caiaphas belonged to a powerful and influential family, and may have had a son named Elioeneiai ben ha-Qayyaf.[135]

In 1990, a rock-hewn tomb was accidentally unearthed on the north side of the modern neighborhood of Talpiot, a couple of kilometers to the south of ancient Jerusalem. Excavations were immediately undertaken by Israeli archaeologist Zvi Greenhut. It was a typical tomb of the first century, nothing lavish, with a roughly rectangular central chamber with a standing pit, and with four *kokhim*, or burial recesses, in its walls. There were twelve ossuaries, five of them inscribed, and two of them were particularly exciting. One had a scratched inscription reading "Yehosef bar Qayafa" (Joseph son of Caiaphas) and "Yehosef bar Qafa" on the other side. Another ossuary was simply inscribed "Qafa," or Caiaphas.[136] Undoubtedly, this tomb belonged to the priestly family of Caiaphas. It may even have had a prominent monument outside that could be seen from a distance. None has been found, but it might have been dismantled in antiquity or even have been accidentally bulldozed before excavations began. Similarly, the tomb monuments in the Kidron Valley are impressive, whereas the actual hewn burial chambers attached to them are quite simple. So I am not too bothered by the simplicity of the tomb as an argument for it not being the Caiaphas family tomb.

In the Gospel of John, Jesus is taken to Annas (or Ananus I), the father-in-law of Caiaphas, before being led to the High Priest himself. Jesus is subsequently interrogated by Caiaphas in front of an impromptu assembly. One of Jesus's disciples, Simon Peter, is able to observe the proceedings from within the compound of the High Priest's house. Caiaphas hears witnesses, one of whom reports Jesus as saying, "I will destroy this Temple . . ." (Mark 14:57–58), but the evidence is seen to be unclear. When Jesus confirms he is the Son of God, Caiaphas is said to have torn his garment as an expression of grief over this perceived blasphemy, and it is decided that Jesus is "worthy of death" (Mark 14:64). On the following morning, the entire council comes together and following a consultation decides to turn Jesus over to Pilate for trial. Luke presents things a bit differently: Jesus being interrogated in the morning and without witnesses.

While there has been some scholarly debate regarding the extent and limits of the Sanhedrin's powers, the present-day opinion is that the principal Jewish authoritative body in Jerusalem would undoubtedly have been able to exercise full judicial powers on social and religious affairs at the time of the Roman prefects and procurators. Even in matters of serious crimes, the Sanhedrin was able to have transgressors executed, but only in accordance with the methods they advocated: namely stoning, strangulation, burning, and even beheading. Crucifixion was not one of them.[137] Stephen is one person who suffered the fate of stoning, as we hear in Acts, in accordance with Jewish law as it was deduced from Deuteronomy (17:5–27). The later High Priest Annas (or Ananus II) also convened the judges of the Sanhedrin to condemn James, the brother of Jesus, according to the writings of Josephus.[138]

While the Sanhedrin was a form of high court or senate, it is unclear whether the *full* forum of this body would have convened specifically to deal with the matter of Jesus, especially since it was just before the Passover festivities. The Sanhedrin would normally convene at the Chamber of Hewn Stone near the Temple, but never at night.[139] If this meeting did take place, which was highly unusual, then perhaps it was just an ad hoc assembly of select members of the Sanhedrin (the "Council," *bouleutes*, in Mark 15:43) that convened in order to determine whether or not Jesus should be charged with blasphemy based on the reports by "witnesses" coming from the Temple Mount and the Pools. Alternatively, this last-minute meeting may have been arranged by concerned members of the Council, perhaps even instigated by Joseph of Arimathea himself, to see if Jesus might be willing to admit to a lesser charge so that he need not stand trial with the Romans on the more serious charge of sedition or terrorism.[140] This might explain why following his arrest Jesus was not led directly to the Roman barracks for imprisonment and to await trial, but was first brought to the home of the High Priest. Ordinarily, the Sanhedrin should have been concerned with the preservation of human life, as one learns from rabbinical writings such as the Mishna (m. Makk. 1:10), but Jesus clearly had enemies on the Council who were not at all sympathetic to him, and Joseph of Arimathea may have been his only friend there.

What is absolutely certain is that the Sanhedrin had no jurisdiction on matters of sedition or insurrection, and this could only have been dealt with by the Romans. For this reason John says, "the Jews said unto him [Pilate] it is not lawful for us to put any man to death"

(18:31). What John probably meant by this is that since the assembly of the Sanhedrin was unable to find Jesus guilty of blasphemy—for which he could have been put to death if they wished—the only alternative was for him to be charged with sedition, which, ultimately, was a Roman matter and one that needed to be decided upon by the Governor or by someone appointed by him to handle such cases.

What would the house of the High Priest Caiaphas have looked like? We have the brief description of his dwelling in the Gospels, as well as a wealth of comparative archaeological remains.[141] If John is not mistaken when he says Jesus was taken to Caiaphas only after first being brought to his father-in-law Annas, then we may assume they both lived in the same residence, which would probably have been a large, extended, and multi-roomed household. Households of extended families are known from many different periods in ancient Palestine. The Gospels imply that from the street in front of the house there was a porch leading into an open courtyard (John refers to a door), where a fire was lit and where people huddled around. From there, Jesus was taken inside the house proper, apparently to the first floor.

Palatial houses, some belonging to priestly families, have been uncovered in excavations in the Jewish Quarter of Jerusalem, including one that belonged to the priestly family of Kathros, since a stone weight was found in the excavations bearing the Aramaic inscription "[of] Bar Kathros."[142] This family was one of the reviled priestly families mentioned in the Talmud and Tosefta ("Woe unto me because of the house of Kathros, woe unto me because of their reed pens").[143] These houses had stepped ritual bathing pools (*miqwa'ot*) in their basements, lavish mosaic floors, and walls covered with exquisite painted designs.

Additional houses of the period were uncovered in the area of the traditional "House of Caiaphas" within the Armenian property of Saint Saviour on the summit of Mount Zion.[144] Some of the wall paintings from these excavations—depicting parts of buildings, stylized wreaths, birds, and orchard branches with figs—were of a very high standard of craftsmanship. Indeed, they were of such good quality that they might have looked respectable in any Roman town house, even at Pompeii. These paintings raise serious questions as to where first-century Jews in Jerusalem actually drew the line in terms of their supposed anionic stance condemning figural decorations, based on the requirements put forward in Exodus (20:4).[145] The houses on Mount Zion were destroyed with the rest of the city by Titus and his legions in 70 CE. Among the finds was an exceptional artifact: a sword still in its leather scabbard. Near these excavations is a Crusader-period chapel with a small room regarded by the Armenians as the traditional "prison of Jesus," the place he was held before being brought to trial. Further downslope is the Church of Peter in Gallicantu; excavations around and below it also revealed houses from the first century CE. The "prison of Jesus" is pointed out there as well.

From the point of view of the Romans, Jesus was a subversive troublemaker and a leader of a potentially dangerous group of agitators and malcontents. Passover was always a difficult time—celebrating as it did the Israelite release from Egyptian bondage (a point of view that would not have been lost on the Romans)—and Jerusalem was always bursting to its brim with pilgrims from all over the country coming to attend the Temple. The last thing the Romans wanted was unrest on the streets, since this might lead to riots and anarchy. Pontius Pilate would not have been particularly bothered by the Jewish accusations of blasphemy leveled against Jesus. But he may have been concerned with the portrayal of Jesus in some quarters as some kind of anointed king or Messiah, and would have seen this as posing a direct challenge to Roman leadership since only they could appoint local kings (such as, for example, Herod the Great in 37 BCE). Hence, independent claims of kingship would not have been tolerated and claimants were firmly stamped out.

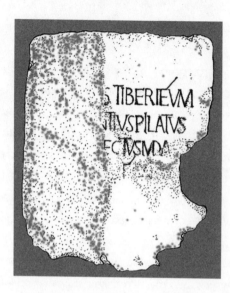

Figure 4: Inscription from Caesarea mentioning Pontius Pilate.

Jesus was bound and brought to Pontius Pilate, who was the supreme Roman authority at that time in Judaea (26–36 CE).[146] What was Pilate's official title? In the Gospels he is simply called "Governor," but Josephus, as well as Tacitus (*Annales* XV.44:3), refer to him as "procurator." For many years it was debated whether the first Roman governors of Judaea, between 6 and 41 CE, were procurators or prefects. In the end an important archaeological find was made at Caesarea Maritima in 1961 by an Italian excavating team that helped solve this problem once and for all. A stone fragment of a monumental Latin inscription was discovered reading "[Po]ntius Pilatus / [Praef]ectus Iuda[ea]e," indicating that Pilate's correct title was not procurator, after all, but *praefector* of equestrian rank over the province of Judaea. This dedicatory inscription was apparently for an edifice at Caesarea called the "Tiberieum," which was built by Pilate in honor of the emperor Tiberias (14–37 CE).[147] This edifice may have been a lighthouse on the edge of the harbor, or perhaps a building associated with the Roman imperial cult.[148] It is not surprising that Pilate would have wanted to embellish Caesarea with buildings since his official residence was situated there at the *Praetorium*, in the area of the old palace of Herod the Great, remains of which have been uncovered in recent excavations.[149]

Josephus is one of the primary historical sources on Pilate and he depicts him as a cruel, ruthless, and brutal person. Philo also describes him as guilty of "venality, violence, robbery, assault, abusive behaviour, frequent executions without trial, and endless savage ferocity" (*Legatio ad Gaium* 301–302). Pilate was definitely not the sort of person you would want to antagonize at any time. But the picture of Pilate provided in the Gospels is quite different. He is portrayed there as an indecisive and compassionate man, and surprisingly also a believer in Jesus's innocence. This is not at all credible.[150] He was undoubtedly a hard and manipulative man, and this comes across in the devious way in which he conducted the suppression of a protest made by the inhabitants of Jerusalem who accused him of misusing the *korban* Temple funds for the construction or restoration of the water aqueduct to Jerusalem: "Large numbers of the Jews perished, some from the blows they received, others trodden to death by their companions in the ensuing flight. Cowed by the fate of the victims, the multitude was reduced to silence" (*War* II.177). There is also the reference in Luke (13:1) to Pilate being involved at some point in the spilling of Galilean blood in Jerusalem. Six years after the death of Jesus, in 36 CE, Pilate used inordinate violence by massacring Samaritans and with the killing of several of their leaders; this brutality eventually led to him being recalled to Rome (*Antiq.* XVIII.85–87).

In view of his propensity for violence as a means of achieving his ends, would Pilate even have bothered giving a low-ranking individual such as Jesus a trial, when this matter might conceivably have been dealt with by a Roman subordinate? Perhaps at any other time of the year this might have been the case, but because of the sensitivities of the Passover week, it is more than likely Pilate would have wanted to deal with the matter himself so as to ensure a *firm* outcome. The assembly of the Sanhedrin had seemingly not been able to resolve the matter, and so it was up to Pilate to sort things out and to show an example. He was probably afraid that if he was not seen as decisive, unrest on the street might quickly turn into a full-blown insurrection. Pilate would not have wanted a long drawn-out trial, insisting instead that Jesus be dispatched immediately to his death.

The fact that Pilate was wary of the inhabitants of Jerusalem and at times did try to take heed of the mood of the crowd is made clear from the episode when he removed the Standards, bearing the Imperial image. Pilate's soldiers arrived in Jerusalem—probably entering through the Gate of the Essenes—for winter encampment; they brought with them their Standards and entered the city at night.[151] The soldiers would have gone directly to the barracks adjacent to the *Praetorium*, which might even have had provision for a special shrine (*sacellum*) to contain the Standards. The soldiers did not intend to transfer them to the Antonia fortress, which in its proximity to the Temple might have caused severe offense to Jews.[152] The inhabitants of Jerusalem, we are told by Josephus, were in an uproar because they felt their "laws [that] permit no image to be erected in the city" had been broken (*War* II.169–174). Hence they made their way to Caesarea, where they protested *en masse* against the Standards. Pilate finally capitulated and had the Standards removed from Jerusalem.

According to Mark, Jesus was led in front of Pilate and asked whether he was "King of the Jews." Jesus was evasive and did not provide a clear denial, which probably more than anything else sealed his fate. All Pilate now had to do was to condemn him to death. However, Mark then goes on to relate how Pilate offered clemency for a prisoner in view of the upcoming Passover holiday, hoping the crowd would choose Jesus. Many scholars do not regard this story as historical.[153] In fact, no sources suggest that such clemency existed at times of festivities in Judaea or elsewhere, but this still does not mean it is untrue. What is clearly unlikely, however, is that the Romans would have provided freedom to a man (Barabbas) convicted on charges of insurrection and murder, and who was therefore the equivalent of what one would call today a "terrorist." To allow Barabbas back on to the streets of Jerusalem would have been a foolhardy act of the Roman authorities, to say the least, and so must be unlikely. Hence, Barabbas was most likely executed—clemency or no clemency.

Setting aside the complications and contradictions about the trial as set forth in the Gospels, what is certain is that Jesus was ultimately condemned to death by Pilate, who was the supreme Roman authority in Jerusalem at that time, and then summarily executed by crucifixion, which was a Roman and not a Jewish method of execution. In this regard, Josephus, writing in the years following the fall of Jerusalem in 70 CE, provides a clear, albeit concise, reference to these events that is in my opinion entirely believable: "Pilate, upon hearing him [Jesus] accused by men of the highest standing among us, had condemned him to be crucified . . ." (*Antiq.* XVIII.64). Tacitus, writing about eighty or so years after the death of Jesus, also says the sentence was carried out by Pilate: "Christus, the founder of the name, had undergone the death penalty in the reign of Tiberius, by sentence of the procurator [sic.] Pontius Pilate, and the pernicious superstition was checked for a moment, only to break out once more, not merely in Judaea, the home of the disease, but in the capital [Rome] itself . . ." (Tacitus, *Annales* XV.44:3).[154]

According to the Gospels, the trial of Jesus was held at the *Praetorium.* At the time of Jesus there were two main locations in Jerusalem controlled by Roman soldiers: the Antonia Fortress, which was situated on a high rocky outcrop at the northwest corner of the Temple Mount, and a military barracks situated within the complex of the old palace of Herod the Great, which was used as the seat of the Governor whenever he was in Jerusalem. From medieval times it was assumed the *Praetorium* was at the Antonia Fortress and for this reason the traditional Via Dolorosa—the route Jesus took to the place of the crucifixion—extended from that area on the northeast of the Old City and westward as far as the Church of the Holy Sepulchre. However, it is unlikely Jesus was tried at the Antonia since it served primarily as a military observation tower with a very specific function: to keep an eye on the activities of the Jewish worshippers on the Temple Mount and to prevent rioting or demonstrations there. It was to this spot, we will remember, that Paul was brought, having been saved from the Temple mob (Acts 21:30–36). The tower was too cramped to serve as the residence and headquarters of the governing official. As a controlling maneuver, this was the place where the Romans kept the High Priest's vestments. Josephus reports an act of insensitivity toward Jewish worshippers at Passover when a Roman soldier exposed his buttocks "and made a noise in keeping with his posture" (*War* II.224). Archaeological work shows that little has survived of the actual structure of the Antonia Fortress except for the rock-cut base itself on the northwest of the Temple Mount. Judging by the very limited size of the rock base which I have measured (90 x 40 meters) it would appear that this "fortress" was no more than a very large and high tower with turrets at its corners, and with a flight of broad steps leading down into the Temple area.

Today, a consensus of opinion exists among scholars that Herod's palace on the west side of the city was the same as the *Praetorium* and that in its immediate vicinity Jesus was tried and condemned to death (Mark 15:16).[155] The fact that Herod's palace was used by Pilate as his residence, and was the center of his military and civic headquarters in Jerusalem, is very clear from the episode of the votive round shields (of *clipeus* type) that were dedicated "in honor of Tiberias" in 32 CE, as related by Philo of Alexandria (*Legatio ad Gaium* 299–305).[156] Herod's palace lay at the northwest angle of the Upper City, in the area spanning the distance between the present-day Citadel, *Kishle,* and Armenian Garden. The palace precinct was protected by a strong fortification system with three tall and impressive towers that were inserted at intervals. Herod the Great named these after friends and a former wife: Hippicus, Phasael, and Mariamne. The massive base of one of these towers (probably Hippicus) is visible today in the Citadel near the Jaffa Gate.[157] Josephus wrote that "adjoining and on the inner side of these towers, which lay to the north of it, was the king's palace, baffling all description: indeed, in extravagance and equipment no building surpassed it" (*War* V.176–183).

The palace itself consisted of twin apartments or wings (the Caesareum and Agrippium) elevated upon a massive podium, parts of which have been uncovered in archaeological excavations in the Armenian Garden.[158] It is disappointing that so little has been recovered of the superstructure of the palace complex. It would appear that the magnificent palace was pulled down and dismantled down to its foundations in the Byzantine period, in the fifth century CE, to make way for Christian chapels and monastic dwellings. Sufficient features of the palace have however survived, enabling us to provide for the first time a fairly good reconstruction of where the palace was situated and what it looked like. The size of the actual palace building complex appears to have been 140 meters from north to south, judging by a set of broad rock-cut steps in the Citadel moat, which ran along the north side of the building and by the podium boundary wall delimiting it to the south. Since, according to Josephus, the palace consisted of two wings, we may suggest that the palace was a square building with an equivalent distance of 140 meters from east to west. The service buildings, with kitchens, installations, and storerooms, were located north of the palace in the area of the present-day courtyard of the Citadel. This area was enclosed to the northwest by the fortifications of the city and Hippicus and Phasael, the two monumental towers that were inserted into the line of the defense wall. The principal road running today through the Armenian Quarter roughly marks the central line dividing the two wings of the palace. The southeast corner of Herod's palace falls roughly beneath the complex of the present-day Armenian Church of St James. The southwest corner of the palace was marked by a large tower named Mariamne, remains of which have been found in archaeological excavations.

Herod established a magnificent formal garden to the south of the palace that was regarded as one of the marvels of Jerusalem:

". . . all around were many circular cloisters, leading one into another, the columns in each being different, and their open courts all of greensward; there were groves of various trees intersected by long walks, which were bordered by deep canals, and ponds everywhere studded with bronze figures, through which the water was discharged, and around the streams were numerous cots for tame pigeons" (*War* V. 180–181).

Beyond it was the camp (*stratopedon*) in which a garrison of soldiers was lodged; I estimate that it was situated immediately within the west gate and to the south of the garden.[159]

After the grandeur of the Jewish Temple, Herod's palace was reportedly the most amazing building complex in Jerusalem. Josephus provides a description of the "Old" or "First" fortification wall, which partially surrounded the palace, and mentions two landmarks associated with the section of defense wall running from the Hippicus tower southward, namely "Bethso" and the "Gate of the Essenes." The first of these two landmarks is a feature connected with Herod's palace. The second feature, as we shall see, is crucial for understanding the true location of the trial of Jesus. In Josephus' day the Western Hill was identified as Mount Zion (*War* V.137). Josephus wrote: "Beginning at the same point [i.e., the Hippicus Tower] in the other direction, westward, it descended [i.e., the Old or First Wall] past the place called Bethso to the gate of the Essenes, then turned southwards above the fountain of Siloam . . ." (*War* V.145).[160] It stands to reason that Josephus would not have mentioned these locations had they not been significant features in the urban landscape.

The meaning of the word "Bethso" has been debated, but the assumption is that it was a designation for *bet tso'a* ("place of sewers" or "house of excrement"). In the Temple Scroll the location of the toilets in the idealized City of the Temple is situated on the northwest of the city: "And you shall make a place for a 'hand' (*mqwm yd*), outside the city, to which they shall go / out, to the northwest of the city—roofed houses [*btym mqwrym*] with pits within them, / into which the excrement [*htso'a*] will descend, [so that] it will [not] be visible at any distance (*rhwq*) / from the city, three thousand cubits [1.5 km]" (11QTemple col. XLVI, lines 13–16).[161] While the Temple Scroll does not reflect the actual Jerusalem of that time, the writer of the words *btym mqwrym* ("roofed houses") may have been inspired by the fact that in his day there were covered drainage tunnels existing on the northwest of Jerusalem, i.e., structures carrying sewage hidden underground.

In archaeological excavations conducted near the Citadel a monumental drainage tunnel was uncovered to the south of the southern moat, extending outward from beneath the line of the "First Wall" fortification.[162] I had a part to play in the uncovering of this tunnel in 1982–83. The western sloping part of the tunnel has two parallel walls with capping slabs of stone, but its interior could not be excavated owing to the instability of the side walls. Further excavations were conducted beneath the *Kishle* building to the east and much more of the tunnel was traced.[163] Together the two parts of the tunnel have a length of about 40 meters. The inner tunnel when cleared proved to have a width of about 1.5 meters and a height of more than 6 meters from floor to ceiling. A rock-cut channel in the floor of the tunnel contained a layer of grey clayey silt, clearly dried sewage. Archaeologists tend to make rich pickings in ancient cess pits, toilets, and sewage channels—even in the *Praetorium* people were losing things! The tunnel was no exception to the rule and when excavated the contents contained ceramics of first century CE date, a hoard of metal objects, and a few coins dating from the time of the Roman

Procurator Antonius Felix (52–60 CE). The very small aperture, only 20 centimeters wide, at the western end of the tunnel, which served as the tunnel's exit point, confirms that it can only have been used for the disposal of waste products. Clearly the tunnel drained away the sewage from the entire complex of Herod's palace and from the subsequent *Praetorium*.

The full extent of the tunnel to the east is unknown, but its lower western extension was apparently uncovered by a nineteenth-century antiquarian, Conrad Schick, beneath the area of the present-day buildings of Khutzot Hayotser in the upper Hinnom Valley.[164] Schick recorded finding a tower and tunnels, one of which is likely to have connected up with our tunnel, at the point where it made a turn southward running toward the pool known as Birket Sultan. Not surprisingly, during archaeological work there in the 1970s by an Israeli archaeologist, Amos Kloner, a deep plastered drainage tunnel was uncovered at the base of Birket Sultan extending to the south.[165] If the three segments of tunnel are indeed part of one combined sewage system (with a total length of more than half a kilometer) from the first century CE, this would fully negate the generally accepted opinion that Birket Sultan is the Serpent's Pool mentioned by Josephus (*War* V.108), since, clearly, one cannot conceive of a situation where waste products would be allowed to run freely and unchecked along the bottom of a water pool. Indeed, the structure of Birket Sultan is almost certainly of medieval date (known in the Crusader period as "Lacus Germani") and we should follow the suggestion that the Serpent's Pool was actually situated on the north side of the city.[166] A rock-cut pool situated just outside the present-day Damascus Gate— below and west of the mouth to the subterranean cave of Solomon's Quarries—and recorded by various explorers in the nineteenth century, may indeed be that same pool.

Another subterranean tunnel was investigated beneath Christ Church on the northern side of Herod's palace, just inside Jaffa Gate, but it had a different purpose altogether and served to bring water into the city. The tunnel was first studied by Charles Wilson and other explorers in the mid-nineteenth century, but its exact location disappeared until an engineer from Haifa in the late 1980s accidentally located the opening to a vertical shaft (13 meters deep) descending to the tunnel. I newly investigated the tunnel in the late 1990s together with the archaeologist Rafi Lewis and the historian Kelvin Crombie. Anyone suffering from claustrophobia should not consider entering such a tunnel system; it is difficult to breathe inside and there is no space to stretch arms and legs. The tunnel system runs for 80 meters parallel with the stretch of the First Wall fortification line, which marks the separation between the northern end of the Upper City and the hill of Golgotha. The tunnel was seen to cut through two existing ritual pools (*miqwa'ot*) and so was most likely built at the time of the siege of Jerusalem between 66 and 70 CE. It may have been one of the "underground passages" mentioned by Josephus in which notables and priests attempted to hide from the Romans (*War* II.429).

In an archaeological excavation conducted in the 1970s by Israeli archaeologist Magen Broshi along the western Old City wall of Jerusalem—in the 280-meter stretch between the southern moat of the Citadel and the present-day southwest angle of the Old City—an amazing discovery was made, which I believe sheds enormous new light on the trial of Jesus. At the time of the excavation, in which I too participated, the true significance of the find was not fully understood.[167] The excavations revealed a monumental gateway with the remains of a large courtyard situated between two fortification walls. On the northern side of the courtyard was a rocky outcrop and on top of it was a small rectangular built platform with steps. Having studied these remains in detail in recent years, it seems to me that the gate should be identified as the Gate of the Essenes. It struck me that these finds also fit very well the description in the Gospel of John regarding the place of the trial of Jesus: "When Pilate therefore heard

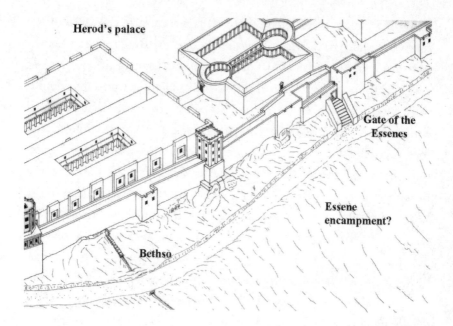

Figure 5: Reconstruction drawing of the Palace of Herod the Great / Praetorium.

these words he brought Jesus out, and sat down on the judgment-seat (*bema*) at a place called the pavement (*lithostrotos*), but in Hebrew, *gabbatha*" (19:13).[168]

Could the Place of Judgment and the Gate of the Essenes be one and the same? The exact location of the Gate of Essenes has been a matter of uncertainty among scholars. Some proposed it be located at the southeast end of the First Wall on the lower slope of the traditional Mount Zion, at a point where it led to the Kidron Valley and toward the Judean Desert.[169] Indeed, a gate of first-century CE date was uncovered at this spot by the explorers Frederick Bliss and Archibald Dickie in the nineteenth century, and was later re-excavated by British archaeologist Kathleen Kenyon in the 1960s. Others, however, were more circumspect, suggesting the gate should be sought somewhere on the west of the city, not far from the Hippicus Tower, but without providing any exact location.[170]

Many scholars were of the opinion, however, that the Gate of the Essenes should be identified with the one excavated at the southwest angle of the First Wall, on the slope of the traditional Mount Zion, by Bliss and Dickie in 1894–97.[171] The gate was found in a wall with a length of 45 meters and built of smooth-faced stones without margins, dressed with a comb-pick and laid in lime.[172] The construction style of this wall resembles quite a few fortification wall segments uncovered around Mount Zion that are dated to the Byzantine period. The recent excavation by the Israeli archaeologist Yehiel Zelinger of the core of one of the towers of the same fortification wall, further to the southeast, brought to light coins that do not post-date 455 CE. This supports the view that the wall was built by Eudocia in the mid-fifth century CE, though we cannot ignore the possibility that the wall was also rebuilt—or at least certain portions of it—in the early Islamic period, i.e., in the seventh and eighth centuries CE and even later.[173] The gate (2.40 meters wide) was at the southeast end of the wall with a series of superimposed thresholds, all representing separate stages of use in the Byzantine and early Islamic periods.[174] The area of the gate was re-excavated in the 1980s with the dating of the earliest gate to the first century on the basis of potsherds from the period in a small probe beneath the fills of the adjacent paving.[175] This dating, however, seems doubtful on methodological grounds, since the potsherds are most likely to have been residuals in a consolidation fill poured beneath the Byzantine paving.[176] In other words, the pottery material does not date the construction of the gate, which, in my opinion, is most likely to be from the Byzantine period—mid-fifth century CE at the earliest.

The best identification for the Gate of the Essenes has to be the gateway complex uncovered in excavations midway along the western Old City wall. The gateway complex consists of an inner (Hasmonean) and outer (Herodian) fortification wall, with respective gates, and a central courtyard open to the sky between the walls. The courtyard

(30 by 11 meters) was originally paved on its south side and it had a rocky outcrop on its north. The pavement was unfortunately seriously robbed of its paving stones in the Byzantine period. The gateway was flanked by two large towers (20 x 9; and 19.5 x 13.5 meters) and it had an external stepped approach (8 meters wide) broad enough to accommodate carts and horses. The paved steps were laid on a sloping embankment, bordered on either side with thick plastered stone walls, leading up to the gate in the outer wall. Here too the stones belonging to the threshold of the outer Herodian gate were robbed out in the Byzantine period with pits extending down to the foundations of the wall. It appears that the width of the inner Hasmonean gate was about 3 meters wide, suggesting that the gate in the outer wall had a similar width. The excavation of the fills and collapsed stone debris on top of the paved steps of the gateway approach indicates the gate complex was destroyed by the Romans in 70 CE. The excavation of an area under the steps of the gateway approach, and of additional patches of stone pavements outside the outer wall, suggest it was built in the latter part of the first century BCE, probably at the time of Herod the Great.

Since the gateway led directly into the private compound of Herod the Great's palace, it is hardly likely that it would have been used as a public thoroughfare by the city inhabitants or by the Essenes. The reason for the construction of the gate in the first place may have been as a direct response to a nasty experience Herod the Great had at one of the public gates of the city, which irked him considerably. It was on the occasion of the death of Antipater (c. 43 BCE) when the Jewish High Priest Hyrcanus refused Herod entrance into Jerusalem on the grounds that some of his non-Jewish soldiers might accidentally contaminate the purity of the Jewish pilgrims gathered in the city for a festival. Josephus tells us that "it was not proper to admit a crowd of foreigners when the people were in a state of ritual purity" (*Antiquities* XIV.285; cf. *War* I.229). Although Herod did in fact manage to gain entrance into the city by stealth, he must have realized that possessing one's own private entrance into the city would definitely have made things easier.

But why was the gate named after the Essenes, instead of as the "Gate of Herod" or the "Gate of the Palace"? One likely explanation is that this is because the Essenes were favored by the Herodian dynasty, as the ancient historians Philo and Josephus attest.[177] The story is that an Essene prophet named Menachem predicted that Herod the Great would rule over the Jews, and "from that time he [Herod] continued to hold all Essenes in honor." We may even suggest the Essenes were the same as the mysterious religious group referred to in the Gospels, known as the "Herodians" (Matthew 22:16; Mark 3:6; 12:13).

The presence of Essenes in Jerusalem is not surprising, since we hear from Josephus that the Essenes "occupy no one city, but settle in every town" (War II.124). Because of the royal privilege extended to them by Herod, members of the Essene community may have been allowed to establish themselves outside the palace gate—perhaps even in an enclosed encampment of their own to ensure communal purity—and this resulted in the gate being named after them. The slope below the gate and above the upper Hinnom Valley would have been one possible location. The fact that Essenes tended to live in separate communes is mentioned by Philo and Josephus.[178] Indeed, gates in antiquity were ordinarily named after features or places *outside* the cities, not inside them. In 1975 the famous Israeli archaeologist and general Yigael Yadin proposed that the gate was named after the Essenes because, unlike the rest of the inhabitants, they were obliged to "ease" themselves in latrines situated outside the city for reasons of ritual purity. The frequent comings and goings of the Essenes, according to this theory, ultimately led to the gate being named after them. I think this highly unlikely for the simple reason that the gate led directly into the property of the palace of Herod the Great (and the later *Praetorium*), with its extensive gardens and military barracks. Neither Herod nor the Roman governors would have allowed the constant movement of Essenes within the privacy of their grounds.[179] I think we can also reject the hypothesis put forward by some scholars that there was a separate Essene Quarter in the southern part of the Upper City and in the area of the traditional Mount Zion.[180] This assumption was made based on what was perceived to be an unusual proliferation of ritual bathing pools (*miqwa'ot*) on Mount Zion. However, ritual bathing pools are now known from many different parts of the city and they are a sure indicator for Jewish houses, but nothing else.

Now that we have shown that the gate uncovered on the west side of Herod's Palace is likely to be the Gate of the Essenes, what historical evidence may be adduced to support the idea that the courtyard situated within the gate was the place where Jesus was tried? Luckily, as we shall see, there are a number of historical attestations for a tribunal set up at the *Praetorium* and, more particularly, on its western side.

First, when Pilate used Temple funds for the purpose of building or restoring an aqueduct to bring water to Jerusalem, the local inhabitants, we are told by Josephus, "formed a ring round the tribunal of Pilate, then on a visit to Jerusalem, and besieged him with angry clamor" (*War* II.175–177; cf. *Antiquities* XVIII.60–62). Clearly this episode took place close to the *Praetorium* but not inside it. Signaling from his tribunal, Pilate had many of the protestors beaten and killed by his soldiers, some of whom had previously infiltrated the crowd. Since Josephus describes this as an uprising in which many thousands took part, it cannot have taken place within the inner precincts of the *Praetorium,* which was a closed compound surrounded by a wall. Hence, a place on the outside to the west and in full view of the tribunal would fit the location outside the gate perfectly. The barracks for the soldiers had to be close by. This military camp (*stratopedon*) is mentioned by Josephus (*War* II.329) as

Figure 6: Reconstruction drawing of the Gate of the Essenes where it is suggested the trial of Jesus took place.

adjoining the palace or *Praetorium*, just inside the gate area, and to the south of Herod's gardens. We should also mention the incident in which Herod Agrippa I seized Peter during Passover and threw him into prison in Jerusalem (Acts 12:3–9). This cannot have been at the Antonia Fortress but must have been at the *Praetorium*. The prison apparently had an "iron door which led into the city" (Acts 12:10) and since it gave access to a street it was probably located on the east side of the camp facing the city.

The second mention of a tribunal at the *Praetorium* is in the story of the outbreak of the First Jewish Revolt in 66 CE against Rome. Florus, who was at that time the Procurator, arrived at Jerusalem from Caesarea in an attempt to suppress the uprising. According to Josephus, Florus lodged at Herod's palace and "on the following day had a tribunal placed *in front of the building* and took his seat; the chief priests, the nobles, and the most eminent citizens then presented themselves before the tribunal. Florus ordered them to hand over the men who had insulted him, declaring that they themselves would feel his vengeance if they failed to produce the culprits" (my italics; *War* II.301–309). When they refused to do so, Florus had his soldiers sack the Agora/Upper Market and the residential quarter, which were in the close vicinity of the palace.

> "There ensued a stampede through the narrow alleys, massacre of all who were caught, every variety of pillage; many of the peaceable citizens were arrested and brought before Florus, who had them first scourged and then crucified. The total number of that day's victims, including women and children, for even infancy received no quarter, amounted to about three thousand six hundred. The calamity was aggravated by the unprecedented character of the Roman cruelty. For Florus ventured that day to do what none had ever done before, namely to scourge *before his tribunal and nail to the cross* men of equestrian rank, men who, if Jews by birth, were at least invested with that Roman dignity."

Since crucifixion was unlikely to have taken place within the city, the passage implies that the tribunal was set up adjacent to the palace/*Praetorium* and next to, or alongside, the western city wall, with the crosses set up outside but still at a visible distance.[181] This fits perfectly the suggested location of the tribunal inside the courtyard of the Gate of the Essenes.

How does this new information about the setting of the Roman tribunal fit in with the trial of Jesus as recorded in the Gospels? Mark does not tell us very much about the location of the trial of Jesus, accept that at one point the crowd "went up" to Pilate, perhaps indicating that he was seated at an elevated spot inside the gate. The soldiers brought Jesus to the *Praetorium*. Matthew adds that Pilate "was sitting on his judgment-seat" and there was a crowd "gathered together" at the tribunal (27:17–19). Pilate's judgment-seat may have been similar to the one used by Herod the Great's son, the Tetrarch Philip. Josephus wrote that during Philip's travels, "the throne on which he sat when he gave judgment accompanied him wherever he went. And so, whenever anyone appealed to him for redress along the route, at once without a moment's delay the throne was set up wherever it might be. He took his seat and gave the case a hearing" (*Antiquities* XVIII.107).

Unlike Mark and Matthew, Luke does not say anything at all about the place of the trial or its setting. John, however, provides a lot of additional information about the location of the trial. Jesus was led from the House of Caiaphas "into the *Praetorium* and it was early, and they [the priests] themselves entered not into the *Praetorium*, that they might not be defiled, but might eat the Passover" (18:28–29). Pilate "therefore went out to them" to find out what the accusation was. This description makes it clear that the place was situated outside the *Praetorium* proper, and that Jesus was in a prison inside the adjacent camp. The priests might have ventured within the outer gate but no further for fear of becoming ritually impure. We are then told that Pilate went in and out of the *Praetorium*, with Jesus being scourged, and then he "went out again," all of which suggests that the actual trial took place in an open space (18:33, 38; 19:4, 13). Jesus was eventually brought out to the place of the tribunal wearing a crown of thorns and purple robes, which enflamed the crowd, and then was taken back into the *Praetorium* camp with Pilate following (19:5, 9). John tells us that Pilate subsequently brought Jesus outside again and that he then sat on his judgment-seat (*bema*) at an elevated place (*gabbatha*) next to the place called the stone pavement (*lithostrotos*). The information provided by John fits well with what we gather from Josephus regarding the Roman tribunal being situated at an elevated location on the west side of the *Praetorium*.

The discovery of a well-defended gateway—probably the Gate of the Essenes—which has an inner courtyard paved with flagstones and

Figure 7: Reconstruction drawing of the Gate of the Essenes where it is suggested the trial of Jesus took place.

with a rocky outcrop on one side corresponds perfectly with the situation of the place of the Roman tribunal as suggested by Josephus and John. Hence, while it is a fair assumption the gate was used mainly as a private entrance into the *Praetorium*, this does not exclude public activities from taking place *inside* the gate and within the large courtyard situated between the walls. Indeed, this spot would have been ideal as the place for proclamations and public trials, and crowd control would have been pretty easy owing to the fact that it was so well defended. The trial at the gate was probably very carefully monitored by the Roman soldiers from the *Praetorium* camp. The crowds that were allowed to observe the proceedings may have been angry, but they were powerless. Once Jesus had been condemned to death by Pilate, the milling crowds would have been ordered to move quickly beyond the gate outside, under the watchful eyes of the heavily-armed Roman soldiers situated on the adjacent towers. Crowd control would have been extremely tight. Jesus was most likely taken back to the prison of the *Praetorium* barracks and from there would have been paraded down the streets of the Upper City to the Gennath Gate, where he was led out of the city to Golgotha.

Since medieval times the Via Dolorosa (the "Way of Suffering") has been traced by Christians in an entirely different part of the city, with its starting point close to the Antonia fortress on the northwest side. This is a tradition that has no historical basis whatsoever. I think there is now strong evidence to suggest that the newly excavated Gate of the Essenes on the west side of the Upper City and the Palace of Herod the Great is the actual place where the trial of Jesus took place. The astonishing thing is that thousands of Christian travelers and pilgrims pass by this site while visiting Jerusalem without realizing its significance. If my identification of the place of the trial of Jesus is correct, many believing Christians will need to think again about the exact spot where it was proclaimed: "Ecce Homo: Behold the Man!" (John 19:5).

But is this how Jesus was crucified? What do we know about the practice of crucifixion in first-century Jerusalem? One major source of information is Josephus, who referred to crucifixion in many of his writings, describing it as "the most pitiable of deaths" (*War* VII.203).[183] Crucifixion was occasionally practiced by Jewish rulers even before the arrival of the Romans. The Hasmonean Alexander Jannaeus (103–76 BCE) is reported to have had 800 Pharisees crucified in Jerusalem at one time, with "their wives and children butchered before their eyes, while he looked on, drinking, with his concubines reclining beside him" (*War* I.97). The fact that they were executed "in the midst of the city" not far from the Jewish Temple would have been regarded by the inhabitants as an additional outrage. We do not hear of crucifixions in Jerusalem during the reign of Herod the Great (37–4 BCE), but since he was notoriously cruel, we may suppose he did this only to avoid upsetting Jewish sensibilities. Execution by crucifixion was regarded as a Roman method and was abhorred by Jews. The traditional method of execution among Jews at that time was stoning, with burning, beheading, and strangling all fairly common as well.[184] Following the Roman suppression of the rebellion that broke out after the death of Herod the Great, 2,000 people were crucified by Quintilius Varus, apparently most of them in the vicinity of Jerusalem.

In Josephus' description of the Roman siege of Jerusalem by Titus, which ended with the capture of the city and its destruction in 70 CE, he wrote that some of the inhabitants of the city were "scourged and subjected to torture of every description, before being killed, and then crucified opposite the walls." Titus hoped that these crucifixions, about 500 per day, would serve as a deterrent to the Jewish inhabitants still held up inside the city and that some of them might be induced to surrender.[185] This didn't work. Josephus goes on to describe the rage of the Roman soldiers who "amused themselves by nailing their prisoners in different postures; and so great was their number, that space could not be found for the crosses nor crosses for the bodies" (*War* V. 450–451). Josephus also wrote about the crucifixions in the immediate aftermath of the capture of the city. In describing his return to Jerusalem after visiting the village of Tekoa, Josephus writes, "[I] saw many prisoners who had been crucified, and recognized three of my acquaintances among them, I was cut to the heart and came and told Titus with tears what I had seen. He gave orders immediately that they should be taken down and receive the most careful treatment. Two of them died in the physician's hands; the third survived" (*Life* 420).

There can be no doubt that many thousands of people from Jerusalem lost their lives through crucifixion during the course of the first century. This figure probably swelled in the wake of the failed revolt against the Romans, which ended with the fall of the city in 70 CE. These executions were made by nailing and tying people to wooden crosses, which was the Roman practice for dealing with deserters, captured enemy soldiers, and rebels at the time of war, and during peacetime for criminals of the lower classes, for thieves, brigands, and slaves.[186] While the practice of crucifixion was loathed by some Roman lawmakers, it was probably also deemed a necessary evil in order to prop up weakened ruling authorities and especially those in the provinces. It was there that the Roman procurators had the jurisdiction to impose the death penalty in peacetime. The crucifixion was frequently preceded by the act of scourging, with the victim tied to a column and beaten with a *flagellum,* which was a stick with attached leather cords or thongs with hard iron or bone tips.[187] The beating was not allowed to be life-threatening since the victim still had to have enough strength to carry the horizontal wooden crossbeam on his shoulders to the site of the crucifixion. The victim was taken there by soldiers, one of whom held the *titulus,* which was an inscription bearing the name of the criminal and his offence; it would later be affixed to the cross above the dying man.[188]

Taking into consideration the fact that many thousands of Jews were executed by Romans in first-century Jerusalem, we should expect to find ample archaeological evidence of crucified remains at sites in the immediate outskirts of the ancient city, with mass burial pits and numerous trench graves, but nothing like this has come to light. We could argue that this is because the crucified were left unburied as in other countries under Roman dominion, with the dead bodies serving as carrion for wild animals and birds of prey. But there is no evidence that this was how things were done in first-century Jerusalem, at least not in peacetime.

An important discovery was made in June 1968 when the remains of a crucified man were recovered from a first century burial cave accidentally unearthed during modern construction work in the new neighborhood of Giv'at ha-Mivtar in north Jerusalem.[189] The archaeologist Vassilios Tzaferis was sent out by the Israel Department of Antiquities to investigate this tomb and three others, to retrieve the finds inside, and to bring the artifacts back to the headquarters in the Rockefeller Museum. Inside one of the stone ossuaries, the physical anthropologist Nicu Haas found the bones of a 24- to 28-year-old crucified man, mixed with the bones of a child. The evidence consisted of a right heel-bone (*calcaneum*) with an iron nail (11.5 cm long) firmly embedded in it.[190] This was a unique find and nothing like it has been found since.[191]

The tomb of the crucified man was carved into a layer of soft limestone. Its forecourt was damaged by the bulldozers, but the small plug-like stone door (*golal*) was found intact. The main burial chamber had a pit in its center enabling family members to move around the tomb without stooping down. There were burial benches on three sides on which bodies could be laid out, and *kokhim* (horizontal burial recesses) in the walls. An additional doorway, also blocked with a stone door, led to another, lower chamber, which also had *kokhim* in its walls.

Nine of the twelve *kokhim* had skeletons in them, with three containing ossuaries covered with lids. One ossuary contained the bones of a 50-year-old man with an inscription in Jewish script identifying him as Simon, "[a] builder of the Temple."[192] Josephus notes that 10,000 skilled workmen and 1,000 trained priests took part in the construction of the Temple (*Antiq.* XV.390). Simon was probably one of them. The general Jewish practice in the first-century CE was to allow the body of the deceased to decompose for at least one year and then for the bones to be collected into an ossuary. The tops of some of the bones in the ossuaries were found sprinkled with a thin layer of black or brown pigment, perhaps the dried remnants of oil used to anoint the bones during the secondary reburial.[193] Ossuaries may have been used by Jews with a firm belief in the resurrection of the dead, but this does not explain why mixed and even incomplete sets of bones of different individuals are found together in ossuaries.[194] It is more likely that ossuaries were used as containers for the bones of some but not all of the dead, following the decomposition of their bodies. Since many of those buried in the tomb were not in ossuaries, we have to assume they were originally used only for the privileged few. Eventually, as pressure built up on space within the tomb, the bones of additional bodies would be gathered up into the ossuaries, or, alternatively, placed into bone pits cut into the floors or benches. This explains the mixed or incomplete sets of bones. Some of the ossuaries in the tomb were decorated and the double rosette was a favorite motif. Quite possibly these are abstract renderings of the winged cherubim (Exodus 25:18–20; 37:7–9), the idea being that these celestial creatures might in some way protect the bones of the dead.

The anthropological study of the osteological remains from the Giv'at ha-Mivtar tomb made by Haas showed that early death was experienced by many in the family, with five children dying before reaching the age of seven, and with only two adults living beyond the age of fifty. This sounds quite shocking, but one has to remember that the nail and the right heel-bone came to be preserved together. There were also remnants of a thin plaque made of olive wood between the head of the nail and the bone. The reason why the executioners chose to put the nail through the heel bone in the first place is because it is the largest bone in the foot. An additional examination of the bones in the ossuary did not find evidence for nails penetrating the wrists or forearms, suggesting that the crucified man's arms were tied to the crossbeam with ropes.

The physical anthropologist who did the original examination of the bones, Haas, reached a number of conclusions particularly in regard to the reconstruction of the crucified man. These conclusions were later shown to be unsustainable in a follow-up study made by the anthropologist Zias, who described the reconstruction by Haas as "anatomically impossible on the basis of the available evidence."[199] In the new reconstruction the crucified man is shown slumped forward with his arms tied with ropes to the crossbeam, and with each leg affixed laterally to the vertical stake. Recent work on the heel bone and nail by Israel Hershkovitz, however, using modern medical scanning equipment, indicates that the actual piecing together and gluing of the shattered heel bone (*calcaneum*) by Haas in 1968 may have been incorrect—if this is so, it might affect the way we reconstruct the crucifixion of the Giv'at ha-Mivtar man.[200] Unfortunately, most of the crucified man's bones were transferred to the Jewish religious authorities in Jerusalem for reburial, and so are no longer available for further research.[201]

Crucifixion was an extremely cruel form of death penalty. As mentioned, the victim was sometimes scourged or flogged beforehand, but not to the extent that he lost consciousness.[202] The person was crucified naked, thereby enhancing the overall humiliation to him and his family. There was probably not one consistent form of crucifixion; Josephus reports that people were crucified in different postures and in accordance with the different types of wooden stakes and beams

Figure 8: Reconstruction drawing showing the way the man from the Giv'at ha-Mivtar tomb was crucified.

available.[203] Some of these may have been typically cross-like in appearance (*crux immissa*), but others may have been put together in the shape of a T (*crux commissa*). If the vertical post (*stipes*) of the cross was already erected at the place of the execution, all the soldiers needed to do were to take the victim, whose arms were already bound to the *patibulum* (crossbeam), and attach him to the vertical post. The scarcity of wood around Jerusalem probably meant that vertical posts and crossbeams were frequently reused. Unsuitable types of wood, such as the knotted olive, would also occasionally be used. Looped ropes and iron nails held the victim's legs to the stake.[204] In some cases the victim was roped and nailed to the cross before it was set vertically in position. Owing to the fact that the victim had no way of supporting his body, death ensued within a matter of hours, accompanied by muscular spasms and asphyxiation. To prolong agony and the moment of death, the Romans placed the victim on a kind of wooden seat or crotch support (*sedile*) halfway down the cross, which gave the victim something to lean against but no relief. A foot support (*suppedaneum*) was also sometimes provided. The nailing of feet to the cross inflicted pain and had a function similar to that of the deliberate breaking of legs in that it hastened death.[205] Crucified criminals are described by Pseudo-Manetho as follows: "punished with limbs outstretched, they see the stake as their fate; they are fastened (and) nailed to it in the most bitter torment, evil food for birds of prey and grim pickings for dogs" (*Apotelesmatica* 4.198).

A description of the crucifixion of Jesus appears in all four Gospel accounts, as well as in the apocryphal Gospel of Peter.[206] Once the decision had been made by Pontius Pilate to put Jesus to death, he was taken by soldiers from the prison at the *Praetorium* to the place of execution outside the city. Josephus wrote: "Pilate, upon hearing him [Jesus] accused by men of the highest standing among us, had condemned him to be crucified . . ." (*Antiq.* XVIII.64). Scholars have debated whether the passage about Jesus is a later interpolation

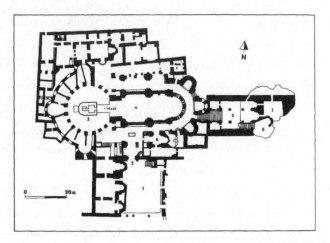

Figure 9: Map of the Church of the Holy Sepulchre in Jerusalem: 1) forecourt; 2) main entrance; 3) Edicule / Tomb of Jesus; 4) Calvary / traditional Place of Crucifixion; 5) Chapel of St Helena; 6) Cave of the Invention of the Cross; 7) Chapel of St Vartan.

or, alternatively, whether it is an embellishment of an authentic account.[207] Either way, this specific sentence about Pilate condemning Jesus to crucifixion seems right and is quite different from the rather ambiguous statements on Pilate's responsibility in the Gospels.

The location of the place of the crucifixion needs now to be considered. Archaeology, as we shall see, has much to contribute on this subject. Tacitus (*Annales* II.32:2) makes it clear that certain areas were usually set aside for crucifixion outside a city, and in the case of Rome this was at a place known as Campus Esquilinus, where slaves were frequently crucified and which was a favorite feeding ground for vultures. For such a place to serve as a deterrent it had to be topographically visible from the walls and houses of the adjacent city or town, or at the very least close to a main highway or road leading from that place. Quintilian wrote that "whenever we crucify the guilty, the most crowded roads are chosen, where the most people can see and be moved by this fear. For penalties relate not so much to retribution as to their exemplary effect" (*Declamationes* 274). The nineteenth-century explorer Charles Warren relates that this was exactly the reason why

the public executions of criminals, including beheadings, was undertaken in his day outside the Jaffa Gate in Jerusalem and close to the
main road leading to Jaffa.[208]

The exact location where Jesus was crucified is annoyingly vague
in the Gospels.[209] They are, however, in agreement that Jesus was
brought to a place called *Golgotha*, which is said to refer to "the place
of the skull." John adds that it was situated sufficiently close enough
to the city for passers-by to be able to make out what was written
on the *titulus* above Jesus's cross (19:20). The name of the place was
derived from the Aramaic *golgolta* or *gulgulta* ("skull") and not from
Hebrew, as John asserts. Moreover, since it was regarded as "the place"
of the skull, we may surmise that the full Aramaic name for this area
in the first century was *meqom golgolta*. As a result of the Latin translation of Luke (23:33), the site also came to be known as Calvary (Latin
calva = skull). Today, the Rock of Calvary is pointed out to pilgrims
and visitors, immediately on the right when entering the Church of
the Holy Sepulchre. This rocky outcrop rises to a height of 9 to 13
meters above the surrounding quarry floor and its top is narrow and
confining (only 3.5 x 1.7 meters). At the time of the Greek Orthodox
excavations in 1988, when the marble covering dating from 1810 was
removed, I was very lucky, together with my colleague Joan Taylor, to
be given the chance to make a thorough examination of the entire top
surface of the Rock of Calvary, something very few people have been
able to do. At the invitation of the engineer Theodossius Mitropoulos,
we clambered around the summit of the rock, examining the various
hewn features and depressions in its surface and signs of plaster. Assuming the rock received its present shape by the time of Jesus and
no later, we reached the conclusion that the summit was too narrow
to permit three crosses to be placed there and its sides were too steep
to allow easy access.[210] While the rock may have been a monument
marking the general place of Golgotha—almost like a signpost—it
was definitely not the actual *place* of crucifixion.

The execution site of Golgotha must have been an easily identifiable topographical landmark close to Jerusalem, a low promontory perhaps, known to the city inhabitants by a name akin perhaps to the later Arabic usage of the word *ras* ("head") for a prominent, but not exceptionally high, hillock or knoll. The implication from the Gospel references is that it was a place people had easy access to and it could be seen from afar, which suggests a conspicuous location rather than a small rocky outcrop. More importantly, it was situated adjacent to a path or road leading to the city, along which Simon of Cyrene was "coming [to the city] from the country" (Mark 15:21), and which, understandably, led directly to a gate (Hebrews 13:12). The Gospel of John provides another piece of topographical information in that Jesus's tomb is said to be located close to the place of the crucifixion: "Now in the place where he was crucified [i.e., Golgotha] there was a garden; and in the garden a new tomb . . . There then they laid Jesus" (19:41–42). While in the non-canonical Gospel of Peter, Golgotha is not mentioned by name, the tomb where Jesus was buried is stated to have been at a spot "called Joseph's Garden" (6:24).[211] Clearly, Golgotha was a well-defined locality outside the city, with gardens and tombs, and with an execution place—perhaps enclosed within a stone fence—situated not far from a road leading to a gate in the city wall.

As we shall see, there are many arguments in favor of accepting the location of the tomb of Jesus with the one beneath the present-day Church of the Holy Sepulchre. Eusebius, writing in the late third century CE on Golgotha, states that the place of the crucifixion was pointed out in Aelia Capitolina—the name of Jerusalem from the time of Hadrian—"right beside the northern parts of Mount Zion."[212] This means we need to seek Golgotha somewhere to the northwest of the city as it existed at the time of Jesus, near the angle where two fortification walls joined, namely the "First" and "Second" walls. These fortifications are described by Josephus, who says the Gennath ("Gardens") Gate was situated along the northern stretch of the First

Wall close to where the Second Wall began in the south (*War* V.146). Remnants of a fortified gate dating from this period were uncovered in the Jewish Quarter in the northern stretch of the First Wall by Israeli archaeologist Nahman Avigad, who identified it convincingly as that of the Gennath Gate.[213] If this identification is correct (and I believe it to be so) then the gate would have had to be the point of departure for the Second Wall. Since the nineteenth century the exact course of the Second Wall has been debated by scholars, but today there is some consensus as to its general alignment.[214] It ran north from the gate just mentioned and then turned eastward, where it joined up with the fortress of Antonia, situated at the northwest angle of the Temple Mount. According to Josephus, the northern end of the Second Wall had "upper gates" (*War* V.337). For this reason we should assume a road or path ran parallel to the Second Wall from the outside, extending from the Gennath Gate northward, passing the upper gates, and then reaching the main highway leading northward along the watershed in the direction of the city of Nablus.

Two other factors need to be mentioned before we deal with the possible topographical identification of Golgotha. First, a valley existed on the north side of the First Wall and extended eastward down to the Tyropoeon Valley. It is referred to by scholars as the Transversal Valley, but is not mentioned in ancient sources. Second, at the top of this valley, to the west, there was a very large open reservoir of water, known as the Amygdalon ("Towers") Pool, mentioned by Josephus (*War* V.468). The situation of this pool would have made it fairly easy to establish terraced orchards and gardens, irrigated with channels leading from the pool, descending in serried fashion down the length of the upper Transversal Valley towards the Gennath Gate. These terraced gardens would have been the reason for the name of the gate.

We may assume that a road or path ran parallel to the northern stretch of the First Wall, from the outside, ascending along the edge

of the Transversal Valley westward where, after passing Herod's old
palace (or the *Praetorium*), it joined up with the main highway leading westward in the direction of Emmaus and distant Jaffa. This
may have been the road traversed by Simon of Cyrene. Archaeological excavations have shown that much of the area on the north side
of the Transversal Valley and as far north as the Church of the Holy
Sepulchre served as a major quarry for extracting blocks of building
stone in antiquity. Some of these stone quarries were open to the sky,
but there were also subterranean caverns in which stone blocks, made
from the higher quality *meleke* stone layer, were removed by masons,
leaving the inferior *mizzi hilu* stone layer as a roof. These quarries
appear to have had a long history dating back to the eighth century
BCE, but it is likely they continued to be maintained and used until
the area came to be enclosed within the Third Wall around 44 CE.
Indeed, these quarries may very well have supplied considerable quan-

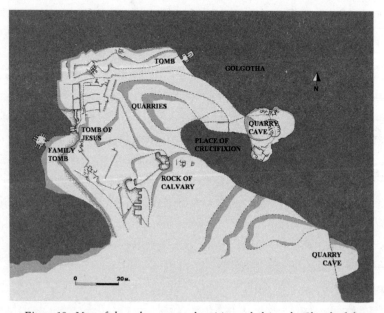

*Figure 10: Map of the rocky areas and cavities underlying the Church of the
Holy Sepulchre.*

tities of stone blocks needed for the construction of the Second Wall of Jerusalem, probably at the time of Herod the Great.

The sheer rock-cut scarps left by the quarrymen were ideal for burial caves to be cut into them. Eventually, the lower quarried areas were abandoned and filled in with soil and quarry debris, with some abandoned quarry areas being converted into garden patches and orchards. Hence, we should reconstruct this area at the time of Jesus as a large rocky knoll with an expanse of rock-hewn cavities and subterranean indentations at many different levels.[215] The size of this locality appears to have spanned at least 200 meters from north to south and 150 meters from east to west. The depressions in the ground, especially where the quarrying activities had ceased, were partly used for horticulture or arboriculture. Some of the rocky scarps were pierced with openings leading to burial caves. This combination of burial caves, stone quarrying, and agricultural activities at the same spot was a common phenomenon in the first century CE as we can learn from archaeological finds in the city's surroundings.

This rocky area should in my opinion be identified as Golgotha.[216] It was here, not far from the road extending along the Transversal Valley (from the direction of the *Praetorium*) and close to the Gennath Gate, that the execution grounds would have been situated. If we accept the testimony of John, Jesus was also buried in the vicinity. We may surmise that the exact situation of Golgotha was passed down from generation to generation among Jesus's supporters, even when the place itself came to be hidden beneath the pavement of the Forum and Temple of Venus in Aelia Capitolina, which was built after 135 CE to replace the ruins of Jerusalem. This is clear from Eusebius, an erudite and learned scholar writing in the late third century, who noted that the "Place of the Skull" was still "pointed out in Aelia" on the northern side of Mount Zion, indicating that knowledge of the whereabouts of Golgotha had been maintained from 70 CE and until his day. Present-day visitors to the Church of the Holy Sepulchre are shown the Rock of Calvary and told that this is where the crucifixion took place. I have already shown that to place a crucifixion on the top of this narrow mass of rock would not have been feasible. The rock is therefore a finger-like "marker" representing the general place of the crucifixion, but nothing more. Instead, Christian writers and travelers from the fourth century CE onward, such as the Bordeaux Pilgrim, Cyril of Jerusalem, and Egeria, make it clear that they understand Golgotha to be a very large expanse of rock spread beneath the large basilica, or the "Martyrium," built at the instigation of Constantine the Great to the east of the Tomb of Jesus. The actual place where a patch of the rock of Golgotha was shown to visitors and venerated was probably located at the west end of the building within the area of its domed apse. The foundations of part of this apse were discovered during an excavation in the choir of the Katholikon in 1971; unfortunately, the central part of the apse, in the area in front of the steps leading down to the Chapel of St Helena, has not yet been excavated so we do not know what the rock looked like.[217]

The Gospels provide slightly contradictory accounts of the crucifixion, but they are consistent in not providing details as to the exact manner in which Jesus was attached to the cross, the shape of the cross, the way his arms and legs were placed on it, whether ropes were used in addition to nails to hold his arms in position, and so forth. Nails are not mentioned in any of the Gospels in connection with the crucifixion of Jesus. However, John does refer to the marks seen on the hands of Jesus resulting from the nails (20:25), and in the non-canonical Gospel of Peter we hear: "And then the Jews drew the nails from the hands of the Lord and laid him on the earth" (6:21).[218] There is agreement in the Gospels that Jesus was offered wine mixed with myrrh before being crucified, as an act of mercy, perhaps to dull the effect of the ensuing crucifixion, but it was refused. His garments were divided up and lots were cast over them by the soldiers. There are two "malefactors" or criminals who were crucified with Jesus on either side. A *titulus* is set up on top of the cross reading

"King of the Jews," and Jesus is mocked. He may still have been wearing the crown of thorns.[219] Darkness descends; this is probably not an eclipse but the result of gathering clouds and a brewing storm. Jesus is given a sponge with vinegar (or soured wine) which is placed on a reed for him to drink. A lance is plunged into his side to ascertain that he is dead before being removed from the cross. There are many potential causes that may have contributed to Jesus's death. The earlier scourging would undoubtedly have led to a massive loss of blood and the effect of carrying the heavy crossbeam on his shoulders to Golgotha would also have brought about substantial dehydration and exhaustion. Hence, it is not surprising that Jesus did not last very long on the cross, perhaps 3 to 6 hours at the most.[220]

It is unclear who exactly attended the crucifixion, with Luke mentioning that "the people [of Jerusalem] stood beholding" (Luke 23:35). This crowd was sympathetic to Jesus and did not mock him.[221] Luke says that after Jesus died the "multitudes that came together to this sight, when they beheld the things that were done, returned smiting their breasts. And all his acquaintance, and the women that followed with him from Galilee, stood afar off, seeing these things." (Luke 23:48–49). The women who stood afar are identified in Mark and Matthew as Mary, the mother of Jesus, Mary Magdalene, and Salome, with John also referring to the presence of the wife of Clopas, saying also that they stood close to the cross. A Centurion, as one of the executioners, is deeply shaken by the events and according to Luke states his belief that Jesus is innocent. It is possible that Simon of Cyrene, a Jewish pilgrim in Jerusalem for the Passover holiday who helped carry the cross of Jesus, was also part of the multitude observing from the road. Interestingly, an ossuary is known from the Kidron Valley in Jerusalem bearing the Greek inscription "Alexander [son of] Simon" and in Jewish script "Alexander [the] Cyrene." Since we know that Simon of Cyrene had two sons, Alexander and Rufus, it is quite likely that this ossuary belonged to his son.[222]

Figure 11: Ossuary inscription mentioning "Alexander {the} Cyrene" written in Greek and in Jewish script.

There was a rush to remove Jesus from the cross so that he could be buried before the beginning of the Sabbath. This was such a concern that John relates the inhabitants of Jerusalem asked for special dispensation from Pilate to allow them to have the legs of the three crucified broken, so that they might die faster. The apocryphal Gospel of Peter goes even further and has Joseph of Arimathea and Herod Antipas asking Pilate for the body of Jesus even before the crucifixion has begun: "And Herod said, 'Brother Pilate, even if no one had begged him, we should bury him, since the Sabbath is drawing on. For it stands written in the Law: the sun shall not set on one that has been put to death" (2:3). Even Josephus points out that this was normal procedure in his day: "malefactors who have been sentenced to crucifixion are taken down and buried before sunset." (*War* IV.317).

The ignoble demise of Jesus by crucifixion was a fact his followers in subsequent centuries found difficult to explain. This led to pagan opponents accusing Jesus's followers of worshipping a criminal and, even worse, a cross, a charge that was hard to contradict in the context of a society in which crucifixion was deemed both scandalous and shameful. For those from a Jewish background it is unlikely that they could ignore knowledge of the biblical curse laid upon anyone hung upon a tree, as set forth in Deuteronomy, and in later centuries the notion of a crucified messiah was particularly offensive to them.[223] Early pagan critics claimed Jesus could not have been the son of God. After all, the argument went, how could a son of God be executed as a criminal? Hence, Justin in his rebuttal of this criticism wrote about such claims: "they say that our madness consists of the fact that we put a crucified man in second place after the unchangeable and eternal God, the Creator of the world" (*Apology* I.13:4). But

Jesus's dishonorable end remained difficult to explain in subsequent centuries. Even Paul made it clear to his readers that to preach about a Christ crucified is to Jews a "stumbling block" and to Gentiles a "folly" (I Corinthians 1:23). As the scholar Martin Hengel wrote: "A crucified messiah, son of God or God must have seemed a contradiction in terms to anyone, Jew, Greek, Roman or barbarian, asked to believe such a claim, and it will certainly have been thought offensive and foolish."[224]

So we are left with the question as to how the followers of Jesus were able to convert people to their belief system, when the idea of a crucified messiah was somewhat anathema to all those around them. Clearly those from the lower classes and slaves, who suffered from crucifixion, would not have wanted association with a religion that constantly reminded them of their fears. What the followers of Jesus were able to offer, however, was something different and of a higher order: a promise of a better afterlife and an immediate entrance into the Kingdom of Heaven. This is what made Christianity palatable, especially to the educated classes. It was this concept that was strongly highlighted by the apologetics in response to those mocking the idea of a crucified God.

SEVEN

THE BURIAL OF JESUS

"When evening had come, and since it was the day of Preparation, that is, the day before the Sabbath, Joseph of Arimathea, a respected member of the Council, who was also himself waiting expectantly for the Kingdom of God, went boldly to Pilate and asked for the body of Jesus. Then Pilate wondered if he were already dead; and summoning the Centurion, he asked him whether he had been dead for some time. When he learned from the Centurion that he was dead, he granted the body to Joseph. Then Joseph bought a linen cloth, and taking down the body, wrapped it in the linen cloth, and laid it in a tomb that had been hewn out of the rock. He then rolled a stone against the door of the tomb."

(Mark 15:42–46).

The exact whereabouts of the tomb of Jesus is the greatest mystery. We cannot be certain where he was buried. The assumption has always been that he was buried *next* to the place of crucifixion at Golgotha based on the Gospel of John (19:41), but there is no mention of this in the other three Gospels.

Today, the traditional tomb is pointed out close to Calvary at the Church of the Holy Sepulchre within the Old City of Jerusalem. Is this the tomb of Jesus? Thousands upon thousands of Christian pilgrims flock to this place while visiting the Holy Land, lining up to get a brief glimpse of the hallowed spot. But what they actually see is a built structure known as the Edicule, adorned with lamps and candles, in the circular part of the church known as the Rotunda, and many go away disappointed that nothing can be seen of the original tomb. Have the ecclesiastical authorities and visiting pilgrims been misled? Are they worshipping at the wrong location? In the previous chapter I argued for the probability of this location as Golgotha, where Jesus was executed, but what about it also being the place of his tomb? While the tradition connecting this location with his tomb can be traced back to the early fourth century, how was the tradition maintained by Jesus's followers during the two hundred years or so when the tomb was not even visible but buried beneath tons of rubble below the foundations of the Temple of Venus and the adjacent Roman Forum of Aelia Capitolina?

A number of alternatives have been proposed for the location of the Jesus tomb. Some suggest it was situated to the east of Jerusalem on the Mount of Olives, while others say the Hinnom Valley to the south of the city might be a more appropriate location.[225] But these proposals are not backed up either by archaeology or history. Recently, the tomb of Jesus was identified in a cave at Talpiot, a modern suburb south of the city, and it received a lot of press attention (see Excursus, p. 175). In the nineteenth century, a more solid argument was made for an alternative Golgotha at a rocky promontory to the north of the city and an ancient burial cave was identified at the spot. Many visitors who visit this place—now known as the "Garden Tomb"—are told that this might actually be the place of Jesus's burial. But is it?

Over the past three decades I have been puzzling over where Jesus was actually buried, taking into consideration all available archaeological and historical data. I have also tried to keep an open mind on the ideas about the location of the tomb, some quite outlandish, put forward by a myriad of investigators since the nineteenth century. The search for the tomb of Jesus is a fascinating detective story; there are many twists and turns and red herrings.

We will consider the archaeological and historical reasoning for the proposed identification of the place of burial later on. But what do the Gospels actually say about the death and burial of Jesus?

Admittedly, the Gospel accounts are not very informative about the circumstances of the burial.[226] No information whatsoever is provided in regard to the *exact* topographical position of the tomb in relation to the ancient city, except that John says it was close to the place where Jesus was crucified at Golgotha (19:41). Later, following the construction of the Third Wall fortification by Agrippa (41–44 CE), the area of Golgotha was included in the "suburbs" of the expanded city, which had, in Josephus' words, "gradually crept beyond the ramparts" (*War* V.148). These suburbs were sparsely settled judging by archaeological finds, except for the built-up area around the Bethesda Pools and to the west of it—an area referred to by Josephus as Bezetha. The establishing of this "new town" and the use of parts of it for market purposes (e.g., the "timber market" referred to by Josephus, *War* II.530) and as encampment grounds for pilgrims for the Jewish festivals (an area referred to as "the plain" in *War* II.13), would have necessitated the emptying of the burial caves in this area—including those at Golgotha—and their reburial elsewhere, as was the custom at the time. The rabbinical injunction was that "carcasses, graves, and tanneries may not remain within a space of fifty cubits [i.e., approximately 25 meters] from the town" (m. Baba Bathra 2:9). Indeed, a few Iron Age tombs were found beneath the line of the western stretch of the First Wall and it would appear their contents were cleared out at the time this fortification wall was built by the Hasmoneans in the late second century BCE, showing that the injunction was something that was actually heeded.[227]

The Gospels do say that the body of Jesus was removed from the cross *late* on Friday afternoon, which was on the eve of the Jewish Sabbath, and then taken to the place of burial. As we have seen, the crucifixion most likely took place close to the city walls and owing to the rapid onset of the Sabbath, with a concomitant need for rapid burial, we may assume that only a short distance was traversed to the place of his tomb.

Joseph of Arimathea is a key figure in this story. Arimathea is the name of the place Joseph originated from, but its exact whereabouts are unknown. It is thought to have been somewhere in the western foothills since Eusebius later identified Joseph's hometown at Rentis close to Diospolis or Lod.[228] Joseph is said to have received special permission from Pontius Pilate to bury Jesus in his newly-cut tomb. According to Mark, Pilate required that a Centurion check first to ensure that Jesus had indeed died before granting the body to Joseph, who then supervised the actual physical removal of the body from the cross. The fact that Jesus, who was a stranger in Jerusalem, was buried in a tomb belonging to a local inhabitant clearly indicates the importance of Jesus as a charismatic figure who was appreciated beyond the inner circle of his followers. Joseph of Arimathea is said to have been a person of some standing in Jerusalem society—a "rich man," according to Matthew (27:57; cf. Mark 15:43)—otherwise he would hardly have been granted a private audience with Pilate, let alone receive from him special dispensation to bury the body of a crucified criminal who was not even a member of his own family. The fact that Joseph's tomb was *newly-cut* (Matthew 27:60; Luke 23:53; John 19:41) leads us to infer that his family had not been living in Jerusalem for very long and that his older relatives were buried in the village or town of Arimathea, which explains why his tomb did not house previously deceased members of the family. Indeed, Luke makes it very clear that the tomb was a place where "never man had yet lain" (23:53). Why would a person of Joseph's status have owned a tomb at Golgotha, which was ostensibly a place designated for the crucifixion of bandits and murderers? Golgotha was a large knoll with an expanse of rock on the northwest of Jerusalem, but only one small part of it need have been set aside as a place of execution. Owing to the importance of land ownership at that time and the fact that land close to Jerusalem was at a premium, this would have been an ideal spot for Joseph to establish a family tomb. Depending on the size of the plot of land in which the tomb was hewn, the area around it could also have been used for other activities like stone quarrying, or even as a place for a pottery kiln or tannery.

We wonder what Joseph's arguments were when he stood in front of Pilate, whom the Gospel of Peter says was his "friend" (2:3).[229] Confessing that he was a disciple of Jesus (Matthew 27:57) would not have gone down well with Pilate, but as an elected member of the "Council" (*bouleutes*) or Sanhedrin (Mark 15:43) Joseph's plea on religious grounds would not have been ignored by the Roman authorities. Josephus testifies to the fact that the Romans did not require their Jewish subjects to violate their religious laws (*Against Apion* II.73). I surmise he would have argued that respect be accorded to the executed man based on the prevalent Jewish custom of the time that dead bodies must not be left exposed to be eaten by wild animals and buzzards. It was vital that the body of Jesus be buried before sundown and the beginning of the Sabbath when burials were prohibited. Instructions are provided in Deuteronomy: "And if a man has committed a sin worthy of death, and he is to be put to death, and thou hang him on a tree: his body shall not remain all night upon the tree, but thou shalt in any wise bury him that day . . ." (21:22–23).[230]

Rabbinical writings actually make it clear that the bodies of executed criminals were kept at that time in two places not far from the Sanhedrin court, one for the beheaded and strangled, and one for the stoned or burnt (m. Sanhedrin 6:5–6). Crucifixion is not mentioned in this context because it was a Roman method of execution. The fact that Jesus was crucified and his body was not subsequently placed in one of the tombs designated by the Sanhedrin for the executed clearly indicates they did not condemn Jesus to death. Legal jurisdiction in this specific case, as we saw in the previous chapter, was entirely in the hands of the Romans.[231]

Joseph is not reported in any of these accounts as having made an attempt to prevent the crucifixion of Jesus, though he may have attended the special meeting at the High Priest's house the previous evening. Luke does say obliquely that Joseph "had not consented to the counsel and deed of them" (23:51). The Gospel of Peter surprisingly has Joseph asking Pilate for the body of Jesus *before* the crucifixion had even commenced (2:3). Luckily, Joseph provided a tomb for Jesus to be buried in. Had he not done so, what would have happened to Jesus's body? The idea that an executed Jew would have been chucked into a common burial pit after being removed from the cross is unlikely. It may have been the normal practice for criminals of the lower classes and for slaves elsewhere in the Roman Empire, but it is unlikely to have been practiced in Jerusalem because of Jewish religious sensibilities. The truth is the Roman authorities would have wanted to keep the Sanhedrin and locals agreeable.[232] In fact, as we have seen, the only remains of a crucified man ever found in Jerusalem were not found in a pit, but inside a rock-cut family tomb at Giv'at ha-Mivtar to the north of Jerusalem, belying the notion that crucified criminals were subsequently buried disgracefully like dogs and without the dignity of a final repose. It was vital to Jews that on death they were buried with their family members, as is made clear in the biblical expression that on burial a person "slept" or was "gathered to his fathers" (e.g., Judges 2:10; I Kings 15:8).

The fact that Joseph makes such a late appearance in the story of the final days of Jesus might suggest that he had nothing to do with the deliberations over his fate. As mentioned, he probably did attend the council meeting at the High Priest's house the evening before the crucifixion and may even have been appointed at that meeting to see to it that Jesus received a dignified burial. But why would Joseph have aligned himself so publicly with Jesus by providing him with his own tomb? The answer given by Mark is that this is because Joseph was a person "waiting for the Kingdom of God" (15:43), but this is rather vague and may even be a late gloss. It could also mean that Joseph was simply a highly religious person with a personal concern for the honor of the dead. However, the text in the Fourth Gospel indicates quite emphatically that Joseph was a disciple of Jesus (John 19:38). Hence, we cannot ignore the possibility that Joseph was in some way inculcated into the teachings of Jesus. But this seems unlikely for the simple reason that there is a complete lack of clarity regarding Joseph's relationship to Jesus in the other three Gospels. The explanation may be straightforward: Joseph wanted to protect the honor of a man labeled as a criminal, perhaps personally believing Jesus to be a man of religious conviction who had unwittingly threatened the ruling establishment (both Jewish and Roman). We shall never know for certain. The fact is, after Jesus's burial Joseph completely disappears from the Gospel accounts, which is quite telling. One possibility is that Joseph was held responsible by the Roman authorities for the disappearance of the body of Jesus from his tomb on the Sunday after the burial, and that he suffered dire consequences as a result of this.

Would Jesus's body have been placed in a rock-cut tomb as the Gospels say? We can argue that Jesus was only buried in Joseph of Arimathea's rock-cut tomb as a last-minute resort, since there was not enough time to dig a common trench grave before the incoming Sabbath.[233] This is the theory put forward by the American scholar Jodi Magness. However, there is no archaeological or historical evidence to suggest that this was the intention. The theory is unconvincing for a number of reasons.

First, I think that concerted digging by a number of strong individuals could easily produce a body-sized trench grave in no time. Second, there is no archaeological evidence for scattered graves from this period in the surroundings of Jerusalem. I would contend that this cannot just be put down to an accident of discovery, i.e., that trench graves are not usually found because they are poor in finds and hence more susceptible to destruction by modern development.[234]

Indeed, land was at a premium and the entire hinterland of the city was given over to intensive and extensive agricultural (olive and vine cultivation) and industrial (primarily rock quarrying) activities. Cemeteries with rock-cut family tombs were not covered over with soil and were specifically established in landscapes where rock outcrops were common. Hence, every patch of land with arable soil was surrounded with a stone fence or terraced and used for cultivation. Scattered areas of trench graves would have been deemed wasteful in terms of the utilization of land resources in the hinterland of Jerusalem.

Theoretically, a number of cemeteries with trench graves may have been established on marginal lands on the distant outskirts of the city. Indeed, a cemetery with trench graves was uncovered at Beit Safafa a couple of kilometers south of Jerusalem. However, it is still the only one found, and the uniqueness of this cemetery is such that it led the Israeli excavator Boaz Zissu to suggest it might even have been used by the Essenes since it resembled the cemetery of the Dead Sea Scroll sect at Qumran on the northwestern shore of the Dead Sea.[235]

There is another consideration. Many Jews at that time would have vehemently objected to placing a body in a trench grave without absolute certainty that the person was dead and not in a comatose state. In certain regions of Israel where trench or cist graves were used for burial, such as the Jordan Valley and Coastal Plain, it would appear the body was first placed in a mourning chapel and that only after a prescribed period of time was the actual burial undertaken. Hence, on the east side of the Qumran cemetery, there is an unusually large structure (Tomb No. 1000) which I believe was not a tomb at all, but a mortuary chamber where a deceased person was placed for three days or so before being transferred to a trench for burial.[236] No such structure was found at the Beit Safafa cemetery, but the full extent of the cemetery was not revealed and it may have been bulldozed away during the earlier building operations at the site.

No Jewish person would have been placed into a trench grave until there was absolute certainty that he was dead, and this would have been especially true in the case of a man crucified on the Friday before the Sabbath. In my opinion, the intention to bury Jesus in a rock-cut tomb existed all along and had Joseph of Arimathea's burial chamber not been available, Jesus would have been buried in another cave. The main problem Joseph needed to contend with, when granted an audience with Pilate, was whether he would actually be permitted to take away the body of Jesus *before* sundown and the beginning of the Sabbath: "Then Pilate wondered if he were already dead; and summoning the Centurion, he asked him whether he had been dead for some time. When he learned from the Centurion that he was dead, he granted the body to Joseph" (Mark 15:44–45).

As we have seen in regard to Lazarus, the phenomenon of someone being declared dead and then reviving was actually quite common in antiquity. In the case of an immediate burial in a trench grave, if someone did revive, the chances of their getting out alive were very slim indeed. Such a problem did not of course arise in regard to rock-cut tombs. Hence, the door to the tomb of Lazarus could be rolled away and his shrouded body easily examined to see whether he had revived. This was also the reason for the visit made by the two Marys to the tomb of Jesus on the Sunday morning after the Sabbath was out. They were there to check on the body of Jesus and we must take this as reflecting common practice among Jewish families in Jerusalem at that time, i.e., with the ritual mourning period lasting for three days (I Corinthians 15:4). Hence, it is not surprising to read in the rabbinical *baraita* of Semahoth about the custom of visiting a tomb three days after a deceased person had been buried: "one should go to the cemetery to check the dead within three days and not fear that such smacks of pagan practices; it once happened that a [buried] man was visited and went on to live another twenty-five years" (8:1).[237]

According to the Gospel accounts, Joseph of Arimathea is said to have tied or wrapped the body of Jesus in a linen burial cloth (*sindon*), known in Hebrew as a *takrik* and in the rabbinic sources as a *sadin*. Mark says the shroud was bought specially for this occasion and Matthew adds that it was clean. Various garments and wrappings were used as shrouds in this period, some even made of expensive and imported cloth. It is only from the second century that shrouds made exclusively of linen were used for the dead, whether rich or poor, judging by rabbinic sources. According to the Gospel of Peter (6:24) the body was first washed before being wrapped in a linen burial shroud.[238] This was in accordance with the Jewish custom of washing the body of the deceased in water—while propped up so that impurities from the area of the feet should not reach the other parts of the body—and then anointed with oils and perfumes before finally being wrapped in a shroud. Family members probably heated up water for the washing while attending the dead at the tomb entrance or courtyard, which explains why vessels described as "cooking" pots are sometimes found inside tombs of this period.[239] Small juglets are frequently uncovered in tombs and they probably contained oils and perfumes. Spices were also wrapped in the shroud.[240] In John we hear that Jesus's body was wrapped in cloths and that in the preparation of Jesus's body Joseph was helped by a second person named Nicodemus bringing with him "a mixture of myrrh and aloes, about a hundred pounds" (19:39), which seems an exaggerated quantity. Nicodemus may very well have belonged to a charitable town association (*haver ir*) that dealt with duties such as the preparation of a body for burial, similar to those mentioned in later rabbinical sources.[241] John goes on to say that they bound the body of Jesus in "linen clothes with the spices, as the custom of the Jews was to bury" (19:40). Vessels such as heating pots, storage jars, and juglets that were used during the preparation of the body for burial evidently could not be taken back home owing to their impure state and so were left in the tomb.

Rabbinic sources indicate that the jaw of the deceased would have been closed and bound before the head was covered, and that the arms were arranged down the sides of the body and the feet tied together at the ankles, before wrapping the entire body in a shroud. A separation was clearly made between the body shroud, made out of a single sheet or from strips of cloth (or even from clothes), and the cloth used to cover the head. This is evident from the description of the burial garments of Lazarus (John 11:44). Similarly, in the description of Peter stooping to look into the empty tomb of Jesus, we hear of the "linen wrappings [*othonia*] lying there, and the cloth [*soudarion*] that had been on Jesus's head, not lying with the linen wrappings but rolled up in a place by itself" (John 20:6–7). We may conclude that the Gospel writers referred to a single linen cloth or *sindon* for the body of Jesus and a separate napkin-sized cloth for his head.

At this point, it is worthwhile saying something about two shrouds: the Turin Shroud, which is purported for many centuries to be the shroud of Jesus, and the Jerusalem Shroud, which is the only one of its kind from the time of Jesus dug up in the Jerusalem region. The subsequent investigation of the burial cave in which the Jerusalem Shroud was found has provided a great deal of information on burial practices in first-century Jerusalem.

The consensus of opinion is that the famous Turin Shroud dates from between 1260 and 1390 based on radiocarbon determinations, which is quite damning for those who believe it was the shroud of Jesus. Furthermore, its characteristic twill weave does not match up with the simple weave of shrouds known from the Roman period in the Near East. Undoubtedly, the Turin Shroud is a unique artifact, and scientists worldwide have attempted to fully understand what it represents.[242] The actual "Jesus" image, which is seen on it, was probably created either by a deliberate process of oxidation and dehydration of the cellulose fibers of the linen itself, or the result of the application of pigments, paints, dyes, or stains. While there is still a lot of mystery about how it was made, the medieval date for this shroud is fairly secure. In any case, the Turin Shroud consists of one single sheet, which supposedly was used for covering the entire body (back and front), whereas, as we have seen, the evidence from the Gospels shows that Jesus was provided with a separate shroud for the body and another cloth to wrap the head. This was also a general practice for all burials of the first century, partly, as we have seen, so as not to prevent a person placed in a tomb from suffocating should he happen to revive.

On a blustery grey morning in January 2004 I attended a lecture in the auditorium of San Salvatore in the Old City of Jerusalem. This lecture was given by Professor Giuseppe Ghiberti from the Vatican in Rome on the subject of the Turin Shroud. The occasion was hosted by the Franciscan Biblical School and the talk was about the results of new conservation work done on the Shroud and about a recent photographic scan of its entirety, a copy of which Ghiberti brought with him to Jerusalem. I could see a full-scale reproduction of it hanging on the left wall of the auditorium. The lecture was given entirely in Italian, of which I speak not one word. Luckily, seated next to me was a friend, Anna de Vincenz, and she bravely translated the pertinent points of Ghiberti's lecture, whispering some parts of it to me word for word. Fidgeting in the seat to my right was Don Antonio Scudu, Head of the Bet Gemal Monastery, whom I know quite well. When a reference was unexpectedly made by the speaker to the recent discovery I had made of a shrouded body in a first-century tomb in Jerusalem, Don Antonio exhaled and gestured excitedly with his hands. Quickly making his way up to the front of the hall, he told one of the organizers that the said archaeologist who had dug up the new shroud was actually present. Suddenly, I was invited to the podium, where Professor Ghiberti wrung my hand warmly, asking me if I was willing to say a few words about the new discovery. I was happy to do so.

The Jerusalem shroud is physically very different from that of the Turin Shroud, first because it was found in pieces and is incomplete, and, secondly, because it is fully oxidized—i.e., it has a blackened appearance—and there are no signs whatsoever of any image existing upon it. The shroud was found entirely by chance. It was during an excursion I made in 2000 with a colleague, James Tabor, and some of his students to the well-known ancient cemetery of Akeldama situated in the lower Hinnom Valley, at the foot of Mount Zion in Jerusalem. The reason for the excursion was to acquaint the students with Jewish burial customs practiced in the first century CE, and to give them a visual context for their reading about the burial of Jesus in the Gospels.

There are more than seventy rock-cut tombs in this cemetery and some of them have marvelous decorated interiors; scholars have remarked on them since the nineteenth century, and a number have been excavated.[243] This is the place of the traditional Akeldama, the "Field of Blood," the potter's field that was bought with the thirty pieces of silver that Judas cast down in the Jewish Temple (Matthew 27:3–8; Acts 1:19). Some traditions suggest this is also the place where Judas in his remorse hung himself. One of the students, Jeff Poplin, drew our attention to something interesting next to the external wall of the Monastery of Saint Onyphrius. While clambering along a rocky scarp in the lower Hinnom Valley, below a large vaulted building from the Crusader period, known as the "Charnel House," he spied broken stone ossuaries lying scattered about outside a tomb entrance. Closer examination showed that the ossuary fragments had fresh breaks, indicating they had been smashed fairly recently and that professional tomb robbers were most likely the culprits.

This meant that a more detailed look of the interior of the cave was needed. I crawled into the cave. Inside the upper chamber I was confronted with a scene of devastation: many large fragments of broken and crushed ossuaries, some bearing incised decorations of rosettes

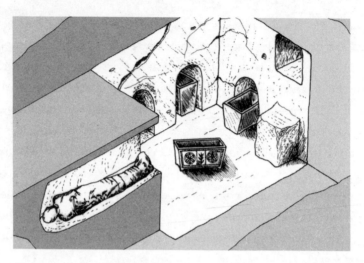

Figure 12: Reconstruction drawing showing the interior of the Shroud Tomb at Akeldama.

and other chip-carved decorations. In the walls of the chamber I could see tunnel-like burial recesses (*kokhim* or loculi) and apse-like niches higher up in the walls used for bone collection purposes. In one of the corners of the chamber, I could see a shaft leading down to a lower chamber. Climbing down to this lower chamber I could make out many more broken ossuaries. The devastation was the result of the tomb-robbing that had taken place in the cave. It was evident that those ossuaries the clandestine diggers had not wanted to take away with them were purposefully smashed up. It made me feel ill.

Unfortunately, the robbing of ancient tombs has been going on in this area since the nineteenth century. Keeping track of and trying to stop all this illegal activity is a sometimes impossible task undertaken by the Israel Antiquities Authority with its anti-robbery unit headed by Israeli archaeologist Amir Ganor. Later I found out our specific tomb had first been opened by tomb robbers in 1998, and that after preliminary recording by archaeologists it was blocked up again with boulders to prevent further destruction. There was also a fear of possible public disturbances by the local Ultra-Orthodox Jewish community who oppose the excavation of burial caves. They demonstrate and try to prevent archaeological work by committing acts of violence. I was once publicly cursed by these extremists in connection with my archaeological work at Tell el-Ful (Gibeah of Saul), with posters plastered on the walls of the Mea Shearim neighborhood, detailing the curse that would befall me—that my hands would wither and fall off.

It was while clambering around in the lower chamber of the cave that I noticed the blackish remains of what looked like a shroud, mingled with a layer of fragmentary human skeletal remains, in one of the side loculi. At the far end of the loculus I could see a clump of reddish-brown human hair. I immediately realized that a relatively well-preserved burial shroud in a first-century tomb in Jerusalem would be a unique find. Shrouds have not been found in Jerusalem before, except for a small scrap of a woolen garment excavated by the French explorer De Saulcy in the autumn of 1863 at the Tomb of the Kings, but the early date of this piece of fabric is said by some to be doubtful, and even smaller fragments of a hair net and a piece of felt found in the Tomb of Jason by the Israeli archaeologist Levy Yitzhak Rahmani.[244] The realization that this discovery at Akeldama might be of major significance for scholarship, combined with the fact that the remains we found were rapidly deteriorating owing to the influx of oxygen into the cave, as well as the fear that tomb robbers might easily return and destroy the evidence, led us to conduct an emergency digging operation, together with our colleague archaeologist Boaz Zissu, on the day of the discovery. It was an operation that lasted through the night.

The tomb has all the typical features of first-century tombs known around Jerusalem. A simple entrance cut into a quarried scarp led to a square rock-cut chamber with loculi (*kokhim*) cut into the walls and with a number of apse-like bone-collecting niches (*ossilegium*) in the upper parts of the walls.[245] White plaster seen around the edges of the loculi openings and around the niches clearly indicates that they were originally sealed with slabs of stone. The closing of loculi with stone slabs is well known in Jerusalem tombs, but the use of hard white sealing plaster is quite rare. A passage in one corner of this chamber led down to a lower chamber, which also had loculi, as well as a bone-collecting niche in one of the walls, and two adjacent small rooms (perhaps used as storage areas for ossuaries).

The two burial chambers were full of shattered ossuaries made of soft limestone, and one complete ossuary made of hard limestone.[246] It is likely that complete examples and those with clear inscriptions on them were removed by tomb robbers in 1998 before archaeologists arrived at the scene. The complete ossuary made of hard limestone was abandoned by the tomb robbers because it was too heavy for them to transport. A project of restoring the shattered ossuaries and their lids was successfully undertaken by British conservator Noël Siver. There were more than twenty ossuaries, many plain in appearance, but some had carved decorations on their sides, mainly of pairs of rosettes and with chip-carved border designs. They had flat or arched lids. Four inscriptions were visible on the ossuaries scratched with a nail or stylus: three in Jewish script (Mary; Shimon ben [son of] Shulai; and Salome) and one in Greek (Phineas) which was on the ossuary of a child.

The extraordinary preservation of the shroud and the large clump of human hair were due to an unusual combination of factors. First, the loculus containing the shroud was placed not at floor level but at a higher level in the wall of the cave. The reason for this is that the original tomb masons attempted to avoid a natural fissure extending obliquely through the wall of the cave and this resulted in the positioning of this specific loculus at a higher level above the surrounding floor. Water infiltrating the cave drained within the natural fissure and *beneath* the loculus. Inevitably, this led to much dryer conditions within the loculus, and this was good for the preservation of organic materials. Second, the opening to the loculus was originally tightly closed with a fitted stone slab and sealed hermetically with a coat of very hard white plaster along its edges. These two factors effectively created the right environmental conditions for the preservation of the shroud. As anybody who has excavated ancient tombs in Jerusalem will know, the high level of humidity in this region usually means that organic remains—such as hair, skin and flesh tissue, and shroud wrappings—are not found in first-century tombs, whereas the skeletal material tends to remain fairly well preserved. Conversely, the conditions of preservation within this loculus were exactly the opposite, with badly preserved skeletal material and very well-preserved organic materials. We can only assume that the body acids of this specific individual reduced the bones to almost nothing.

Shroud fragments were seen extending the entire length of the loculus, with a clump of hair with skull and shroud fragments adhering to it at the back, and with the bones of the feet close to the opening. On the basis of the bones alone it was not possible to identify the sex of the individual; however, it was definitely an adult since the bones were scattered over a length of 1.6 meters. The skeletal material was examined by the physical anthropologist Debbie Sklar, who was able to identify a metatarsal bone showing signs of pathology on it—indicating that the person suffered from a disease that basically affected not just the soft tissue of the body but also the actual bones. This was an important observation, as we shall see shortly. Careful dry sifting of the soft fill on the loculus floor by flotation expert Egon Lass showed that it was not actually soil but decomposed bone. He also detected small carbonized wooden twigs mixed with the bone shreds and possibly these are the remains of incense materials used when the body was wrapped in a shroud. Another possibility is that they represent twigs derived from a bier made out of tree branches on which the body was placed when it was brought to the tomb.

The excavation of the shroud was a painstaking operation lasting four hours, with the material being transferred the next morning into the safekeeping of the ancient textiles expert Orit Shamir at the organic laboratory of the Israel Antiquities Authority. I should point out that during the excavation the shrouded material was labeled separately according to the various parts of the body. The largest piece of shroud from the head region was about 16 cm in size. The first thing we needed to establish was the exact date of the shroud. Perhaps this was a shroud from a later Byzantine re-use of the cave? Alternatively, perhaps this tomb had been robbed out a couple of hundred years ago and the cloth was left there by the robbers? We needed some certainty on this matter. Hence, a sample of the cloth was sent for radiocarbon dating at the AMS radiocarbon laboratory in Texas. The test was run by the scientist Doug Donahue and it revealed without question that the shroud was from the beginning of the first century CE.[247]

With the antiquity of the shroud now certain, Shamir began her research and ascertained that the shroud was made of good-quality one-to-one plain-weave textiles made of wool. Laboratory molecular testing of the cytochrome b gene of the woolen textile indicated that it was of *Ovis sp.* (i.e., the genus of sheep and goats). A second textile was identified by researcher Kim Vernon in the head region of the shroud made of fibers of plant origin characterized by a cellulose staining dye (calcoflour), and this is most likely to have been linen. Since both the woolen and linen parts exhibit a type of warp that was both Z-spun and S-spun, this means the shroud was composed not of two but of at least *four* separate pieces of textile, if not more. Hence, we are not talking about a single shroud, but of shroud wrappings. In addition, another type of textile with an open weave was identified (perhaps a very fine hair-net?) and it too may be of plant origin.

According to Shamir's research, the textiles with the Z-spun warp could not be of local manufacture and had to have been imported into the Palestine region from a production center in Syria or Anatolia or perhaps even from further afield, from Greece or Italy. Although at least three instances of closing-cords were identified, the overall shape and size of the original shroud wrappings could not be determined.

The rock surface at the top of Calvary in the Church of the Holy Sepulchre.

The apse of the Constantinian church marking Golgotha in the Church of the Holy Sepulchre.

A reconstruction showing a shrouded corpse in a first-century CE tomb.

An ossuary
decorated with
carved rosettes
from the
Shroud Tomb.

Remnants of shroud and human hair from the Shroud Tomb.

Subterranean rock quarries discovered beneath the Church of the Holy Sepulchre.

The façade of the Church of the Holy Sepulchre.

The so-called Tomb of Joseph of Arimathea in the Church of the Holy Sepulchre.

The Edicule / Tomb of Jesus with a shaft of light coming through the domed ceiling of the Rotunda in the Church of the Holy Sepulchre.

The façade of a first-century CE rock-cut tomb at Akeldama with John Dominic Crossan (*right*) and the author.

The façade of the Talpiot Tomb in a recent photograph.

The use of clothes or a combination of wrapping garments as shrouds is a phenomenon already known from other burial contexts dating from the first and second centuries CE, notably a textile fragment found in a burial cave at Jericho and shroud garments of various materials (including leather) from the cemetery at Khirbet Kazone in Jordan.[248] In addition to the use of single-linen shrouds for the dead in the second century, there is also historical evidence for burial with multiple garments judging by references in rabbinic sources.[249] The use of imported woolen textiles suggests the deceased was someone of wealth and a person of some social standing in first-century Jerusalem society.

The next stage of the project was to initiate a series of scientific studies of materials derived from the cave. This was done at the Hadassah Medical Unit of the Hebrew University in Jerusalem, under the general supervision of the scientist Chuck Greenblatt.[250] The tests began with a microscopic examination of the skeletal fragments, hair, and organic layers of material, and were then followed by procedures using scanning electron microscopy (SEM) and molecular analyses for human DNA, sex identification, and pathogenic DNA. As a result of these tests, we can now be certain that the individual wrapped in the shroud was a male of adult age. The tests were also able to show that the human bones belonged to one individual and that the loculus had not served as a repository for the secondary burial of bones derived from other individuals. Furthermore, the shroud undoubtedly belonged to the skeleton found in the loculus and it had not been dumped there at a later stage. Analysis of the well-preserved locks of hair showed that it was free from head lice. The man's hair was well-kept, trimmed with scissors, and very clean, indicating the person had been a very well-groomed individual.

Mitochondrial DNA extracted from bone material of eleven skeletons from different parts of the tomb indicated that the shrouded man was definitely maternally related to at least five other individuals in the burial cave. Hence, this was without doubt a family tomb. Genetic analysis made of the shrouded individual—replicated separately in laboratories in different parts of the world—identified the positive presence of pathogenic *Mycobacterium tuberculosis* DNA. Three other tomb occupants, two of whom were infants, were also shown to have suffered from tuberculosis. The shrouded man probably died of his tuberculosis affliction, but the DNA testing was also able to show that he suffered from leprosy (Hansen's disease), a disfiguring and debilitating disease. Co-infection with *Mycobacterium tuberculosis* and *Mycobacterium leprae* is not uncommon in some parts of the world today. As previously discussed, this identification of Hansen's disease in the shrouded individual would appear to be the first scientific evidence of the oldest appearance of this disease in Israel. As with victims of the modern-day HIV disease, which is only deadly insofar as it attacks the human immune system, it was not the leprosy that killed our shrouded man but the aggressive and debilitating tuberculosis co-infection.

The discovery of a first-century shroud in a Jewish tomb at Akeldama is of major significance not only for archaeologists studying the burial practices of first-century Jerusalem, but also for scholars wishing to understand the exact procedure by which Jesus was buried. The man buried in the Akeldama tomb was undoubtedly a person of some importance in first-century Jerusalem, judging by his clean hair and by the quality of his woolen and linen shroud, notwithstanding the fact that he suffered from leprosy, which was a disease that evidently extended across social boundaries. The shroud wrappings appear to have consisted of a number of woolen and linen textiles, but there is no evidence that any of these were woven together. Hence, there was no defiance of the injunction in Deuteronomy that "you shall not wear clothes made of wool and linen woven together" (22:11). The close proximity of our tomb to other tombs of importance, notably the Tomb of the High Priest Ananus (cf. Josephus, *War* V.506) near the foot of the Upper City, suggests it belonged to a priestly or aristocratic family. The fact that our shrouded individual suffered from leprosy and succumbed to tuberculosis, both diseases that can cause extreme physical deformities and pain, means it is likely the lepers Jesus encountered during his healing procedures suffered not just from *psoriasis* (or scaly skin) but also from Hansen's disease.

In this chapter we were able to establish the general context for the burial of Jesus in Jerusalem in 30 CE by examining the manner in which his body might have been prepared for the final rites. Archaeology has a lot to contribute in this regard, and especially in the light of the discovery of the Shroud Tomb. In the following chapter we will examine the location of Jesus's burial. Was it at the traditional place of Golgotha, or somewhere else?

EIGHT

WHO MOVED THE STONE?

"Early on the first day of the week, while it was still dark, Mary Magdalene came to the tomb and saw that the stone had been removed from the tomb. So she ran and went to Simon Peter and the other disciple, the one whom Jesus loved, and said to them, 'They have taken the Lord out of the tomb, and we do not know where they have laid him.' Then Peter and the other disciple set out and went towards the tomb. The two were running together, but the other disciple outran Peter and reached the tomb first. He bent down to look in and saw the linen wrappings lying there, but he did not go in. Then Simon Peter came, following him, and went into the tomb. He saw the linen wrappings lying there, and the cloth that had been on Jesus's head, not lying with the linen wrappings but rolled up in a place by itself. Then the other disciple, who reached the tomb first, also went in, and he saw and believed."

(John 20:1–8)

Is it possible to suggest an exact location for the tomb of Jesus? The Gospels provide us with information about the aftermath of the crucifixion, how Jesus was buried, and about the empty tomb. However, they say nothing about the situation of his tomb, except for John, who says it was at Golgotha (19:41). The traditional tomb is pointed out within the Church of the Holy Sepulchre in the Old City of Jerusalem, but many are dissatisfied with this location. Since the nineteenth century a number of proposals have been made for locating the tomb: that it was on a rocky knoll just north of the present-day

Old City (the so-called "Garden Tomb"); that it was somewhere on the slopes of the Mount of Olives; that it is in one of the rocky scarps situated in the lower Hinnom Valley; and more recently that it was to the south of Jerusalem in the present-day neighborhood of Talpiot (see Excursus, p. 175).

We can easily dismiss the Mount of Olives and Hinnom Valley identifications since they are not based on serious archaeological or historical considerations, but what about the Garden Tomb claim? The site is visited by many thousands of Christians who believe this to be the place of the tomb. Have they got it wrong? The story began when in 1867 a rock-hewn cave was cleared out by a peasant in a plot of land situated on a prominent hillock on the north side of the present-day Old City. The southern scarp of this rocky knoll is distinguished by a remarkable quarry-cave known as the Grotto of Jeremiah and opposite it is the Cave of Zedekiah ("Solomon's Quarries").[251] Luckily, the site of the tomb was immediately inspected by the resident antiquarian Conrad Schick and he provided a brief description of the finds made there, though at the time of his visit he expressed no thoughts as to its possible interpretation. This came later in 1883 with the arrival in Jerusalem of General Gordon. Gordon later became well known when he suffered a dramatic death in Khartoum at the hands of the Mahdi, two days before a relief expedition arrived from England to save him. Although not a biblical scholar, Gordon was impressed by the appearance of the hillock above the Grotto of Jeremiah and thought it might be Golgotha (hence "Gordon's Calvary"). The idea was that topographically the hillock represented the head of a skeleton, with the body extending the length of Mount Moriah, and with the feet ending up at the Pool of Siloam. As far as we can tell, Gordon did not identify any one tomb on this hillock as the tomb of Jesus. This was largely down to Schick. In archaeological terms, the tomb was undoubtedly used during the Byzantine period, in the fifth or sixth centuries, judging by red-painted crosses on its walls and by human bones found within, but there is nothing to suggest that this was not just another Christian tomb like many others known in the vicinity of Jerusalem.[252] Indeed, recent research has shown, quite conclusively in my mind, that this tomb was originally hewn in the Iron Age (eighth–seventh centuries BCE).[253] If we accept that Joseph of Arimathea's tomb was "newly-cut" (based on Matthew 27:60; Luke 23:53; John 19:41), then this must render the Garden Tomb an unlikely candidate for the tomb of Jesus.

The most likely spot for Golgotha, as we have seen, was in the area situated immediately north of the Western Hill (traditional Mount Zion) and the angle formed by two fortification walls (the First and Second Walls), leaving it *outside* the city at the time of Jesus (30 CE). Golgotha had the characteristics of a low hillock extending down to the Transversal Valley with stone quarries and tombs, and with gardens in the deeper quarried areas that may have been irrigated from the Amygdalon Pool. Eventually this area was included within the city when construction of the Third Wall began at the time of Herod Agrippa (41–44 CE). We assume that before the urbanization of this area began, the contents of all the tombs located there were transferred elsewhere, so as to uphold the Jewish notion of purity, which did not allow burials within the city walls. Pilgrim encampments were also situated there at the time of the Jewish festivals. When the construction of the new Roman city of Aelia Capitolina was begun by Hadrian (circa 135 CE) to replace the city destroyed by the Romans in 70 CE, the immediate parts of Golgotha and the surrounding areas sloping southward toward the bed of the Transversal Valley were ultimately filled in with thick deposits of rubble and soil. Deep consolidation walls were also built extending down to bedrock, so as to level this area and to create an artificial platform (a podium) on top of which a Forum and a Temple of Venus were established.[254]

The substantial building operations made by Hadrian's architects radically changed the appearance of the area. If we accept that the tomb situated beneath the Church of the Holy Sepulchre is the correct location for the Jesus tomb, this raises a question. How did the followers of Jesus remember its exact location during the centuries when the tomb was hidden from sight beneath the foundations of the Roman Forum and until it was discovered by Bishop Macarius in 325/326 CE? A difficult question, but I think there is a solution. One part of the general region of Golgotha I believe always remained visible in the Roman city was the upper part of a rocky outcrop, which is now known as the Rock of Golgotha or Calvary. Indeed, Melito of Sardis (circa 190 CE) refers to the place of the crucifixion being pointed out to him in the "middle" of the street in the city.[255] This must mean that he was shown something; it may have been the summit of the rocky outcrop. There may even have been a cultic pagan statue placed on top of the rock. In a sense, the rocky outcrop served as a marker for the general location of the tomb of Jesus until the early fourth century, one that would have been clearly visible to the followers of Jesus,

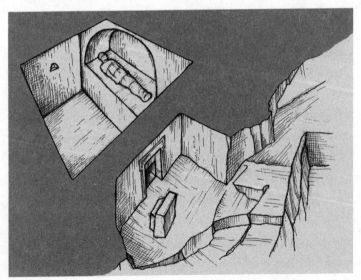

Figure 13: Reconstruction drawing showing the layout of the Tomb of Jesus.

even if the tomb was not. This is why when Constantine the Great acceded to a request made at the council of bishops at Nicaea in 325 CE to allow for the recovery of the tomb of Jesus, Bishop Macarius knew exactly where to look for the tomb. Otherwise, his reputation would have been in jeopardy, especially since the area of the Forum was *within* the city and there was no assurance that tombs might be found in the rock below it. An eyewitness to the excavations, Eusebius, stated that the tomb discovery was "contrary to all expectation," but this was surely an exaggeration; the Emperor himself declared that the discovery "surpassed all astonishment."[256]

The tomb of Jesus is pointed out today beneath the Church of the Holy Sepulchre, but nothing of its original rock-cut state is now visible. At the time of Constantine, the mass of rock surrounding the tomb to the west was cut away and the tomb itself was housed within a small structure (Edicule), situated in front of a large basilica (Martyrium) dedicated in 335 CE.[257] Hardly anything of the original tomb has survived owing to the destruction of the tomb by Caliph Hakim in 1009, and later in a devastating fire in 1808. The plan of the tomb interior and its small dimensions, combined with information about rock levels in its vicinity, is all that we have to go on when it comes to reconstructing the appearance of the traditional tomb of Jesus. A broad sweep of the area extending northwest and southwest of the tomb had already been quarried for blocks of stone in the Iron Age, some 600 or 700 years before the time of Jesus. Hence, access to the tomb that was cut into the eastern scarp of the quarry must have been via a path. The entrance to the tomb was from the east with a small courtyard or porch hollowed out in front of it, judging from the description by Cyril of Jerusalem who wrote about a "rock shelter" in front of its door (*Cat.* 14:9); this feature was not a separate tomb chamber as some scholars have suggested. The inner chamber was rectangular with a single bench on its north side (probably within an *arcosolium*) on which the body of a deceased person could have been placed. All of this does not in any way contradict the description of the tomb as it appears in the Gospels. The modern structure of the Edicule (built after the fire of 1808) has been the focus of a recent study. It was clad with iron scaffolding at the time of the British Mandate over Palestine in order to prevent collapse, when major fissures opened up in the side walls of the Edicule. It is amazing that so many people visit the tomb without being aware that the structure above it is precarious and in a state of collapse.

On the western side of the Rotunda, not far from the traditional tomb of Jesus, is a rock-hewn tomb with features that undeniably date it to the first century CE. This cave has a number of loculi and part of a standing pit and is known as the "Tomb of Joseph of Arimathea."[258] Because of its close proximity to the Tomb of Jesus, I would like to suggest that, contrary to the accepted identification, it was used not for Joseph of Arimathea but for the burial of some of the immediate or extended members of the family of Jesus. We do not know where Joseph and Mary, the parents of Jesus, were buried, but it could very well have been in this tomb. The Gospels also tell us about Jesus's brothers (or half-brothers), James, Joses (or Joseph), Judas, and Simon (Matthew 13:55; Mark 6:3), and since many of them eventually became important figures among the Nazarenes based in Jerusalem, it would not be surprising to find them being buried in a tomb *close* to the tomb of Jesus. The family tomb would have been shifted to yet another location following Agrippa's construction of the Third Wall (40–44 CE), when the area of Golgotha was included within the city defenses for the first time. James appears to have been buried in a tomb in the Kidron Valley.[259] It would make sense for members of the family of Jesus to want to be buried in Jerusalem since this was the last place Jesus was seen. Many believe that the natural place for a tomb of the *family* of Jesus would have been in his hometown at Nazareth. But there are three reasons why this does not make sense: First, the Gospels report that the body of Jesus disappeared in Jerusalem and so it was not possible for his family to transfer his bones in an ossuary back to his hometown. Second, the inhabitants of Nazareth had cast Jesus out of their village and even threatened him with physical harm (Luke 4:28–29), and so I cannot believe Nazareth would have been the natural resting place for the family members of Jesus, even after his death. Third, Jerusalem was the city of the Temple and was where many Jews aspired to be buried. It is unlikely that Jesus's family would have thought otherwise.

So what did the actual tomb of Jesus look like? Based on the limited information from the Gospels we can conclude that the tomb had a square inner chamber (approximately 2 x 2 meters) and at least one bench (2 x 0.50 meters) along one of the walls, on which we are told quite explicitly the shrouded body of Jesus was "laid out" by Joseph (and Nicodemus). This would not have been done on the floor of a burial cave. In addition, the body was not said to have been placed inside a coffin or into a loculus. Ordinarily, there would have been simple benches for the dead on all three sides of the cave resembling the couches (*klinai*) of the living and arranged in *triclinium* fashion. Jesus's tomb might conceivably have had a full supplement of three benches, but this seems unlikely. It is also possible that the bench was hewn in a wall beneath an arched recess (an *arcosolium*), but again we cannot be certain of this. Most tombs with benches also have loculi (*kokhim*) cut into their walls. Since Joseph's tomb was newly cut, it is unlikely that the stone masons had got around to adding these features, since the practice of the time was to cut out additional tomb features only gradually and when the need arose. The fact that the tomb had at least one bench also implies it had a standing pit, allowing people entering into the cave to stand upright without having to bend. This is what Simon Peter is reported to have done (John 20:6). Access to the tomb would have been via a forecourt, which is where family members and mourners would gather. This is the place where

Mary stood weeping and from there "stooped and looked into the tomb" (John 20:11; cf. John 11:31).

What can archaeology tell us about burial caves at that time in Jerusalem? As many as 1,000 rock-cut tombs (if not more) are known to have existed in the close vicinity of first-century Jerusalem. These tombs are generally simple in appearance, with a small forecourt leading to an entrance, an inner chamber with benches along the walls (with occasional arched recesses known as *arcosolia*), a standing pit, and characteristic tunnel-like loculi (*kokhim*) hewn into the surrounding walls. Research has shown that while these tombs possess most or many of the features just enumerated, they also have certain individualistic characteristics making no two tombs alike.[260]

It has been argued that no exact parallel for the Jesus tomb arrangement may be found among the tombs of Jerusalem.[261] I would contend, however, that this is because there was no absolute uniformity to the system of hewing tombs in the first century even if there were general principles to follow. The bottom line is that there were always exceptions to the rule and individualism was pronounced. That tombs were hewn out in stages, according to need and not at one time, and over a period of a couple of generations, also helped to contribute to this culture of individualism.

The door leading into Jesus's tomb would have been quite small (0.40 x 0.60 meters), meaning access was gained only by crawling in on one's hands and knees, or feet first. Jesus was laid out on a bench inside the rock-cut tomb, and the entrance to the cave was closed with a large stone (*lithos*) which was rolled (*prosekulisen*) in front of it.[262] What would this stone have looked like? The traditional view is that it would have been a large circular stone, similar in shape to a circular stone used in an oil press or flour mill.[263] It would have been kept slotted in a rock-cut groove to one side of the entrance, and when needed was rolled forward, thus sealing the doorway. Such stones could not, however, have been moved by one person alone. Both Mark and Matthew say Joseph was able to handle the rolling of the stone by himself, and so it cannot have been too large. Another problem is that rolling stones of this kind are only known in very large and monumental tombs of the first century, whereas Jesus was reputedly buried in a small and modest single-chamber tomb with one bench to one side. Small chambers of this kind were exclusively blocked with a rectangular or square block of stone, almost plug-like in appearance, known as a *golal.*[264] We could argue that because of his wealth Joseph of Arimathea's masons intended from the outset to cut a multi-chambered tomb, but that their plan was thwarted owing to the urgency to use it for the burial of Jesus, after they had managed to cut out only one chamber. Thus, the intention might have been to create a monumental tomb with a circular closing stone at its entrance, similar to the Nicophorieh Tomb (sometimes incorrectly known as Herod's Family Tomb) near the King David Hotel in Jerusalem. However, I think this unlikely, and from my own (back-breaking) experience in archaeological excavations with the opening of stone doors of tombs, it is clear to me that even a rectangular or square stone had to be "rolled" in and out of position when a tomb was being closed or opened. There are hundreds of examples of tombs from this period in the Jerusalem area, with small entrances sealed with rectangular or square doors. In addition to the tomb door there may have been other methods of sealing. We are told by Matthew that the blocking stone at the door of the tomb was secured and sealed by a Roman guard in response to fears among the Pharisees that the body of Jesus might be spirited away at night. According to the Gospel of Peter, Pilate sent Petronius the Centurion with soldiers to join others in the watch over the tomb. They "rolled thither a great stone and laid it against the entrance to the sepulchre, and put on it seven seals, pitched a tent and kept watch" (8:31–33; cf. 9:37).[265]

What about the general necropolis of Jerusalem and how different were the tombs of the rich and poor? Could the family of Jesus have afforded a burial cave if they wanted to be buried close to the tomb of Jesus? The first-century necropolis surrounded the city on all sides; as far as we can ascertain, its layout was not the result of rational planning by city authorities, but of complicated issues around ownership of land, on the one hand, and religious concerns regarding the impurity of the countryside for pilgrims coming to the city for the holidays, on the other. Jewish law (*halakha*) prescribed that tombs should be outside the city walls at a distance of no closer than 50 cubits (approximately 25 meters). It may be assumed that this was also the distance prescribed between tombs and the highways leading to Jerusalem, as was the case with other locations deemed "impure" such as tanneries and industrial kilns. The appearance of the roads leading to Jerusalem differed considerably from those that led to Roman cities in Italy, which tended to be packed cheek-to-jowl with tombs and their monuments.

There was no continuous band of tombs spread evenly around the city. Instead, the necropolis comprised a series of cemeteries with a light scatter of tombs in between. This is the only way we may explain that at Akeldama (the traditional "Field of Blood") there is a very dense concentration of tombs—more than seventy are known—above the southern lower Hinnom Valley, with only a sparse scattering of tombs along the upper Hinnom Valley. There are also noticeable differences in the style and rock-cutting techniques used in the preparation of tombs in individual cemeteries. Further research, however, is necessary in order to elucidate these differences fully.

Although rock-cut tombs with simple entrances are ubiquitous in the vicinity of Jerusalem, only a very small number of tombs with rock-cut monuments and decorated façades are known. Hence, by comparison to the cemeteries at Petra or Palmyra, for example, such tombs are rare on the ground and exceptional. Pilgrims and visitors to Jerusalem, including Jesus, would have observed these unique monuments in the landscape around the city almost like solitary signposts. Examples include the Kidron Valley tombs, the so-called Tombs of the Apostles and Ananus at Akeldama, the Tomb of the Kings, Jason's Tomb, the Nicophorieh Tomb, and so on. In terms of ownership, the assumption is that the length of time needed to quarry out tomb chambers—the skill that was required from an artisan or mason (*lapidarius*) to decorate façades and to cut or build an adjacent monument—must have been costly and could only have been met by the elite and ruling class of Jerusalem.

The fact that there are so few tombs of this kind would also support the notion they were made for the *very* wealthy. Indeed, the so-called "Tomb of the Kings" situated to the north of Jerusalem belonged to Helena, Queen of Adiabene and her son Izates, and can be dated to the second quarter of the first century CE. This tomb was distinguished by three pyramids.[266] Josephus tells us about the monuments of the Hasmonean rulers Jannaeus and John Hyrcanus that were apparently situated to the north and northwest of the city, but they have never been found. He also mentions the monument of Ananus, situated along the lower Hinnom Valley, apparently in the area of the Akeldama cemetery.[267] But not all important families had impressive tombs, it would appear, at least judging by the tomb identified as belonging to the priestly family of Caiaphas, which is a fairly simple rock-cut tomb. I would argue, however, that even this tomb might originally have possessed an impressive monument next to it, which disappeared at some later date.

The ordinary rock-cut tombs found in their hundreds around Jerusalem are assumed to have belonged to the middle class of the city, but in my opinion this is incorrect. Indeed, as we have seen, archaeology has not been able to adduce any evidence whatsoever for the existence of trench graves for the lower classes in the immediate vicinity of the city. I have already mentioned that the cemetery of trench or cist graves found at Beit Safafa, a couple of kilometers to the south of the city, remains unique in the hinterland of Jerusalem. Within the immediate area of Jerusalem, only a few ossuaries found on the lower slope of Mount Zion above Birket Sultan have been identified as belonging to members of the lower class. However, the fact that even these finds were made on prime land only a stone's throw away from the royal palace of Herod makes it unlikely they were the burials of the "poor."

I believe we must seriously consider the possibility that simpler forms of rock-cut tombs could be afforded by members of the lower classes. My research has shown that a professional mason can carve out a cubic meter of soft chalk in a period of four days of work. Hence, an average-sized chamber of 2 x 2 meters, with benches and a standing pit, could be hewn according to my calculations within twenty days, with an additional eight days to cut the forecourt and entrance. Four days must be allowed for the hewing of each individual loculus (*kokh*). Assuming that a typical tomb has six *kokhim*, then we must add to the total an additional twenty-four days of work. We may conclude, therefore, that a total of about fifty days of work was ideally needed to prepare a normally shaped rock-cut tomb. However, we may substantially reduce the time factor for the obvious reason that tombs were never ready-made all at once, but were hewn, extended, and adapted in stages over generations, depending on the number of deceased needing burial within a given family. Half-finished tombs turn out to be characteristic of the Jerusalem necropolis. The tombs I surveyed with my colleague Boaz Zissu, in the Akeldama cemetery to the south of Jerusalem, were all "works in progress." The idea of a large lower-class family employing a stone mason for one or two months is not far-fetched, especially since many tombs were hewn in stages, depending on the income status of the family and, of course, on necessity. Hence, we may assume that the *complete* appearance of a given tomb was only reached after two generations or so of use.

Clearly the poor in Jerusalem were not as poor as they were thought to have been. They were probably quite well off by the standards of several villages in Judea, excluding perhaps those in the hinterland of Jerusalem. This was the result of the special status of Jerusalem as the home of the Jewish Temple, which made it the constant object of Jewish veneration and pilgrimage. Jerusalem became a very rich city from the time of Herod the Great (37 BCE) and it remained that way until the destruction of the city by Titus (70 CE). The argument that is sometimes made that Jesus's supposed humble origins would inevitably have precluded him from being buried in a rock-cut tomb, and that his family should have counted themselves lucky to benefit from Joseph of Arimathea's generosity, is without basis. After all, the family of Lazarus, who regarded themselves as friends of Jesus, were able to afford a rock-cut tomb, so why not the family of Jesus?

It is important to note that the façades of the ordinary rock-cut tombs were never covered up and were visible from a distance. It is quite possible that tomb façades were even whitewashed so that they should stand out from a distance, as is implied in Matthew (23:27). Since the Jewish custom of the time was not to place possessions and valuables next to the deceased inside a tomb, as archaeology confirms, this means the problem of tomb robbing was not such an acute problem as it was with the rich tombs in some neighboring cultures of the Near East and around the Mediterranean. If the doorway of a tomb was not hidden but was actually highlighted, this means that knowledge of the exact location of the tomb of Jesus could easily be maintained up to 70 CE and perhaps even until 135 CE when the pagan city of Aelia Capitolina was built and the tomb was covered by buildings and hidden from view. Personally, I am a strong advocate of the strength of oral tradition, and see no reason why the place of Jesus's tomb, even when hidden underground, could not have been remembered by his loyal followers.[268]

The importance of the appearance of the simple tomb façade as a flag of ownership—however modest—should not be overlooked. In northeast Jerusalem an example exists of a very well-cut and finely chiseled tomb façade, but strangely nothing of the interior chamber had been cut out. Perhaps the owner was not able to start working on the interior of the tomb owing to the destruction of Jerusalem in 70 CE, even though recent work in the area of Shu'fat clearly shows continuity of Jewish settlement there until 135 CE. Ordinarily, when a tomb is discovered during construction work around Jerusalem, only the tomb chamber itself and its entrance are preserved. Due to the vagaries of the salvage operations, it is rarely possible to investigate the landscape surrounding the given tomb. The study made of the Akeldama cemetery shows that the tombs had an intricate and varied system of external features with courtyards and mourning areas with benches—some that were jointly used, suggesting even clan (rather than just family) ownership. There were also washing basins but no ritual bathing installations (*miqwa'ot*), access routes and steps between the various topographical levels, and areas used as quarries that were contemporary with the use of the tombs. This is what the area around Jesus's tomb would have looked like.

So what does all this tell us about the inhabitants of Second Temple period Jerusalem? Well, the fact that graves of commoners have not been found must indicate I think that almost all the inhabitants of the city were able to afford rock-cut family tombs. The middle class—constituting the majority of the population—probably owned the better-hewn tomb complexes and were able to choose burial plots at better locations close to the city, but this in itself is no surprise. The wealthy of the city, however, were clearly ostentatious, and the tomb monuments they erected were necessary to boost their prestige. They were probably hated by the main population. They would have been among the people mocked by Matthew (23:27–29) whom he likens to "sepulchres which outwardly appear beautiful, but inwardly are full of dead men's bones." He goes on to denounce their manipulative ways: "Woe unto you. . . for ye build the sepulchres of the prophets, and garnish the tombs of the righteous . . ."

Clearly the tombs with decorated façades and monuments had more to do with the living than with the dead and with matters of preferred fashion and social standing rather than with perceptions of religious tradition and the afterlife.[269] In regard to prestige and tomb monuments, we should remember the character of Habinnas, the tomb designer and builder, who attends the feast given by his wealthy patron Trimalchio, as described in *Satyricon* by Petronius, who was writing at the time of Nero. During the dinner conversation the design of his tomb came up and Trimalchio, turning to Habinnas, said, "And, thanks to you, I'll be able to live on after my death."

At the time of Jesus's burial, his family and disciples were not clustered around the tomb as we would expect, but kept at a distance. Mark says the preparation of Jesus's burial was done without any assistance from his mother Mary or Mary Magdalene, both of whom are said to have observed the proceedings from a distance. According to Luke, spices and ointments were prepared by the "women of Galilee" (which included the two Marys, Joanna, and some others) before the Sabbath, but only so they could be used early Sunday morning for an expected secondary anointing of the body of Jesus.[270]

The story of the events that took place on the Sunday morning differs from Gospel to Gospel quite dramatically. A common thread to all the stories is that the family members and disciples are all taken aback and surprised by the empty tomb. Mark has Jesus's mother Mary and Mary Magdalene arriving after sunrise with spices so that they can anoint the body, but on arriving they find an empty tomb. Inside the tomb they see a young man who indicates to them the place where Jesus's body had originally lain. They flee. Matthew has the two Marys appearing at the tomb early in the morning, but with an earthquake occurring and with an angel descending and sitting upon the blocking stone of the tomb. The angel shows the women the place where Jesus had originally lain, and then the women leave to notify the disciples. Luke also has the two Marys arriving with the spices and finding the stone rolled away from the entrance, but in this case they are joined by Joanna and some other women. Inside the tomb they see two men in dazzling clothes. They leave and seek out the disciples. Simon Peter then goes to the tomb, but all he can see in the tomb are the linen shrouds.

According to John, Mary Magdalene arrives by herself at the tomb when it is still dark, finding that the stone has already been moved. She runs to find Simon Peter and the other disciples, claiming that unidentified persons have taken away Jesus's body "and we know not where they have laid him." Simon Peter goes to the tomb with another unnamed disciple, stoops in and sees nothing but linen shrouds. Subsequently, Mary arrives and she also looks into the tomb, seeing two angels on either side of the place where Jesus's body had lain. A variation of this story, but with a great more detail, is provided in the Gospel of Peter (9:36–13:56). The events begin on the Saturday evening with the heavens opening up and two men descending to the tomb which they then enter after the stone covering the entrance has rolled away. The soldiers guarding the tomb see not two men but *three* men emerging from the tomb, and this is what they report to Pilate, who, for some inexplicable reason, commands them not to say anything about what they have seen. On the Sunday morning Mary Magdalene and some other women come to the tomb and find the entrance open. On entering they see a young man who shows them the place where Jesus's body had lain.

The surprise and confusion ensuing among the family and disciples of Jesus as a result of the discovery of the empty tomb, as relayed by the Gospel writers, seems to me to be quite authentic. There is nothing in the accounts to suggest the body of Jesus was taken away in the middle of the night by those close to him, or that he had somehow been revived and walked away, unless we believe the testimony of the apocryphal Gospel of Peter with two people going into the tomb and three emerging. The preliminary scourging, the crucifixion itself, and the final lance wound in Jesus's side would make it unlikely that he could have regained consciousness.[271] In Matthew we hear that already on the Sabbath certain Pharisees had expressed their fears to Pilate that the disciples might be planning to try and spirit away the body of Jesus from the tomb, so that this might confirm Jesus's words, "after three days I [will] rise again." (27:62–66; cf. the Gospel of Peter 8:29–30). For this reason Pilate provides a guard. We wonder why Pilate didn't simply send for Joseph of Arimathea to get him to account for these rumors. Perhaps he did and this is the reason why Joseph disappears from the Gospel accounts. Various strange and outlandish theories have been put forward to try to explain away the empty tomb, but they are all based on nonsense. One theory has it that Jesus was drugged, revived, and secretly smuggled out of the tomb, and that subsequently he led a revolt against the Romans and ultimately perished fighting. Another amusing theory is that Jesus put himself into a death-like trance, was revived, got married, and sired children in the Galilee before trekking off to India. Archaeology and history cannot prove or disprove the possibility that Jesus's body was smuggled out by persons unknown, but this is a matter of speculation. The reality is that there is no historical explanation for the empty tomb, other than if we adopt a theological one, i.e., the resurrection. I leave it up to the reader to make up his own mind.

CONCLUSION

Some readers might think it presumptuous of me, an archaeologist, to write about the character, achievements, and goals of such an important figure as Jesus. After all, billions of people across the planet worship him as Christ the Savior, and as the Son of God. But my views are expressed here honestly based on an analysis of archaeological and historical data available to me; I have no personal or religious axe to grind, one way or another, and I definitely have no wish to offend anyone, even though some of the things I say may be radical and controversial. I hope readers will appreciate that I have tried to provide a balanced assessment of the final days of Jesus in Jerusalem, during the crucial week preceding the Passover festival in 30 CE, which culminated with his crucifixion.

My method of work in writing this book was straightforward: archaeological and historical analysis, combined with serious and thoughtful deduction. First, I established a comprehensive picture of the Jewish cultural context into which Jesus was born. Second, I examined how he fit in or diverged from the environment in which he lived and that influenced him. Third, I attempted to analyze the logic of the decisions Jesus took in going up to Jerusalem and the actions he made that ultimately brought him into conflict with the Jewish and Roman authorities.

The only written sources available to us about Jesus's final days are the Synoptic Gospels (Mark, Matthew, and Luke) and the Fourth Gospel (John), as well as the apocryphal Gospel of Peter, but none of them are straightforward witness accounts. These texts were adapted, embroidered, and changed by redactors, and so using them uncritically and indiscriminately can be dangerous. The earliest of these was written some forty to sixty years after the death of Jesus, and their compilation and dissemination must be seen against the background of conflict that arose between the followers of the Jesus group and the overall Jewish community, on the one hand, and the separation or parting of ways with the followers of the Baptist group, on the other. What I have tried to do is to reckon with the many thousands of scholarly studies written on the historicity of the Gospel narratives and on the life of Jesus. I have examined the complexity of the archaeological data in some detail, though I am sure there will be a few studies I have inadvertently overlooked. There are numerous books available to readers on the historical Jesus—thousands, in fact—from Farrar to Crossan, but with a few exceptions archaeology tends to play second fiddle in these endeavors, which mostly rely on a critical textual and literary analysis of the Gospels. I hope my book goes that extra mile.[272]

I have just come back from a long day of digging on Mount Zion in Jerusalem, where we are working in the general area of the "House of Caiaphas" of Byzantine tradition. Where exactly the first-century house of the High Priest was situated we cannot be sure, but the area we are digging undoubtedly had palatial houses from that period. It is great fun to thread the soil through one's fingers, digging up fragments of cooking pots and storage jars, occasionally hitting upon a coin, but ultimately the main thrill is in being able to reveal the outline of the households, kitchens and installations, dining halls and bedrooms, dating back some 2,000 years. Archaeology deals intrinsically with the extrapolation of evidence through a process of careful excavation, survey, and research, but there are limits to exacting knowledge from the ground. Historical reconstructions of the past may ultimately be proposed, but these need to be constantly verified as new discoveries and further scholarly research become available.

A lot of hard work has gone into the gathering of these archaeological data. Explorations have been made by many hundreds of scholars from the nineteenth century and to the present day, and I want to salute them all for their incredibly painstaking and difficult work.

Jesus's family came from a Judean background, and eventually relocated to the small village of Nazareth in the Galilee where Jesus grew up from 6 BCE. Contrary to accepted wisdom, Jesus's family was not poor—Joseph had a respected profession as a mason and carpenter, and the family could afford regular trips to Jerusalem to attend the festivities there. In later life, Jesus mixed with well-off or wealthy friends or patrons, such as Lazarus, Mary and Martha from Bethany, and Joseph of Arimathea. Jesus spent most of his life in the Galilee in Nazareth and later at Capernaum, where he established his reputation as a rabbi, teacher, and healer.

Jesus was baptized in the Jordan River by John the Baptist. As far as we can tell, Jesus's experience in the river was a private affair and not something that was fully understood by others, including John. John was a radical religious extremist, modeling himself on the morality and demeanor of the old Israelite prophets, leading an austere existence in tough arid environments, and looking to pave the way toward the coming of a Messiah by persuading people to redeem themselves of their sins and to purify their bodies in water. There were no physical enjoyments in his way of life; there were no miracles that he had a part in. Basically, what John promised was an uplifting religious and purification experience at the Jordan River, with the promise of the eventual return of the Messiah, perhaps, as I have suggested elsewhere, through the return of the intermediary in the person of Elijah.[273] According to Jewish belief, Elijah is regarded as the one who will be the forerunner of the Messiah. The reason why John went to the lower Jordan River to baptize in the first place was I think because of its proximity to the Cherith Valley and to the place where Elijah was thought to have ascended into the heavens.

We assume this is also the reason why John left his hometown in the vicinity of Jerusalem and descended to the Jordan River to await the return of Elijah.

I think the relationship between John and Jesus is a key to a proper understanding of what Jesus was hoping to achieve during his final days in Jerusalem. By comparison to John, Jesus was a cosmopolitan individual, a free thinker, and flexible in his ways. He was willing to mix in different social contexts and to express unconventional ideas without adhering to the fetters of religious norm. Jesus also had a good understanding of varying medical conditions, states of catalepsy, skin ailments, and leprosy. Jesus was for a while a key member of John's inner band of baptizers at the Jordan River, but at some point he struck out on his own with a few of his own followers. Jesus did not have the same fascination with the austere existence in the wilderness as John had, and John was probably not interested in Jesus's use of baptism for healing purposes. Judging by the hints in the Gospels it would appear Jesus later developed his own form of baptism, with combined healing and purification procedures, and with the anointing of various parts of the body (notably the head and feet) with oil, with the added mystique of "signs and wonders." Herod Antipas was reputedly struck by Jesus's reputation as a miracle-maker rather than as a teacher (Luke 21:8).

Following John the Baptist's death in 28 CE, Jesus moved ahead to consolidate his position as chief baptizer and healer in Judea, but encountered opposition from the Baptist movement (cf. John 10:41–42), which was strong in the Jordan Valley and in the area close to John's birthplace at Beth Haccerem near Jerusalem. This probably forced Jesus's hand, and in 30 CE his "plan of action" was as follows: (1) Go to Jerusalem with disciples and followers for the Passover festival; (2) along the way visit the Baptist centers in the Jordan Valley and strengthen ties with John's followers there; (3) set up headquarters in Bethany; (4) practice healing and teaching at the major locations of purification in Jerusalem, notably at the Siloam and Bethesda Pools; and, finally, (5) establish a new movement of baptism with healing, centered in Jerusalem with himself as the proclaimed successor of John the Baptist.

So what was it that brought Jesus on a direct collision course with the Jewish and Roman authorities in Jerusalem? Could it have been his "triumphal" entrance into the city? I have argued that this is unlikely, and that his entrance was made modestly and with no public fanfare. It was a low-key event that only had significance for his followers. What about the demonstration made by Jesus with the overturning of tables in the Outer Court of the Temple? Again, I show this was not such an important event, except for Jesus's followers. Indeed, Jesus was allowed to continue teaching there on subsequent days without any interference from the Temple officials, who could easily have banned him had they wanted to do so.

Jerusalem was packed with many thousands of Jewish pilgrims who came to celebrate the Passover festivities and to attend the Temple, from all over the country, and even from far-flung places such as Gaul and Mesopotamia.[274] This must have put an enormous strain on the Jewish and Roman authorities who were trying to maintain order at the main water purification pools at Siloam and Bethesda, since every one of these pilgrims had to be ritually purified, as well as at the gateways into the Temple Mount, where there would have been milling crowds, and in the city streets. Many pilgrims were living in tent encampments not far from Golgotha on the north side of the city, and there were others living in tents on the slopes of the Mount of Olives, or in lodgings in outlying villages, such as at Bethany and Bethphage. The fact that Jesus and his disciples took up lodgings at Bethany, but later encamped on the Mount of Olives opposite the Temple, was very typical of those times. Passover was a time of heightened religious awareness, celebrating the release of the Israelites from Egyptian bondage.[275] It has been suggested that Jesus must have been involved in more serious revolutionary activities to justify the severe action taken against him, perhaps even getting involved in the planning of riots and disturbances as the ringleader of a potential insurrection.[276]

I do not think Jesus had any revolutionary intent. He was trying to establish a new movement of baptism, with alternative purification and healing procedures, centered at the Siloam and Bethesda Pools. Since these were the official purification pools for pilgrims before they entered the Temple area, Jesus would have come into contact with many thousands of pilgrims. Crowds were drawn to him as the supposed successor of John the Baptist. From the point of view of the authorities, this made him dangerous and a threat, and ultimately sealed his fate. Luke wrote about Jesus: "He stirs up the people, teaching throughout all of Judea, and beginning in Galilee even unto this place" (21:5). I suppose members of the Sanhedrin tried to get Jesus to recant after he had been arrested and brought to the house of the High Priest, but without success. Jesus was then passed over to the Roman authorities for trial. As the proclaimed leader of a Baptist group—similar to that led by John the Baptist, who had been beheaded by Herod Antipas—Pilate had no problem whatsoever in charging Jesus with subversion and promptly executing him by crucifixion. The Romans also wanted to maintain calm in the city during Passover and hearing about crowds gathering around Jesus at the pools would have displeased them. Not one of Jesus's disciples was crucified with him, and there are a number of possible explanations. This may be because the disciples fled Jerusalem and went into hiding (Mark 14:50; 16:7) though Simon Peter and John were later questioned (Acts 4:3–6). Alternatively, Jesus's activities may not have been regarded as group-related and so his crucifixion would have sufficed—this is perhaps implied in John: "one man should die for the people" (18:14).

The historical Jesus, I suggest, was a man from an accomplished and well-off rural background in Galilee, trained in matters of ritual purification by John the Baptist, a believer in alternative healing methods and perhaps even in a spot of magic, whose fiery speeches and unconventional teaching scared the Jewish and Roman authorities to such an extent that they decided to take the radical step of putting him to death. Judging by the stories that appear in the writings of Josephus, one could be executed for far less in those days.

THE TALPIOT TOMB AND THE "JAMES" OSSUARY

There was a hushed air of expectancy in the hall when the attendants took away the black cloth covering two stone boxes (ossuaries) that bore inscriptions, so the assembled journalists were told, of
none other than Jesus son of Joseph and Mary Magdalene. You could
have cut the air with a knife when the announcement was made. The
press conference took place in February 2007 at the New York Public
Library and was organized by Discovery Channel, and by Simcha
Jacobovici and James Cameron, the makers of the documentary "The
Lost Tomb." It was indeed a dramatic moment, with a panel of experts
ready to answer questions on the stage, and with the endless flashing
of cameras recording the moment for posterity. The two main questions that hung on every journalist's tongue, in the stunned silence
following the announcement, was whether there was sufficient scientific proof that the family tomb of Jesus had indeed been discovered,
and, if so, how would this ultimately affect Christianity?

I too attended the press conference, even though I had considerable
doubts regarding their controversial interpretation of the Talpiot tomb
as the family tomb of Jesus.[277] But I did think it important for me to
be present, first because I happened to be one of the team members
who excavated the tomb, and second so that I might register my skep-
ticism on the spot and tell journalists a different side of the story.

The tomb was excavated twenty-eight years ago on a westward-facing slope of a hill, within the area of East Talpiot, a new residential suburb which was constructed about 2 kilometers due south of ancient Jerusalem.[278] The area had the appearance of an enormous quarry site, with bulldozers churning up the sides of hills, large trucks trundling around the place, piles of rubble, and clouds of yellow dust billowing in different directions. The general layout of the streets had already been roughly demarcated and the ground was sufficiently flat to allow vehicles access to most areas under construction. The buildings were only partly built, or not at all. There was already a gas station on the corner.

The cave was in the side of a rocky scarp just above the street (later known as Dov Gruner Street) and the gaping hole of the entrance was visible even from a distance. Although the rock-cut façade of the tomb was in the shade, I found it quite striking upon my approach. It was hewn from gleaming white limestone and there were chisel-marks cut diagonally across the entrance that were set off by the orange staining derived from the soil fills removed by bulldozers. Above the doorway was a simple raised carving of a circle and a pointed triangle.

The facts of the discovery are quite straightforward. A blast at the East Talpiot construction site brought to light the tomb and resulted in the destruction of its large external rock-cut courtyard and part of the roofed vestibule. The discovery of the cave was reported separately by two individuals on Thursday, 27 March, 1980, namely by Kerner Mandil, in charge of the supervisory office of the Armon Hanatziv/East Talpiot Project, and by the engineer Ephraim Shohat, of the construction company Solel Boneh. An archaeologist, Eliot Braun, was immediately dispatched on that same day by the Israel Department of Antiquities and Museums to check on the nature of the discovery and he reported back to Amos Kloner, the Jerusalem District Archaeologist. Kloner eventually reached the site himself to check on the situation. Clearly the cave needed to be excavated. The blocking stone to the cave was missing and the interior of the burial chamber had become blocked with approximately half a meter of soil that had been washed in from outside. It is not clear if the tops of the ossuaries were visible. However, a few ossuary fragments were noticed outside the cave entrance, and were reported by Yoseph ("Yoske") Gath, an archaeologist working for Kloner in the Department. It was too late to do any digging so the work was postponed to the following day.

The next day (Friday, 28 March, 1980), Gath began excavating and by noon managed to extract ten ossuaries from the cave, with a special truck arranged to transport them back to the safekeeping of the Rockefeller Museum. These ossuaries were handed over to Curator and Anthropologist Joe Zias and placed into temporary storage, where they were later examined by Chief Curator L.Y. Rahmani. The work had to be undertaken in a hurry, since excavations were not permitted on Saturday and any ossuaries left in the cave might be pilfered by greedy antiquity thieves. Alternatively, members of Jerusalem's Ultra-Orthodox Jewish community might demonstrate and create disturbances and this could lead to a cessation of the excavations altogether. Indeed, this is exactly what happened to another Second Temple period tomb, situated only 20 meters to the northeast of the excavated tomb, which was full of ossuaries (some inscribed). Because of Ultra-Orthodox Jewish objections, it was later sealed and still remains unexcavated.

Not long after the archaeologists left the site that Friday, an eleven-year-old boy named Ouriel, returning from school, entered the building site and saw the cave entrance. This was after he had heard additional blasting at the site. At that time he says there was only one Arab guard and all the construction workers had gone home. He peered into the cave, identified it as a tomb, and then went home to tell his mother, Rivka Maoz. The Maoz family were living in an apartment block they had moved into in 1976 in the older part of the East Talpiot neighborhood, about 100 meters or so to the south of

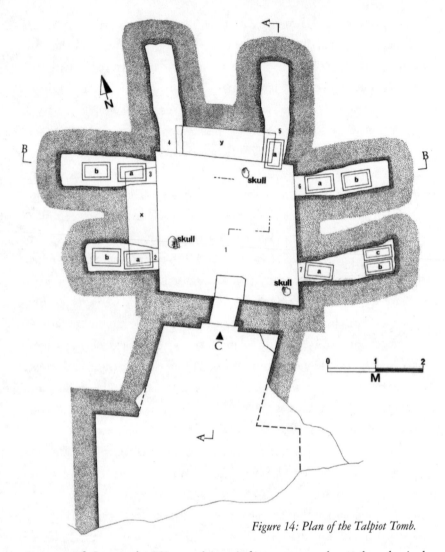

Figure 14: Plan of the Talpiot Tomb.

the area of the tomb. His mother tried to contact the archaeological headquarters at the Rockefeller Museum, but without much success since everyone had already gone home. There were no excavations that Saturday and the guard at the construction site was not very diligent. As a result the tomb was visited by local children who had heard about the tomb and were drawn to investigate it. This resulted in some human bones being taken out of the tomb and removed from

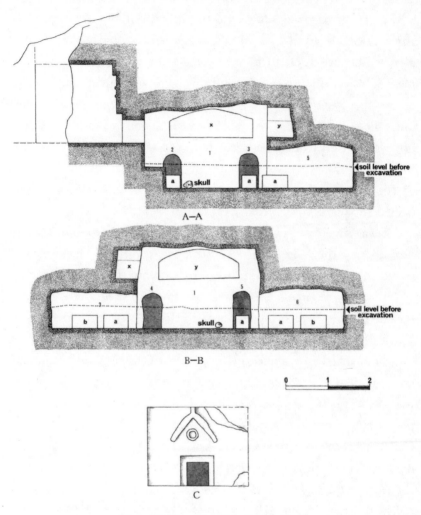

Figure 15: Elevations of the Talpiot Tomb.

the site. Conscientiously, Rivka Maoz, with the help of her son, collected the pilfered bones from the kids and placed them in a plastic bag. When the excavations were resumed on Sunday, Ouriel handed over the bones to the archaeologists.

My involvement with the Talpiot tomb began with a telephone call from Kloner: "Could you go tomorrow morning to Talpioth where Yoske is digging?" he wanted to know. At that time I was working as a part-time archaeological assistant and surveyor in the Department of Antiquities. He wanted me to take measurements and make a drawn plan and elevations of the tomb. I contacted the excavator, Gath, and made arrangements to meet with him the following day on the edge of the new neighborhood. He possessed a rather morose demeanor, quite the opposite of me. "Anything special about this tomb?" I asked him. "Not really," he replied. "Anyhow, you will get a good look at it tomorrow."

The excavation within the cave (IAA Permit No. 938) was conducted in stages with breaks between 30 March to 11 April 1980, and it was supervised by Gath, with the help of three to four workers provided by the Solel Boneh construction company. Having completed the excavation, Gath returned to his office (15 April), wrote up a preliminary report on the excavations, and prepared a File Card for the site, both of which he deposited in the Department's archives.[279] Tragically, Gath died before he was able to publish the results of his excavations, and it was left to Kloner to publish a final report on the tomb in 1996.[280] A major difficulty Kloner had in writing this report was owing to the fact that Gath left behind only sparse and incomplete notes about the results of his excavation. My examination of Gath's notes in the archives at the Rockefeller Museum confirms that his notes are minimalist in content and that a lot of vital information about the tomb has been lost.[281]

The second problem Kloner had was that the human bones from the cave had not been written up; anthropologists Joe Zias and Patricia Smith, who studied material from tombs at that time, both confirm that neither of them examined the human bones from this specific cave. Moreover, the bones were no longer available to Kloner for study since they had been transferred to the religious authorities for reburial, either by Gath himself not long after the excavation had been completed, or in accordance with an agreement made between the Israeli government and the religious authorities who had objected to the storage of human bones within the Antiquities Authority's storerooms.

The original courtyard in front of the tomb entrance had been badly destroyed by the blasting operations. Enough of the vestibule was preserved, however, for me to ascertain its size at the time I was preparing the plan of the tomb. Above the doorway are decorative carvings in raised relief. Gath suggested that these represent an attempt to depict a rosette with a gable above, and that it was left unfinished, perhaps because the local chalky rock (*nari*) was too soft to make carvings in any greater detail. I should point out that these carvings are not at all mysterious, but are known from the rock-cut façades and interior doorways of a number of tombs around Jerusalem. Representations of gabled doors with *acroteria* are known from several tombs within the Akeldama ("Field of Blood") cemetery south of Mount Zion. The circle, however, most likely represents a wreath, and examples are known from the decoration of tombs around Jerusalem, notably from the ceiling of the inner chamber of the so-called "Tomb of Absalom" in the Kidron Valley, and from the lintel of the "Tomb of the Apostles" in Akeldama and elsewhere.[282]

Clambering into the cave I could see that its interior chamber was intact. Toolmarks left by the hewer's chisels were evident on the walls and ceiling. A step led down into the chamber, which was square (2.9 x 2.9 meters) and had a ceiling that was sufficiently high (2 meters) to allow for standing room, so that family members could arrange with ease the burial of their kin on the two shelves positioned within arched burial spaces (*arcosolia*) in the upper northern and eastern walls of the cave. This was where the shrouded bodies were placed as primary burials and left to decompose (a process that took about 1 year), with the bones later gathered and placed within ossuaries. Cut into the lower walls of the chamber were *kokhim* (averaging 1.8 meters in depth and 0.50 meter in width), and there were two in each of the three walls. Except for one, they were used as storage spaces for the ten ossuaries containing human bones in secondary burial.

The cave had evidently been forced open, entered, and ransacked at some point before the modern era by tomb robbers. At the time of the excavation, this disturbance by intruders was clear to Gath owing to the fact that the blocking stone for the door was missing and quantities of soil had later accumulated within the cave, having been washed in from outside. The intruders were probably also responsible for the removal of the stones blocking the *kokhim* (if indeed they originally had them), for the sweeping of the intact primary inhumations from the *arcosolia* shelves, for the smashing of some of the ossuaries (seven were broken and six of these were eventually restored), and with the chucking of two ossuary lids onto the floor of the main chamber.

Gath noticed skulls and large limb bones at two points on the floor and it is feasible that these came from the primary burials that were swept off the *arcosolia* shelves by the intruders. At the time of the excavation, only a thin compacted fill (5 cm thick) of crushed bones was found on the shelves. A third skull was found in the corner of the main chamber and it may have been taken out of one of the ossuaries in the adjacent *kokh*. In addition to this, fragmentary human bones and a few first-century CE potsherds were found scattered throughout the main chamber. The number of interments in the cave is unknown, but, basing himself on data obtained from other tombs that have been studied, Kloner believes that it might have been about thirty-five individuals. Unfortunately, this is mere guesswork since the anthropological remains from the Talpiot tomb were never examined or quantified.

Ten ossuaries were discovered in the Talpiot tomb. In making a measured plan of the cave I recorded the position of the ossuaries according to information provided by Gath. Since Gath did not match up the Rockefeller IDAM accession numbers given to the ossuaries with the attribution numbers as they appear on my plan of the cave, we will never know for certain which ossuary came from which *kokh*,

Figure 16: The ossuary inscription "Ya'aqov {James} Bar Yosef {Joseph}, brother of Yeshua {Jesus}."

and this is unfortunate and represents a major loss of information. In addition, we have no information about the ossuary fragments Gath picked up *outside* the tomb entrance. In total, only three of the ossuaries were found intact; the rest were broken and had to be restored. Six or seven lids were discovered, one gabled and the rest flat in appearance. Five of the ossuaries were plain and five were decorated with double rosette motifs in panels, surrounded by bands with chip-carved zigzag designs, except for one that also has a decoration of vertical rows of small circular disks. Maker's marks were detected scratched on three of the ossuaries.

Only nine of the ten ossuaries from the tomb are at present in the Israel Antiquities Authority storerooms in Beth Shemesh.[283] Where is the tenth missing ossuary? Rahmani in his 1994 catalogue described it as "a plain, broken specimen." Tabor has suggested that it might be the same as the so-called "James son of Joseph, brother of Jesus" ossuary, implying that the ossuary was stolen and eventually ended up in the hands of the collector Oded Golan.[284] The status of this artifact is still unclear. The ossuary is undoubtedly authentic, but the inscription (or part of it) may be a forgery, and the owner is currently in court arguing his case. I am of the opinion that even if the inscription is determined to be authentic, the ossuary is rendered useless for historical purposes since we lack information about its original provenance. Indeed, Ya'aqov (James), Joseph, and Jesus were common

names for males in the first century CE. While I can see how attrac-
tive it would be to link the so-called "James" ossuary with the Talpiot
tomb, it simply cannot be the case because we know for certain that
the tenth "missing" ossuary was plain, undecorated, and uninscribed,
and on top of everything else it was broken. This description does not
fit the "James" ossuary, which is complete and decorated on one side
with double rosettes and on the other with a deeply-carved inscription
in Jewish script. Rahmani, however, recently provided me with an
explanation as to how the tenth ossuary might have become mislaid.
All decorated or inscribed ossuaries, when received in the Rockefeller
Museum in the 1980s, he tells me, were placed on shelves, whereas
broken plain ossuaries, of which there were large quantities, were
stored in the external courtyard of the museum. When the ossuaries were transferred to the new storage facility at Beth Shemesh, the
tenth, broken example was most likely thrown away, owing to a lack
of storage space.

Six of the ossuaries were inscribed (five in Jewish script and one in
Greek). The inscriptions were scratched in different hands with a nail
or stylus. The location of the inscriptions varies: Three were on the
front of the ossuary and another on the back, with two on the short
end of the ossuary and one on the inside. The inscriptions were originally read by L.Y. Rahmani (assisted by L. Di Segni), and published
in a catalogue he prepared on Jewish ossuaries:[285]

(1) Rahmani read the Greek inscription as "Mariamenou Mara"
(of Mariamenon, who is [also called] Mara), with Mariamenon being
interpreted as a diminutive form of Mariamene, a reading he inferred
based on comparisons made with Greek inscriptions of later date
found at the cemetery of Beth Shearim. Mara is interpreted as "honorable lady," but, in fact, the correct form for "honorable lady" should be
Martha. Mara is either the emphatic male form, which sits oddly on a
woman, or a colloquial contracted form. (The Virgin Mary and female

saints are given the title Martha in the later Syriac church.) Recently, a number of scholars have suggested, independently of each other, that the inscription should be read as "Mariame kai Mara," i.e., that it represents the names of two separate individuals, Mariame and Mara.[286] The first name is a variant of two very common Jewish names in the first century CE: Miriam/Maryam and Marya. The second name "Mara" is generally held to be a shortened version of Martha.

(2) There is a deeply incised inscription in Hebrew script, "Yehuda bar Yeshua," on the decorated front of the ossuary. The names "Yehuda" (Judas) and "Yeshua" (Jesus) were very popular names in the first century CE. Rahmani suggested that this person was the son of the "Yeshua (?) son of Yehosef" who appears in an inscription on another ossuary (see No. 4, below).

(3) The inscriptions in Hebrew script are in different hands: "Matya," and "Mata," on the exterior and interior of the ossuary. Both are contractions of the name Matityahu (Matthew). Rahmani suggested that the *yod* of the second name may have been worn away and that it too should be read as "Matya."

(4) A badly scrawled inscription in Hebrew script: "Yeshua (?) son of Yehosef," is in the reading provided by Rahmani and Kloner. The first name, "Yeshua (Jesus)," is not at all clear and it may have been superimposed over an earlier name (as Stephen Pfann has suggested). The first name is preceded by an X maker's mark.

(5) Another inscription in Hebrew script reads: "Yosé." This is a shortened version of Yehosef (Joseph), which itself was a very popular name in the first century CE. This Yosé may possibly have been the father of the individual (identified as Yeshua) who appears in an inscription on another ossuary (see No. 4, above).

(6) Another inscription in Hebrew script reads: "Marya."

There has been a lot of controversy worldwide about the suggestion that the Talpiot tomb might be the family tomb of Jesus.[287] Beyond the general recognition of the similarity between certain names on the Talpiot ossuaries with that of names known from the Gospels (Jesus, Mary, and Joseph), the main thrust of this argument has been that the "Mariamene" named on one of the ossuaries is a form of Mariamne, which should be identified as that of Mary Magdalene, and that the "Yosé" name on another ossuary should be identified as that of Joses, the brother of Jesus (Mark 6:3). This clustering of names, when examined statistically in terms of the appearance of Jewish names of the period, is taken to represent strong evidence in support of the Jesus family tomb hypothesis.[288]

So what should we make of this? The suggestion that the Mariamne name is that of Mary Magdalene is based on an assumed association between the two, as reflected in the *Acts of Philip*.[289] However, since this text dates from the fourth century, and since the only other possible references to Mary Magdalane as Mariamne are in the writings of Hippolytus from the second century CE, we must express extreme caution in the suggestion that Mariamne could have been Mary Magdalene's real name.

However, as mentioned above, the proper reading for the so-called Mariamne inscription appears to be "Mariame kai Mara," as a number of scholars have recently concluded. This would imply that the skeletal remains of two female individuals were placed in the ossuary, a mother and daughter, or perhaps two sisters. If we accept this reading then the entire argument about Mariamene being Mariamne, and Mariamne being Mary Magdalene, evaporates. Moreover, the name "Yosé," on one of the other ossuaries, could actually be a shortened form of Yehosef, and, in my opinion, this is probably the same Yehosef who is the father of Yeshua on another ossuary in the tomb, who, in turn, was the father of Yehuda. Hence, if we discount the Mariamne-Mary Magdalene and Yosé-brother of Jesus connections, then we are simply left with a group of ossuaries bearing common Jewish names of the first century CE. As a result of this, there is nothing to commend this tomb as the family tomb of Jesus. At best, the names of the ossuaries are suggestive but nothing more.

As we have shown, earlier on in this book, the place of the Tomb of Jesus is most likely to have been at the traditional spot beneath the present-day Church of the Holy Sepulchre in Jerusalem.

NOTES

CHAPTER ONE: THE ROAD TO JERUSALEM

1. On the scarcity of archaeological finds at Nazareth dating from the time of Jesus, see: Bagatti 1969. On the agricultural remains dating from the first century: Pfann *et al.* 2007. Nazareth remained a small village even during the subsequent Late Roman and Byzantine periods: Tzaferis 1993: 1103. On the recreation of the village of the time of Jesus: Kauffmann 2005.

2. On whether or not Sepphoris in the first century was a bastion of Hellenism and to what extent Jesus may have interacted or responded to this situation: Meyers 2003; Freyne 2004.

3. Joseph worked not only in the carpentry business but also in masonry: Kee 1992: 15.

4. Celsus Philosophus made a claim (circa 178 CE) that Mary "was turned out by the carpenter who was betrothed to her, as she had been convicted of adultery and had a child by a certain soldier named Panthera. . ." (quoted in Origen, *Contra Celsum* II.32; Stern 1980: 266). For more on this: Tabor 2006: 64–72, who is convinced of the validity of this story.

5. Flusser (1969: 16) was of the opinion that Jesus was born in Nazareth.

6. m. Sanhedrin 6:4.

7. For a summary of the archaeological remains dating from the first century at Capernaum and the "House of Peter", see; Strange and Shanks 2006. See a critical analysis of these remains: Taylor 1989–1990. On Jesus in the Galilee: Freyne 2007: 159.

8. Gibson 2004 a: 133. For alternative dates based on historical (36 CE) and astronomical (29 CE) deductions, see: Kokkinos 1989; and Depuydt 2002.

9. Kokkinos 2002.

10. On the Census of Quirinius: Vermes and Millar 1973: 420–427; and Sanders 1993: 86–87. For an alternative view: Kokkinos 1998: 374–375.

11. Schwartz 1992a: 182–217.

12. On the date of the beheading of John: Gibson 2004 a: 132.

13. Sanders 1993: 290.

14. Mark 10:1, 32, 46; 11:1; Matthew 19:1–2; 20:17, 29; 21:1; Luke 17:11; 18:31, 35; 19:1, 11, 28–29; John 10:40; 11:7, 18, 54; 12:1. On the contradictions and inconsistencies: McCown 1941: 11 ff.

15. John 10:40. On the questionable historicity of the incident of Jesus and his disciples hiding in the Wilderness of Ephraim (John 11:54), see: McCown 1932: 108.

16. Notley 2006: 363.

17. On the marginalization of the Samaritans in early Christian literature: Zangenberg 2006.

18. Avi-Yonah and Gibson 2007: 397, and bibliography there.

19. Dorsey (1991: 12) estimates that a typical day's journey on foot was probably 20 miles. According to Dalman (1935: 233) it would take three days on foot from Tiberias to Jerusalem. Adomnan reports that in the late seventh century CE it took the pious Arculf no less than eight days to travel from the Sea of Galilee to the Dead Sea: Wilkinson 1977: 108.

20. Dorsey 1991.

21. McCown 1932: 124.

22. Wilkinson 1981: 108–112.

23. Abel 1913: 218; Dalman 1935: 233–234; Zertal 2005: 144–147.

24. I visited the site in the company of Jane Taylor. For further information about the site: Gibson 2004 a: 240–241; Gibson 2007a: 145.

25. Gibson 2004 a: 219 ff.

26. Waheeb 2003.

27. On the road from Jericho to Jerusalem: Beauvery 1957; Wilkinson 1975.

28. On such matters: Casey 1998; Chilton 2002; Charlesworth 2002.

29. Hachlili and Killebrew 1999.

30. Netzer 2006: 43 ff.

31. Freyne 2007: 157. See also Barnett 1981; Horsley 1984.

32. This would seem to contradict Mark (14:1) who refers to Jesus at Bethany two days before Passover.

CHAPTER TWO: RAISING A DEAD MAN

33. On the "secondary" relevance of John in regard to the Bethany events: Bultmann (1971: 414, n. 3) who claims the personal names appearing in the Bethany accounts are not historical, and Brown (1971: 428–429) who says the accounts hardly contain any independent historical traditions. But see Coakley (1988) who cogently argues for John's priority as opposed to the Lucan tradition. For the historicity of John's sources re-evaluated: Anderson 2006; von Wahlde 2006.

34. Bethany: Mark 11:1, 11, 12; 14:3; Matthew 21:17; 26:6; Luke 19:29; 24:50; John 11:1, 18; 12:1. Bethphage: Mark 11:1; Matthew 21:1; Luke 19:29.

35. Men. 11:2; Men. 75b.

36. Baedeker 1876: 152.

37. Tsafrir *et al.* 1994: 80; Saller 1957; Pringle 1993: 122–137.
38. Taylor 1987; Taylor 1990; 1993.
39. On the frequency of names: Ilan 2002: 242–248 and 423–424. On the "Mount of Offense" tomb: Gibson and Avni 1998.
40. According to Nesbitt (1961: 120) Simon was possibly the husband of Martha, or at least the father of the family. Sanders (1954–55: 41) suggests that not only was Simon the father of Lazarus, Mary and Martha, but *also* of Judas Iscariot (on the basis of John 6:71; 13:2, 26).
41. See the excellent article by Coakley (1988) and the bibliography there. Also see Dudley and Rowell 1993.
42. Legault 1954: 138; Brown 1971: 451.
43. These are summed up in the article by Coakley (1988: 246–248).
44. tosef. Shabbath 3:16.
45. Gibson 2004 a: 159–166.
46. On cultic uses of oil in general, see Dudley and Rowell 1993: 26–34.
47. On the washing of hands: m. Yadaim 1:1 passim.
48. Eusebius, *Onomasticon* 140; Tsafrir *et al.* 1994: 192; Negev and Gibson 2001: 361; Freeman-Grenville *et al.* 2003: 77, 147.
49. See also Talmud Babylonian Mo'ed Katan, 27a–27b.
50. I am grateful to Rafi Lewis for bringing these quotations to my attention.
51. Kloner and Zissu 2007: 226–227. The tomb was published as Tomb No. 30 by Avigad (1967: 140), but for some inexplicable reason he did not publish a plan of the tomb. Hence, it is published here for the first time. The plan was found in the archives of the Israel Antiquities Authority (IAA).
52. Mas. Semahoth 8:1.
53. See the small cymbals found in a tomb not far from Bethany: Gibson and Avni 1998: 168.
54. Davies 1999.
55. Similarly, the twelve-year-old daughter of Jairus was apparently also an epileptic (Matthew 9:24).
56. The *pardes* or *paradeisus*, cf. I Enoch 60:8. For two excellent books on perceptions of the afterlife: Cooper 1989; Clark-Soles 2006.
57. In 1934 a Greek inscription on a slab of stone was found in Bethany referring to Martha and Mary discussing with Jesus matters relating to resurrection (Saller 1957:366; Hoade 1973:570). I recently examined a photograph of the inscription with Dr Leah Di Segni. It reads: "Here Mary and Martha, listening to the Lord in the Resurrection of [all] the dead. And the Lord. . ." (the rest is illegible). The provenance of the inscription is in the Greek Orthodox Church and Monastery of ed-Jeneneh or Burj el-Ehmar, the place where tradition puts the meeting spot of Martha and Jesus (John 11:29–30). The inscription is probably fourteenth century in date or later.
58. References to lepers: Mark: 1:40; 14:3; Matthew 8:2; 10:8; 11:5; 26:6; Luke 5:12; 7:22; 17:12.

59. John 4:48; Acts 2:22. McCasland 1957.
60. On the importance of the miraculous activities in Luke: Achtemeier 1975.
61. Masterman 1920: 50–55.
62. Crossan 1991: 341–344.
63. Webb 2006.
64. m. Kelim 1:4. See also Betz 1971.
65. Hulse 1975; Zias 1989; Lieber 2000.
66. Alexander Macalister, who was a man of medicine and the father of the famous explorer and archaeologist R.A.S. Macalister, wrote an extremely useful entry on "Leprosy" in the Hasting's *Dictionary of the Bible*, Vol. III, 1903: 95–99. See also Lewis 1987 in regard to Leviticus and on the contrast between priest and leper; and Heller *et al.* 2003 for an alternative view that biblical *tsara'at* was a kind of mould that attacked buildings and the people living in them.
67. Mark 2002.
68. Mariotti *et al.* 2005.
69. Dzierzykray-Rogalski 1980; Zias 1991 a; Zias 1991 b: 149; 2002; Spigelman and Donoghue 2002.
70. Spigelman 2006.
71. Chuck Greenblatt headed this research team.

CHAPTER THREE: FESTIVITIES AT THE HOUSE OF GOD
72. Bahat 1990; Cline 2004.
73. General: Levine 2002: 170 ff.; Lichtenberger 2006; Hippodrome/Amphitheater: Kloner 2000 b.
74. Parrot 1957 a; Comay 1975. For references to Passover sacrifices, see: Num. 9:11–14; II Chron. 30:17.
75. Gibson 2004 b.
76. Jeremias 1969: 62–71.
77. Jeremias 1969: 57.
78. Coakley 1988: 242–243.
79. Jacobson 1990–1991; 1997; Goldhill 2005; Netzer 2006: 137–178.
80. In regard to the construction dates for the Temple and of the Temple Mount (Jos., *Antiq.* XV. 380–390), see Levine 2002: 223–226; Bahat 2006 a: 300.
81. Gibson and Jacobson 1996: 166–172.
82. Bahat 2006 a: 300.
83. On the excavations along the western and southern Temple Mount walls, see Mazar 1975; Ben-Dov 1982; Jacobson and Gibson 1997; Ritmeyer 2006; Mazar 2000.
84. In the exhibition room "Bulevard dels Antiquaris", Barcelona (courtesy of Paul van der Voort).
85. Israeli 1998. The ox-head motif is also known from two first-century tombs in Jerusalem at Akeldama and to the north of the Old City.

86. Dalman 1912; Lewy 1945; Kingsley 2006; Taylor 2008.
87. There are a total of 45 subterranean chambers and cisterns under the Temple Mount: Gibson and Jacobson 1996.
88. Warren 1876; Gibson 2003 a.
89. Demsky 1986.
90. Mark 11:15, 27; 12:35; 13:1–3; 14:49; 15:29; Matthew 21:12, 23; 24:1; 26:55; 27:40; Luke 21:5, 37; John 2:19; 7:28. For references to the Temple at the time of Jesus's death: Mark 15:35, Matthew 27:51; Luke 23:45.
91. Bahat 2006 a: 306.
92. Clermont-Ganneau 1871; Bickerman 1947; Branham 2006.
93. Kenyon 1967: 161 and Fig. 73, 74; 1974.
94. Greenhut 2006.
95. Ben-Ami and Chachnowetz 2007.
96. For a summary of possible second century archaeological remains as the basis for understanding the background to Acts 2:44–45: Murphy-O'Connor 1995.
97. Levine 2002: 139.
98. m. Yadaim 1:2.
99. Gibson 1983; 2003 b.
100. Talmud Babylonian Shabbat 13a.
101. m. Kelim 1:8; Zabim 5:8; Mark. 3:3.
102. Smith 2004.
103. Taylor 2006 b; Bagatti *et al.* 1975.

CHAPTER FOUR: SIGNS AND WONDERS AT
BETHESDA AND SILOAM
104. Walaskay 1975: 87–90.
105. Acts 8:1 Flusser 1988: 575 ff.
106. Acts 2:22. McCasland 1957.
107. Gibson 2005.
108. The following are some of the main relevant sources for the study of *miqwa'ot*: Reich 1991; Reich 1988; Reich 1997; Reich 2000; Amit 1996; Galor 2003; Gibson 2005.
109. m. Miqwa'ot 1:1–8. Ponds, cisterns, ditches, caverns, and puddles that had very little water in them during the dry season, as well as pools with less than forty *se'ah* of water (considerably less than one cubic meter of water), were regarded as unclean and unsuitable for use as *miqwa'ot*, especially those that were situated in the close proximity to a city or village, or next to a road. The validity of *miqwa'ot* was apparently one of the subjects occasionally debated in the "Chamber of Hewn Stone" in Jerusalem: m. Eduyoth 7:4.
110. m. Miqwa'ot 9:2. Avigad 1980: Ill. 175; Galor 2003: 267.
111. Regev 1996.
112. For example: m. Miqwa'ot 2:9–10; 5:6; 6:1, 10:1; cf. Mark 7:4.

113. Berlin 2005: 452, note 92.
114. On the conversion of proselytes: m. Pesahim 8:8. Schiffman 1982; Samet 1993.
115. Gibson and Jacobson 1996.
116. m. Tamid 1:1; m. Miqwa'ot 4:5.
117. tosef. Shekalim 1:2. Mazar 2000: 51.
118. On *miqwa'ot* at agricultural sites: m. Temurah 1:4; m. Tohoroth 10:3. The problem as to the manner in which the *miqwa'ot* at Qumran were originally covered is an acute one (see the discussion in Gibson 2005).
119. Birkat Isra'il situated on the north side of the Temple Mount was not in use during this period and must be of later date (see the argument put forward by Jacobson 1990–91: 37–44). Birket es-Sultan and Birket Mamila are also of medieval date (contrary to Levine 2002: 214–215).
120. Nehemiah 3:15; Josephus, *War* V.145; m. Parah 3:2. Gibson 2003 b: 292–293.
121. Grenfell and Hunt 1908; Schneelmelcher 1991: 94–95.
122. Reich 1980: 225–256. More recently, Bovon (2000) has suggested that the "pool" refers instead to a baptistery, with steps leading in and out, and that it should be set against the background of Christian discussion about water baptism in the second/third centuries CE, and does not refer to anything earlier.
123. Reich and Shukrun 2004: 138.
124. A recent suggestion (Elitzur 2008) that the Siloam Pool, as well as others in the city, served as swimming pools for recreational purposes, seems unlikely. While pools used for swimming are known from Herodian palaces (e.g. at Jericho) this would not be possible inside the city of Jerusalem.
125. For the excavations conducted at the site between 1865 and 1967: Jeremias 1969; Duprez 1970; Pierre and Rousée 1981. Since 1995 I have been involved with a long-term project for the publication of the Pool of Bethesda excavations, together with my colleague Professor Claudine Dauphin, and on behalf of the White Fathers and under the aegis of the French Ministry of Foreign Affairs and of the French General Consulate in Jerusalem. I am grateful to the Community of the White Fathers for their help and assistance over the years.
126. Pierre and Rousée 1981; Bahat 1989.
127. For the later sources on the *probatica*: Baldi 1982: 455–466.
128. Regev 1996.
129. Poirier 2003.
130. There was a limited use in stone vessels from the time of Herod the Great until the mid-first century CE. Thereafter, in the decade or two prior to the destruction of Jerusalem large quantities of such vessels were manufactured: Gibson 2003 b: 287–308; cf. Magen 2002.
131. Gibson 2004 a: 164–165; Milikowsky 2000.

CHAPTER FIVE: THE HEAVY HAND OF THE LAW: A TRIAL

132. Carmichael 1963; Winter 1964; idem 1974; Brandon 1968; Flusser 1969: 116–132; Flusser 1988: 588–592; Horvath 1969; Burkill 1970; Walaskay 1975; Grant 1977: 156–166; Millar 1990; Sanders 1993: 265–274; Crossan 1996: 82–117; Crossan and Reed 2001: 264–271.

133. Crossan 1996: 117.

134. Schwartz 1992 a: 182–217.

135. See references to this family in rabbinical sources: m. Parah 3:5; tos. Yebamoth 1:10.

136. Greenhut 1992; 2006; Zias 1992; Reich 1992; 2006; Flusser 1992. For a critical view of the significance of these finds; Horbury 1994; Evans 2003: 107–108; 2006.

137. m. Sanhedrin 7.1. Burkill 1956; Winter 1974: 63–74.

138. On the stoning of Stephen: Acts 7:58–59; on the condemnation of James: Josephus, *Antiq.* XX.200; cf. Acts 12:1–2.

139. It is unclear whether there was a single Sanhedrin, or, alternatively, two supreme bodies by that name in Jerusalem, a political and a religious one; if so, then the latter was also known as the *bet din ha-gadol*: Mantel 2007: 22–23.

140. Horvath 1969: 180.

141. Mark 14:54, 66–68; Matthew 26:58, 69, 71; Luke 22:55; John 18:15–19.

142. Avigad 1974: 47; Ritmeyer and Ritmeyer 2004: 48.

143. Talmud Babylonian Pesahim 57:1; tos. Menahot 13:21.

144. Broshi 1974: Pl. III.

145. Levine 2002: 389–390, note 75.

146. For the suggestion that Pilate took up office earlier in 19 CE: Schwartz 1992 b: 395–401.

147. Stern 1980: 89, 92; Evans 2003: 45–47.

148. For the suggestion that the Tiberieum was a lighthouse: Alföldy 1999; or a building for the Roman imperial cult: Taylor 2006 a: 564–575.

149. Acts 23:35. For the *Praetorium* at Caesarea: Gleason 1998; Cotton and Eck 2001: 216. Cotton and Eck use the term *Praetorium* to refer not just to the official residence of the Roman Governor in the promontory palace, but to the entire complex of buildings extending between the circus to the north and the city wall to the south. The circus is probably the same as the "great stadium" where Pilate set up his tribunal: Josephus, *War* II.172

150. See the opposing views of Patterson 2004 and Maier 2004.

151. Josephus in *Antiq.* XVIII.55, described these as "busts of the emperor that were attached to the military standards." For a detailed study of the episode of the Standards: Kraeling 1942.

152. Contrary to Kraeling 1942: 280, who assumes that the Standards were taken to the Antonia.

153. Burkill 1970: 327; Crossan 1996: 111.

154. Stern 1980: 89.
155. Benoit 1952; Lémonon 1981: 117–124.
156. Maier 1969; Taylor 2006 a: 575–582.
157. It is generally agreed that the one visible tower in the Citadel known as the "Tower of David" must be Hippicus, though there is less agreement as to where the other two are: Geva 1981; Bahat 1981. I believe Phasael is the southernmost ancient tower uncovered in excavations in the Citadel courtyard, and that Mariamne should be identified with a prominent tower halfway along the present western Old City wall.
158. Gibson 1987; Netzer 2006: 129–132.
159. On the camp and troops garrisoned there: Dalman 1935: 336–337; Millar 1993: 45; Kokkinos 2007: 285. This garrison would have had 500 to 1000 men: Kraeling 1942: 269.
160. Josephus says the First Wall ran *dia* (followed by the genitive) "the place of Bethso", which means it ran "through", or "across" Bethso (see Emerton 1988: 100–101), but not "past" it (as in the Thackeray translation of Josephus).
161. Yadin 1975: 91; idem 1985: 178; Emerton 1988: 94
162. Broshi and Gibson 1994: 153.
163. The *Kishle* building, situated south of the Citadel, was used as an army barracks prior to 1917 and later as a prison attached to the police station.
164. An unpublished plan and section of this subterranean complex made by Conrad Schick in 1899 is in the archives of the Palestine Exploration Fund in London (PEF Archives/Schick/191/1–2).
165. Kloner (2001: 164–165) dated the tunnel to the Late Roman or Byzantine periods, but there is no certainty that the fills within the tunnel date from the time of the tunnel. Hence, an Early Roman (or Herodian) date is quite feasible.
166. On the medieval pool: Boas 2001: 173. On the location of the Serpent's Pool: Broshi 1992; Smith 1907: 114.
167. Broshi and Gibson 1994.
168. *Gabbatha* is actually Aramaic and may have been derived from *gabbeta* meaning "height": Dalman 1935: 335. The Hebrew equivalent for it would have been *gibath* or *gabath*. See its use in the place name Gabath Saul (i.e. Gibeah of Saul/Tell el-Ful) mentioned in *War* V.51, and for additional place names: Elitzur 2004: 177, 297, 300.
169. Avi-Yonah 1956: 307, and Map 10.
170. Yadin 1975: 91.
171. Emerton (1988: 98) has rightly expressed caution about the south-west gate location for the Gate of the Essenes and written: "we cannot be sure that Josephus gives us a complete list of gates and it is possible that there was another gate that would also fit his description."
172. Bliss and Dickie 1898: 14–16.
173. Magness 1991: 212–213; Weksler-Bdolah 2007.

174. The paved street leading from the gate into the city had a standard width of 5.4 m (i.e. 18 feet or *podes*) similar to other Byzantine streets in Jerusalem (Broshi 1977).

175. Pixner *et al.* 1989: 87; Chen *et al* 1994: 79.

176. See also Wightman's comments on this matter (1993: 145).

177. Philo, *Hypothetica* 11:18; Josephus, *Antiquities* XV.371–379. Stegemann 1998: 160–161, 267.

178. Philo, *Prob.* 85; *Hypothetica* 11:1, 5; Josephus, *Antiquities* XVIII.21. Capper (2006: 478) has suggested that the Essene community house at Jerusalem numbered about 100 or 200 individuals, which might be the case.

179. Notley 2006: 368; Yadin 1975: 91; Yadin 1985: 182.

180. For supporters of the Essene quarter theory: Pixner 1976; 1989; 1992a–b; 1997; 2006; Reisner 1989; 1992a–c. For critics: Emerton 1988: 99; Levine 2002: 333; Notley 2006: 368: "Quite simply, there exists today not a single piece of archaeological evidence to demonstrate that an Essene Quarter existed in Jerusalem in Jesus's day"; Gibson 2007 b.

181. Lémonon 1981: 124.

CHAPTER SIX: THE SPLIT IN THE TREE: A CRUCIFIXION

182. For a good summary on the artistic aspects of the crucifixion of Jesus and on the motif of nails, see Hewitt 1932.

183. For additional references to acts of crucifixion in the writings of Josephus: Cohn and Gibson 2007: 309–310.

184. m. Sanhedrin 7.1.

185. Similarly Appian (*Bella Civilia* I.120) relates how in 71 BCE six thousand men were crucified on the Via Appia between Capua and Rome following the defeat of Spartacus and the slave rebellion.

186. Hengel 1977: 87.

187. Edwards *et al.* 1986: 1457 and Fig. 2. There were three grades of beatings in the Roman empire: *fustes*, *flagella*, *verbera*, but the degree of severity between the three is uncertain: Sherwin-White 1963: 27; Walaskay 1975: 90–91.

188. On the *titulus* shown at Santa Croce in Gerusalemme in Rome, see: Thiede and D'Ancona 2000. Contrary to what these authors contend this object is probably a medieval forgery. A radiocarbon date would establish the date of this object, as I pointed out to one of the authors (Thiede) shortly before his death.

189. Tzaferis 1970; Tzaferis 2006.

190. The iron nail has a square-cut and rounded head, with a shaft tapering to a sharp point. According to the published report by Haas (1970: 58) the nail has a length of 17–18 cm, but this must be a mistake. Indeed, in Haas' own archival report he states that the nail has a length of 12 cm (IAA Archives: A-167/1968 excavation file). In a letter written by L.Y. Rahmani, Chief Curator at the Israel Department of Antiquities, to Dr A. a Villa Junipera, of 8 March 1976, the nail is stated to be 10.9 cm: "97 mm to the point of curving,

with about 12 mm in addition to the top", but Rahmani was probably excluding the height of the head of the nail. The nail was once again measured by
J. Zias in the early 1980s who determined that the nail from head to toe was
11.5 cm (Zias and Sekeles 1985: 23); this slightly reduced measurement may
be the result of the cleaning of a skin of corrosion.

191. This find flies in the face of the conclusion reached three and a half decades
earlier by Hewitt (1932: 45) that "there is astonishingly little evidence that the
feet of a crucified person were ever pierced by nails."

192. Attempts to prevent this tomb (in Plot 101) from being destroyed were unsuccessful, even though pleas were made by certain local Jews who were interested in preserving the tomb because it was the last resting place of Simon, a
builder of the Temple, and by Christians who were interested because it was
the place where crucified remains had been found.

193. Corpses were frequently anointed with oils and perfumes in Jewish burials:
Mark 16:1.

194. Strangely, one of the ossuaries contained the bone of a dog and in another
there were two lamb bones mixed with the human bones.

195. Zias and Sekeles 1985; Zias and Charlesworth 1992: 280.

196. Naveh 1970: 35.

197. Yadin 1973. The anthropologist Haas observed that the fine, slender and grac-
ile limb bones of the crucified man indicated the crucified man could not have
been employed in manual labor (IAA Archives: A-167/1968 excavation file).

198. Nails used in crucifixions were regarded as having special healing effects for
epileptics (Pliny the Elder, *Hist. Nat.* XXVIII.36), and for those suffering
from swellings and stings (m. Shabbath 6:10). Iron nails were also found in
first-century tombs at Jericho: Hachlili and Killebrew 1999: 169.

199. Haas 1970; Zias and Charlesworth 1992: 280. See also Møller-Christensen's
attempt (1976) to reconstruct the crucified man's position on the cross, a
theory weakened by the fact that he mistakenly thought the nail had a length
of 17–18 cm (see above, note 190); and Kuhn (1979) who reconstructs the crucifixion based on Haas' supposition that the two heel-bones were attached by
one nail.

200. Israel Hershkovitz is undertaking new research on the crucified man from
Giv'at ha-Mivtar and in an e-mail message to me of 10 February 2008,
wrote: "Based on the skeletal remains, six different positions [for the crucified man] have been suggested: the first three by Haas himself, who made
several mistakes in identifying the *calcaneus* (right/left); the fourth by
Møller-Christensen; the fifth by Zias and Sekeles; and the sixth by Yadin
(based on the interpretation of the name). All reconstructions are merely
speculation, based on false arguments, and are probably wrong."

201. All the bones from the tomb, except for the heel-bone and nail, and some additional fragments, were given over to the religious authorities (to Menashe

Ichler of Hevrat Kadisha Kavod ha-Met) for reburial four weeks after the anthropological work was done: Haas 1970: 39.

202. Scourging could bring about hypovolemic shock, but whether this is what weakened Jesus is not known, see more on this in Edwards *et al.* 1986.

203. Eusebius (*Hist. Eccles.* VIII.8) in the early fourth century indicates that men were sometimes nailed to the cross head down. Crucifixion was eventually abolished by the Roman emperor Constantine in the fourth century because of its Christian symbolism.

204. Pliny the Elder (*Hist. Nat.* XXVIII.4) refers to ropes used in crucifixion. See also Zugibe 1989.

205. Hewitt 1932: 43–44.

206. Mark 15:22–41; Matthew 27:33–55; Luke 23:33–49; John 19:17–37; Gospel of Peter 4:10–6:22: Schneemelcher 1991, I: 223.

207. Grant 1977: 166; Vermes 1987; Vermes 2001: 258–259; Meier 1990.

208. Gibson 2003 a: 30.

209. Mark 15:22; Matthew 27:33; John 19:17; Luke 23:33.

210. Gibson and Taylor 1994: 57.

211. Schneemelcher 1991: 224

212. Taylor 1998: 191; Biddle 1991; 1999: 62–63.

213. Avigad 1980: 69.

214. Parrot 1957 a: 19–23; Avi-Yonah 1968; Wightman 1993: 181–184. A few scholars believe the southern end of the Second Wall ran parallel with the east wall of Hezekiah's Pool (e.g. Bahat 1990: 35), which would mean shifting the location of the Gennath Gate further to the west, but this is unlikely since it would have meant the cultivation of irrigated gardens within the city which was forbidden by Jewish law. The exception were the gardens in the closed compound of Herod's palace.

215. Dalman 1935: 345; Gibson and Taylor 1994: 52.

216. Taylor 1998. For an alternative view placing Golgotha on the Mount of Olives: Kokkinos 1980.

217. Economopoulos 1971; Gibson and Taylor 1994: 74.

218. Schneemelcher 1991: 224.

219. Matthew 27:29; Mark 15:17; John 19:2.

220. It seems to me that recent attempts by medical researchers to clarify the circumstances of Jesus's death are unnecessarily tainted by an unhealthy acceptance of the authenticity of the Turin Shroud (e.g. Brenner 2005; Rehman 2005, but see the sensible remarks by Saliba 2006). This point had already been made by Zias and Charlesworth (1992: 281) in regard to earlier published attempts on the subject (e.g. Edwards *et al.* 1986), but their remarks went unheeded.

221. On the sympathetic crowd, see Flusser 1988: 578.

222. Mark 15:21; cf. Matthew 27:32; Luke 23:26. Evans 2003: 94–96; 2006.

223. For the purpose of clarification one should emphasize that Deuteronomy (21:23) does not refer to a *live* crucifixion. The executed person was only placed on a tree after they had already been killed and subsequently exhibited there for all to see until nightfall (compare with Joshua 8:29; 10:26–27). See also Crossan 1996: 163–164.

224. Hengel 1977: 10.

CHAPTER SEVEN: THE BURIAL OF JESUS

225. For the crucifixion on the Mount of Olives: Kokkinos 1980; Tabor 2006: 226–227; and at the Rock of Tophet in the Hinnom Valley: Haupt 1920.

226. Matthew 27:57–60; Mark 15:42–46; Luke 23:50–56; John 19:38–42; cf. Acts 13:29, and the non-canonical Gospel of Peter 2:3–13:56.

227. Broshi *et al.* 1983: 29–32.

228. In Luke 23:51 it is described as "a city of the Jews." Arimathea was known as Rouma or Arima from "which came Joseph of Arimathaia (sic.) in the Gospels" according to Eusebius (quoted in Freeman-Grenville, Chapman and Taylor 2003: 26, 81; cf. Negev and Gibson 2001: 427: "Ramah"). Joseph of Arimathea appears in a legendary medieval account, which probably dates to no earlier than the thirteenth century, which tells a fabulous story of how he went to England with the Holy Grail and eventually founded there the first church at Glastonbury.

229. Schneelmelcher 1991: 223.

230. See also Acts 13:29 with a follow on from the passage in Deuteronomy, with a reference to Jesus being taken down from a tree and buried in a tomb by his enemies.

231. Flusser 1969: 119.

232. For a dead person to end up in a common pit was anathema to Jews: Lieberman 1965: 515; Kloner and Zissu 2007: 98. However, a jar from the first century CE containing the bones of a baby was found in a cistern at Tel el-Ful to the north of Jerusalem (cf. m. Oholoth 16:5).

233. Magness 2007 a: 5.

234. This argument is made not just by Magness (2007 a: 5) but also by Kloner and Zissu (2007: 95). However, the existing archaeological material (excluding the Beit Safafa cemetery) is undeniably poor: a few ossuaries of unclear context on the western slope of Mount Zion, a few rock-cut cavities within existing cemeteries at Dominus Flevit on the Mount of Olives, and that's about it.

235. Zissu 1998. A very large Nabatean cemetery of some 3500 trench graves of first and second century date was investigated by K. D. Politis at Khirbet Qazone on the eastern shore of the Dead Sea (described by Politis 2001: 419).

236. Because of the size of the structure (Tomb 1000) the excavators Broshi and Eshel (2003) identified it as the tomb of the Dead Sea Sect's *Mevaqqer* (overseer), but I think this is wrong.

237. Safrai (1976: 784–785) notes that those editions of Semahoth which read "thirty days" instead of "three days" are incorrect (cf. Tal. Bab., mas. Shabbath 18). See also Kraemer 2000: 21; Hachlili 2005: 482.

238. See also the washing of the dead body of Tabitha in Jaffa: Acts 9:37.

239. According to Kraemer (2000: 32, 34) post-funeral meals were eaten at the home of the mourner and not at the grave itself, but meals might have been eaten at the grave by members of the family during the first year after death. See also Kloner and Zissu 2007: 124.

240. Hachlili 2005: 480.

241. Mas. Semahoth 12:4–5; cf. Hachlili 2005: 482. See also Mas. Semahoth: 2–5; Tal. Bab., Shabbat, 151a–b, for wrapping procedures.

242. Wilson 1978; Wilson 1986; 1991.

243. Avni and Greenhut 1994. A new survey of this fascinating cemetery was undertaken in 2007 by Boaz Zissu of Bar Ilan University, with my collaboration and with help from Mareike Grosser.

244. The textile fragment is in the collections of the Louvre in Paris, but has not been properly studied as far as I can tell. For a summary of the finds from the "Tomb of the Kings": Kloner and Zissu 2007: 234. For textiles from the Tomb of Jason: Rahmani 1967: 93–94.

245. Matthew 8:22 and Luke 9:60 probably refer indirectly to the practice of *ossilegium*: McCane 1990. On the practice of *ossilegium*: Kraemer 2000: 22; Hachlili 2005: 483–484.

246. On ossuaries, see: Meyers 1971; Rahmani 1994; Hachlili 2005: Magness 94 ff.; Magness 2005; 2007 b.

247. The radiocarbon determination is as follows: 2025 +/– 28 years before the present, and with calibrated calendar date ranges of one sigma: 50 BCE–16 CE and two sigma: 95 BCE–53 CE.

248. On the shroud fragment from Jericho: Hachlili and Killebrew 1999: 169. On the Qazone shrouds, see the brief report by Politis 2001: 419.

249. Kraemer 2000: 78.

250. The scientific analysis and forensic research of the Shroud Tomb was undertaken by the Hadassah Medical Unit at the Hebrew University in Jerusalem headed by Chuck Greenblatt. Members of the team were H. D. Donoghue, I. Findlay, A. Gorski, A. Lahti, C. Matheson, E. Nuorala, M. Spigelman and K. Vernon, and I am grateful to them all.

CHAPTER EIGHT: WHO MOVED THE STONE?

251. For a summary of the circumstances leading to the discovery of the tomb: Parrot 1957 a: 59–65. For the Garden Tomb as the solution for the Protestant search for a "Holy Sepulchre": Kochav 1995.

252. According to Franklin (1911: 88): "There were numerous graves in the vicinity, and during the excavations, which I watched from the beginning, I saw

bones unearthed and carted away with the rubbish. Nearby, the graves were covered with three flat gravestones, which I also saw; two of these contained inscriptions in Greek, one to Nonus, and one to Onesimus, 'deacons of the Church of the Resurrection, buried near my Lord.' These stones have now been let in the ground of the adjoining St Stephen's Church [i.e. the Ecole Biblique grounds of today: S.G.], where they are shown to Catholic pilgrims; but they are not in their original positions, as I witnessed their removal."

253. Barkay 1986; Barkay 2006. For an alternative view regarding the significance of the tomb: Walker 1999: 109–170.

254. For the changes in the area of the Church during the Late Roman Period: Gibson and Taylor 1994: 65–71.

255. Taylor 1998: 189.

256. Hunt 1984: 8.

257. For the archaeological remains at the Church: Parrot 1957 a; Coüasnon 1974; Corbo 1981; 1988; Gibson and Taylor 1994; Ousterhout 2003; Bahat 2006.

258. Clermont-Ganneau 1877; Vincent and Abel 1914:192–193.

259. Eliav 2004.

260. Detailed descriptions of the tombs of Jerusalem have been made since the nineteenth century. More recently an extensive corpus was prepared by Amos Kloner and Boaz Zissu (2007).

261. Kloner 2005: 275; cf. Biddle 1999: 55.

262. Mark 15:46; Matthew 27:60; 28:2; Luke 24:2; John 20:1.

263. Vincent and Abel 1914: 89–96, Fig. 53; Parrot 1957 a: Fig. ix.

264. Kloner 1997.

265. Schneelmelcher 1991: 224.

266. Josephus, *Antiq.* XX.95–96. Pausanius (*Graec. Descrip.* VIII.16:5) also mentions the Tomb of Helena as a remarkable tomb, but was more struck by the mechanism for shutting the door of the tomb than by its pyramids (Stern 1980: 196).

267. On the monuments of Alexander Jannaeus and John Hyrcanus: Josephus, *War* V.304; on the monument of the High Priest Ananus: Josephus, *War* V.506. See Waywell and Berlin 2007.

268. For the use of oral sources and its challenge for historical scholarship: Thompson 1988.

269. For burial practices and social hierarchy in the Roman world, see: Fedak 1990; Cormack 1997; Toynbee 1996; Davies 2004.

270. On the women witnesses: Setzer 1997

271. Schonfield 1967: 163 ff.; idem 1974.

CONCLUSION

272. Farrar 1879; Vermes 1973; 2003; Thiede 2004; Bovon 2006; Borg and Crossan 2006; Crossan 1996. For a religious approach to archaeological evidences, see Kelso 1969. I would recommend the following books on the archaeology

even though they were written more than thirty years ago: Wilkinson 1978; Finegan 1978. See also Wilson 1984. For an excellent modern collection of articles dealing with Jesus and Archaeology, see: Charlesworth 2006. See Reed 2007 for the visual evidences.

273. Gibson 2004 a.
274. Jeremias 1969: 58 ff.
275. Sanders 1993: 269.
276. Carmichael 1963; Brandon 1968: 175–176.

EXCURSUS: THE TALPIOT TOMB AND THE "JAMES" OSSUARY

277. A number of books have been published arguing for or against the identification of the Talpiot tomb as the family tomb of Jesus. The first to express was Tabor (2006: 22–33), following the television production from 1996 made by Ray Bruce (CTVC). The book by Jacobovici and Pellegrino (2007) was written to accompany the showing of the film "The Lost Tomb of Jesus." See Habermas (2007) on the tomb.
278. For a map showing the location of the tomb: Kloner 2000 a: 136. For a summary of the findings at the tomb; Kloner and Zissu 2007: 342–343, and Fig. 237 showing the tomb façade.
279. Gath only published a short report in Hebrew about the discovery of the cave: Gath 1981. A typed report about the excavation written by Gath, as well as other records about the dig is in a file in the archives of the Israel Antiquities Authority at the Rockefeller Museum in Jerusalem. I am grateful to Aryeh Rochman for showing me this material.
280. For the official publication of the tomb: Kloner 1996.
281. For written letters and other archival materials relating to the tomb and to another one situated 20 meters away: IAA administrative archives/ peh/J-M/ bet/8/X.
282. For parallels: Hachlili 2005: 43–54; Gibson 2006; Kloner and Zissu 2007: Fig. 9.
283. IAA Beth Shemesh Registration Nos. 501–508/1980.
284. For a description of the ossuary and its study: Shanks and Witherington 2003. See my published opinion on the "James" ossuary: Gibson 2004 b. On ossuary inscriptions: Kane 1978; Evans 2003. For ossuaries purporting to have "Christian" markings: Sukenik 1947.
285. Rahmani 1994: Nos. 701–706. Similar readings appeared in Kloner 1996: Nos. 1–6.
286. Pfann 2006: 130–131.
287. Tabor 2006: 22–33; Jacobovici and Pellegrino 2007.
288. Feuerverger 2008.
289. Bovon 2002.

ACKNOWLEDGMENTS

I am very grateful to my many friends and colleagues for their help and encouragement while preparing this book for publication, among them Claudine Dauphin, Boaz Zissu, Amos Kloner, James Tabor, Sheila Bishop, Joan Taylor, Rafi Lewis, Nikos Kokkinos, Yehiel Zelinger, James Charlesworth, Claire Pfann, Stephen Pfann, Joe Zias, Leah Di Segni, Ronny Reich, Herb Krosney, Maayan Yatras, Eilat Mazar, Zvi Greenhut, Hillel Geva, Zeev Weiss, Alexander Schick, Israel Hershkovitz, Chuck Greenblatt, and Mark Spigelman.

Scripture quotations at the beginning of chapters are taken from the New Revised Standard Version. Maps for this book were prepared by Vered Shatil. Drawings were made by Fadi Amirah, Leen Ritmeyer, Uwe Beer, Hillel Geva, and Joan Taylor, and photographs were made by Gabi Laron, Duby Tal, Zeev Radovan, Joe Zias, Sandu Mendrea, James Tabor, Jim Haberman, and Daniel Gibson. Regarding archival picture sources I would like to acknowledge the help of Aryeh Rochman and Sylvia Krapiwko of the Archives Division of the Israel Antiquities Authority.

Special thanks to Mareike Grosser, my archaeological assistant, for her help in doing background research and checking references.

Finally, my deep appreciation is extended to my agent, Jonathan Harris, of the Luxton-Harris Literary Agency, London, and to my editor Gideon Weil, Alison Petersen, and staff, at HarperCollins, for all the hard work they put into the production of this book.

My archaeological colleagues need to be thanked for letting me refer to the fruits of their labor—without their discoveries this book could not have been written. The interpretations presented in this book are my own, or at least the radical ones. The mistakes are definitely all mine.

BIBLIOGRAPHY

Abel, F.-M. 1913. "Mélange I, exploration de la vallée du Jourdain." *Revue Biblique* 10: 218–245.

Achtemeier, P. J. 1975. "The Lucan Perspective on the Miracles of Jesus: A Preliminary Sketch." *Journal of Biblical Literature* 94 (4): 547–562.

Alföldy, G. 1999. "Pontius Pilatus und das Tiberieum von Caesarea Maritima." *Scripta Classica Israelitica* 18: 85–108.

Amit, D. 1996. "Ritual Pools From the Second Temple Period in the Hebron Hills." Unpublished M.A. Thesis, Hebrew University, Jerusalem (Hebrew).

Anderson, P. N. 2006. "Aspects of Historicity in the Gospel of John: Implications for Investigations of Jesus and Archaeology." J. H. Charlesworth (ed.), *Jesus and Archaeology*. Grand Rapids and Cambridge: Eerdmans. 587–618.

Avigad, N. 1967. "Jewish Rock-Cut Tombs in Jerusalem and in the Judean Hill-Country." *Eretz-Israel* (E. L. Sukenik Memorial Volume) 8: 119–142 (Hebrew).

Avigad, N. 1974. "Excavations in the Jewish Quarter of the Old City, 1969–1971." Y. Yadin (ed.), *Jerusalem Revealed: Archaeology in the Holy City 1968–1974*. Jerusalem: Israel Exploration Society. 41–51.

Avigad, N. 1980. *Discovering Jerusalem*. Nashville: Shikmona.

Avi-Yonah, M. 1956. "Jerusalem in the Time of the Second Temple: Archaeology and Topography." *Sepher Yerushalyim*, Vol. 1: 305–319. Jerusalem and Tel Aviv: Bialik/Dvir (Hebrew).

Avi-Yonah, M. 1968. "The Third and Second Walls of Jerusalem." *Israel Exploration Journal* 18: 98–125.

Avi-Yonah, M., and Gibson, S. 2007. "Archelais." *Encyclopaedia Judaica*, Second Edition. Detroit: Macmillan. 2: 397.

Avni, G., and Greenhut, Z. 1994. "Akeldama. Resting Place of the Rich and Famous." *Biblical Archaeology Review* 20 (6): 36–46.

Baedeker, K. 1876. *Jerusalem and its Surroundings. Handbook for Travelers.* Freiburg im Breisgau and Jerusalem: Baedeker.

Bagatti, B. 1969. *Excavations in Nazareth.* Jerusalem: Franciscan Printing Press.

Bagatti, B., Piccirillo, M., and Prodomo, A. 1975. *New Discoveries at the Tomb of the Virgin Mary in Gethsemane.* Jerusalem: Franciscan Printing Press.

Bahat, D. 1981. "David's Tower and its Name in Second Temple Times." *Eretz-Israel* 15: 396–400 (Hebrew).

Bahat, D. 1986. "Does the Holy Sepulchre Church Mark the Burial of Jesus?" *Biblical Archaeology Review* 12 (3): 26–45.

Bahat, D. 1989. "The Fuller's Field and the Conduit of the Upper Pool." *Eretz Israel* (Yadin Volume) 20: 253–255 (Hebrew).

Bahat, D. 2006. "Jesus and the Herodian Temple Mount." J. H. Charlesworth (ed.), *Jesus and Archaeology.* Grand Rapids and Cambridge: 300–308.

Bahat, D., [and Rubinstein, C. T.] 1990. *The Illustrated Atlas of Jerusalem.* New York: Simon and Schuster.

Baldi, P. D. 1982. "Piscina Probatica." P. D. Baldi (ed.), *Enchiridion Locorum Sanctorum: Documenta S. Evangelii Loca Respicientia.* Jerusalem: Franciscan Printing Press. 455–466.

Barkay, G. 1986. "The Garden Tomb. Was Jesus Buried Here?" *Biblical Archaeology Review* 12 (2): 40–57.

Barkay, G. 2006. "The Garden Tomb—It Isn't." H. Shanks (ed.), *Where Christianity was Born.* Washington: Eerdmans. 196–211.

Barnett, P. W. 1981. "The Jewish Sign Prophets: A. D. 30–70. Their Intentions and Origin." *New Testament Studies* 27: 679–697.

Barrick, W. B. 1977. "The Rich Man from Arimathea (Matt 27:57–60) and 1QIsaa." *Journal of Biblical Literature* 96 (2): 235–239.

Barth, K. 1933. *The Resurrection of the Dead.* New York: Revell.

Barton, G. A. 1922. "On the Trial of Jesus before the Sanhedrin." *Journal of Biblical Literature* 41 (3/4): 205–211.

Baumgarten, J. M. 1972. "Does *tlh* in the Temple Scroll Refer to Crucifixion?" *Journal of Biblical Literature* 91 (4): 472–481.

Beauvery, R. 1957. "La Route Romaine de Jérusalem a Jéricho." *Revue Biblique* 64: 77–101.

Ben Ami, D., and Chachnowetz, Y. 2007. "An Architectural Complex of the Late Second Temple Period—one of the Adiabene Palaces?" J. Patrich and D. Amit (eds.), *New Studies in the Archaeology of Jerusalem and its Region. Collected Papers.* Jerusalem: Israel Antiquities Authority. 19–24 (Hebrew).

Ben-Dov, M. 1982. *In the Shadow of the Temple. The Discovery of Ancient Jerusalem.* Jerusalem: Harper and Row.

Ben-Dov, M. 2002. *Historical Atlas of Jerusalem.* New York and London: Continuum.

Benoit, P. 1952. "Prétoire, Lithostroton et Gabbatha." *Revue Biblique* 59: 531–550.

Berlin, A. 2005. "Jewish Life Before the Revolt: The Archaeological Evidence." *Journal for the Study of Judaism in the Persian, Hellenistic, and Roman Period* 36 (4): 417–470.

Bernardin, J. B. 1940. "The Resurrection of Lazarus." *The American Journal of Semitic Languages and Literatures* 57 (3): 262–290.

Betz, H. D. 1971. "The Cleansing of the Ten Lepers (Luke 17:11–19)." *Journal of Biblical Literature* 90 (3): 314–328.

Bickerman, E. J. 1947. "The Warning Inscriptions of Herod's Temple." *The Jewish Quarterly Review* 37 (4): 387–405.

Biddle, M. 1991. "Jerusalem: The Tomb of Christ." *Current Archaeology* 123 (XI, 3): 107–112.

Biddle, M. 1999. *The Tomb of Christ*. Stroud: Sutton.

Bliss, F. J., and Dickie, A. C., 1898. *Excavations in Jerusalem 1894–1897*. London: Palestine Exploration Fund.

Boas, A. J. 2001. *Jerusalem in the Time of the Crusades*. London and New York: Routledge.

Boismard, M.-E. 1999. "Bethzatha ou Siloé?" *Revue Biblique* 106 (2): 206–218.

Borg, M. J., and Crossan, J. D. 2006. *The Last Week. A Day-by-Day Account of Jesus' Final Week in Jerusalem*. San Francisco: HarperCollins.

Bovon, F. 2000. "Fragment Oxyrhynchus 840, Fragment of a Lost Gospel, Witness of an Early Christian Controversy over Purity." *Journal of Biblical Literature* 119 (4): 705–728.

Bovon, F. 2002. "Mary Magdalene in the Acts of Philip." F. Stanley Jones (ed.), *Which Mary? The Marys of Early Christian Tradition*. Society of Biblical Literature: 75–89.

Bovon, F. 2006. *The Last Days of Jesus*. Louisville: John Knox.

Brandon, S. G. F. 1968. *The Trial of Jesus of Nazareth*. London: Batsford.

Branham, J. R. 2006. "Penetrating the Sacred: Breaches and Barriers in the Jerusalem Temple." S. E. J. Gerstel (ed.), *Architectural, Art, Historical, Liturgical, and Theological Perspectives on Religious Screens, East and West*. Harvard: Dumbarton Oaks. 6–24.

Brenner, B. 2005. "Did Jesus Christ Die of Pulmonary Embolism?" *Journal of Thrombosis and Haemostasis* 3: 2130–2131.

Broshi, M. 1974. "Excavations in the House of Caiaphas, Mount Zion." Y. Yadin (ed.), *Jerusalem Revealed: Archaeology in the Holy City 1968–1974*. Jerusalem: Israel Exploration Society. 57–60.

Broshi, M. 1977. "Standards of Street Widths in the Roman-Byzantine Period." *Israel Exploration Journal* 27: 232–235.

Broshi, M. 1992. "The Serpent's Pool and Herod's Monument: A Reconsideration." *Maarav* 8: 213–222.

Broshi, M., Barkay, G., and Gibson, S. 1983. "Two Iron Age Tombs below the Western City Wall, Jerusalem and the Talmudic Law of Purity." *Cathedra* 28: 17–32 (Hebrew).

Broshi, M., and Eshel, H. 2003. "Whose Bones? New Qumran Excavation, New Debates." *Biblical Archaeology Review* 29: 26–33, 71.

Broshi, M., and Gibson, S., 1994. "Excavations along the Western and Southern Walls of the Old City of Jerusalem." H. Geva (ed.) *Ancient Jerusalem Revealed.* Jerusalem: Israel Exploration Society. 147–155.

Brown, R. E. 1971. *The Gospel According to John.* London: Doubleday.

Brown, R. E. 1994. *The Death of the Messiah: From Gethsemane to the Grave. A Commentary on the Passion Narratives in the Four Gospels.* London: Doubleday.

Bultmann, R. K. 1934. *Jesus and the Word.* New York.

Bultmann, R. K. 1971. *The Gospel of John.* Oxford: Blackwell.

Burkett, D. 1994. "Two Accounts of Lazarus' Resurrection in John 11." *Novum Testamentum* 36 (3): 209–232.

Burkill, T. A. 1956. "The Competence of the Sanhedrin." *Vigiliae Christianae* 10 (2): 80–96.

Burkill, T. A. 1958. "The Trial of Jesus." *Vigiliae Christianae* 12 (1): 1–18.

Burkill, T. A. 1970. "The Condemnation of Jesus: A Critique of Sherwin-White's Thesis." *Novum Testamentum* 12 (4): 321–342.

Capper, B. J. 2006. "Essene Community Houses and Jesus' Early Community." J. H. Charlesworth (ed.), *Jesus and Archaeology.* Grand Rapids: Eerdmans. 472–502.

Carmichael, J. 1963. *The Death of Jesus. A New Solution to the Historical Puzzle of the Gospels.* Harmondsworth: Penguin.

Casey, M. 1998. *Aramaic Sources of Mark's Gospel.* Cambridge: Cambridge University Press.

Charlesworth, J. H. 1988. *Jesus within Judaism. New Light from Exciting Archaeological Discoveries.* New York: Doubleday.

Charlesworth, J. H. 1992. *Jesus and the Dead Sea Scrolls.* New York: Doubleday.

Charlesworth, J. H. 2002. "Can One Recover Aramaic Sources Behind Mark's Gospel?" *Review of Rabbinic Judaism. Ancient, Medieval, and Modern* 5 (2): 249–258.

Charlesworth, J. H. 2003. "Jesus Research and Near Eastern Archaeology: Reflections on Recent Developments." D. E. Aune, T. Seland, and J. H. Ulrichsen (eds.), *Neotestamentica et Philonica. Studies in Honor of Peder Borgen.* Eiden and Boston: 37–70.

Charlesworth, J. H. (ed.). 2006. *Jesus and Archaeology.* Grand Rapids and Cambridge: Eerdmans.

Chen, D., Margalit, S., and Pixner, B., 1994. "Mount Zion: Discovery of Iron Age Fortifications Below the Gate of the Essenes." H. Geva (ed.) *Ancient Jerusalem Revealed.* Jerusalem: Israel Exploration Society. 76–81.

Chilton, B. D. 2000. *Rabbi Jesus: An Intimate Biography.* New York: Doubleday.

Chilton, B. 2002. "Maurice Casey's Aramaic Sources of Mark's Gospel." *Review of Rabbinic Judaism. Ancient, Medieval, and Modern* 5 (2): 259–262.

Clark-Soles, J. 2006. *Death and the Afterlife in the New Testament.* New York and London: Continuum.

Clermont-Ganneau, C. 1871. "Discovery of a Tablet from Herod's Temple." *Palestine Exploration Fund Quarterly Statement* 3: 132–133.

Clermont-Ganneau, C. 1877. *L'authenticité du Saint-Sépulcre et le Tombeau de Joseph d'Arimathie.* Paris: Gabalda.

Cline, E. H. 2004. *Jerusalem Besieged. From Ancient Canaan to Modern Israel.* Ann Arbor: University of Michigan Press.

Coakley, J. F. 1988. "The Anointing at Bethany and the Priority of John." *Journal of Biblical Literature* 107 (2): 241–256.

Cohn, H. H., and Gibson, S. 2007. "Crucifixion." *Encyclopaedia Judaica.* Second Edition. Detroit: Macmillan. 5: 309–310.

Comay, J. 1975. *The Temple of Jerusalem. With the History of the Temple Mount.* London: Weidenfeld and Nicolson.

Cooper, J. W. 1989. *Body, Soul and Life Everlasting. Biblical Anthropology and the Monism–Dualism Debate.* Leicester: Eerdmans.

Corbo, V. C. 1981. *Il Santo Sepolchro Di Gerusalemme.* Jerusalem: Franciscan Printing Press.

Corbo, V. C. 1988. "Il Santo Sepolcro di Gerusalemme. Nova at Vetera." *Liber Annus* 38: 391–422.

Cormack, S. 1997. "Funerary Monuments and Mortuary Practice in Roman Asia Minor." S. E. Alcock (ed.), *The Early Roman Empire in the East.* Oxford: Oxbow. 137–156.

Cotton, H. M., and Eck, W. 2001. "Governors and Their Personnel on Latin Inscriptions from Caesarea Maritima." *The Israel Academy of Sciences and Humanities Proceedings* 7 (7): 215–240.

Coüasnon, C. 1974. *The Church of the Holy Sepulchre in Jerusalem.* London: Oxford University Press.

Crossan, J. D. 1991. *The Historical Jesus. The Life of a Mediterranean Jewish Peasant.* Edinburgh: Clark.

Crossan, J. D. 1996. *Who Killed Jesus? Exposing the Roots of Anti-Semitism in the Gospel Story of the Death of Jesus.* New York: HarperCollins.

Crossan, J. D., and Reed, J. L. 2001. *Excavating Jesus. Beneath the Stones, Behind the Texts.* New York: HarperCollins.

Dalman, G. 1912. "The Search for the Temple Treasure at Jerusalem." *Palestine Exploration Fund Quarterly Statement* January: 35–39.

Dalman, G. 1935. *Sacred Sites and Ways.* London: Society for Promoting Christian Knowledge.

Danby, H. 1933. *The Mishnah. Translated from the Hebrew with Introduction and Brief Explanatory Notes.* Oxford: Clarendon.

Davies, J. E. 2004. *Death and the Emperor: Roman Imperial Funerary Monuments from Augustus to Marcus Aurelius.* Austin: University of Texas.

Davies, R. 1999. *The Lazarus Syndrome. Burial Alive and Other Horrors of the Undead.* London: Hale.

Demsky, A. 1986. "When the Priests Trumpeted the Onset of the Sabbath. A Monumental Hebrew Inscription from the Ancient Temple Mount Recalls the Sacred Signal." *Biblical Archaeology Review* 12 (6): 50–52, 72–73.

Depuydt, L. 2002. "The Date of Death of Jesus of Nazareth." *Journal of the American Oriental Society* 122 (3): 466–480.

de Vogüé, M. 1864. *Le Temple du Jerusalem. Monographie du Haram-Ech-Chérif, Suivie d'un Essai sur la Topographie de la Ville-Sainte.* Paris.

Dharmendra, R. 1947. "Leprosy in Ancient Indian Medicine." *International Journal of Leprosy* 15: 424–430.

Dorsey, D. A. 1991. *The Roads and Highways of Ancient Israel.* Baltimore and London: Johns Hopkins University.

Dudley, M., and Rowell, G. 1993. *The Oil of Gladness: Anointing in the Christian Tradition.* London: Society for Promoting Christian Knowledge.

Duprez, A. 1970. *Jésus et les Dieux Guérisseurs. A Propos de Jean V.* Paris: Garbalda.

Dzierzykray-Rogalski, T. 1980. "Paleopathology of the Ptolemaic Inhabitants of Dakhle Oasis (Egypt)." *Journal of Human Evolution* 9: 71–74.

Economopoulos, A. 1971. "Archaeological Findings in the Church of the Holy Sepulchre in Jerusalem." Israel Antiquities Authority Archives.

Edwards, W. D., Gabel W. J., and Hosmer F. E. 1986. "On the Physical Death of Jesus Christ." *Journal of the American Medical Association* 255 (11): 1455–1464.

Eliav, Y. Z. 2004. "The Tomb of James, Brother of Jesus, As Locus Memoriae." *Harvard Theological Review* 97 (1): 33–59.

Eliav, Y. Z. 2005. *God's Mountain. The Temple Mount in Time, Place and Memory.* Baltimore: Johns Hopkins University.

Elitzur, Y. 2004. *Ancient Place Names in the Holy Land. Preservation and History.* Jerusalem and Winona Lake: Magnes.

Elitzur, Y. 2008. "The Siloam Pool—'Solomon's Pool'—Was a Swimming Pool." *Palestine Exploration Quarterly* 140: 17–25.

Emerton, J. A., 1988. "A Consideration of Two Recent Theories about Bethso in Josephus' Description of Jerusalem and a Passage in the Temple Scroll." W. Claassen (ed.), *Text and Context: Old Testament and Semitic Studies for F. C. Fensham.* Journal for the Study of the Old Testament Supplement Series 48. Sheffield: Sheffield University. 93–104.

Evans, C. A. 1992. "Predictions of the Destruction of the Herodian Temple in the Pseudepigraphia, Qumran Scrolls, and Related Texts." *Journal for the Study of the Pseudepigrapha* 10: 89–147.

Evans, C. A. 2003. *Jesus and the Ossuaries. What Jewish Burial Practices Reveal about the Beginning of Christianity.* Waco: Baylor University.

Evans, C. 2006. "Excavating Caiaphas, Pilate, and Simon of Cyrene: Assessing the Literary and Archaeological Evidence." J. H. Charlesworth (ed.), *Jesus and Archaeology.* Grand Rapids and Cambridge: Eerdmans. 323–340.

Farrar, F. W. 1879. *The Life of Christ.* Vols. 1–2. London: Cassell, Petter and Galpin.

Fedak, J. 1990. *Monumental Tombs of the Hellenistic Age: A Study of Selected Tombs from the Pre-Classical to the Early Imperial Era.* Toronto: University of Toronto.

Feuerverger, A. 2008. "Statistical Analysis of an Archaeological Find." *The Annals of Applied Statistics* 2: 3–54.

Finegan, J. 1978. *The Archaeology of the New Testament. The Life of Jesus and the Beginning of the Early Church.* Princeton: Princeton University.

Flusser, D. 1969. *Jesus.* New York: Herder and Herder.

Flusser, D. 1988. *Judaism and the Origins of Christianity.* Jerusalem.

Flusser, D. 1992. "Caiaphas in the New Testament." *'Atiqot* 21: 81–87.

Foster, C. 2006. *The Jesus Inquest.* Oxford and Grand Rapids: Kregel.

Franklin, G. E. 1911. *Palestine Depicted and Described.* London: Dent.

Freeman-Grenville, G. S. P., Chapman, R. L., and Taylor, J. E. 2003. *Palestine in the Fourth Century A.D.: The Onomasticon by Eusebius of Caesarea.* Jerusalem: Carta.

Frey, J., and Schröter, J. (eds.). 2005. *Deutungen des Todes Jesu im Neuen Testament.* Tübingen: Mohr Siebeck.

Freyne, S. 2004. *Jesus a Jewish Galilean. A New Reading of the Jesus Story.* London and New York: Continuum.

Freyne, S. 2007. "Galilee as Laboratory: Experiments for New Testament Historians and Theologians." *New Testament Studies* 53: 147–164.

Galor, K. 2003. "Qumran's Plastered Pools: A New Perspective." J.-B. Humbert and J. Gunneweg (eds.), *Science and Archaeology at Khirbet Qumran and 'Ain Feshkha. Studies in Archaeometry and Anthropology* II. Fribourg: Vandenboeck and Ruprecht. 292–230.

Gath, Y. 1981. "East Talpiyot." *Hadashot Arkheologiyot* 76: 24–25 (Hebrew).

Geva, H. 1981. "The 'Tower of David'—Phasael or Hippicus?" *Israel Exploration Journal* 31 (1/2): 57–65.

Geva, H. (ed). 1994. *Ancient Jerusalem Revealed.* Jerusalem: Israel Exploration Society.

Gibson, S. 1983. "The Stone Vessel Industry at Hizma." *Israel Exploration Journal* 33: 176–188.

Gibson, S. 1987. "The 1961–67 Excavations in the Armenian Garden, Jerusalem." *Palestine Exploration Quarterly* 119: 81–96.

Gibson, S. 2003 a. *Jerusalem in Original Photographs. 1850–1920.* London: Stacey International.

Gibson, S. 2003 b. "Stone Vessels of the Early Roman Period from Jerusalem and Palestine. A Reassessment." G. C. Bottini, L. Di Segni and L. D. Chrupcala (eds.), *One Land—Many Cultures. Archaeological Studies in Honour of S. Loffreda.* Jerusalem: Franciscan Printing Press. 287–308.

Gibson, S. 2004 a. *The Cave of John the Baptist.* London and New York: Doubleday.

Gibson, S. 2004 b. "The James Ossuary: A Lost Cause." *Biblical Archaelogy Review* 30 (6): 55–58.

Gibson, S. 2005. "The Pool of Bethesda in Jerusalem and Jewish Purification Practices of the Second Temple Period." *Proche-Orient Chrétien* 55 (3/4): 270–293.

Gibson, S. 2006. "Is the Talpiot Tomb Really the Family Tomb of Jesus?" *Near Eastern Archaeology* 69 (3–4): 118–124.

Gibson, S. 2007 a. *Flights into Biblical Archaeology*. With D. Tal and M. Haramati. Herzlia: Albatross.

Gibson, S. 2007 b. "Suggested Identifications for "Bethso" and the "Gate of the Essenes" in the light of Magen Broshi's excavations on Mount Zion." J. Patrich and D. Amit (eds.), *New Studies in the Archaeology of Jerusalem and its Region. Collected Papers.* Jerusalem: Israel Antiquities Authority. 25–33.

Gibson, S., and Avni, G. 1998. "The Jewish-Christian Tomb from the Mount of Offense." *Revue Biblique* 105 2): 161–175.

Gibson, S., and Jacobson, D. M. 1996. *Below the Temple Mount in Jerusalem. A Sourcebook on the Cisterns, Subterranean Chambers and Conduits of the Haram al-Sharîf.* BAR series. Oxford: Tempus Reparatum.

Gibson, S., and Taylor, J. E. 1994. *Beneath the Church of the Holy Sepulchre Jerusalem. The Archaeology and Early History of Traditional Golgotha.* London: Palestine Exploration Fund.

Gleason, K. L. 1998. "The Promontory Palace at Caesarea Maritima: Preliminary Evidence for Herod's Praetorium." *Journal of Roman Archaeology* 11: 41–52.

Goldhill, S. 2005. *The Temple of Jerusalem.* Cambridge: Harvard University.

Gonen, R. 2003. *Contested Holiness. Jewish, Muslim and Christian Perspectives on the Temple Mount in Jerusalem.* Jersey City: Ktav.

Grant, M. 1977. *Jesus.* London: Rigell.

Green, J. B. 1992. "Death of Jesus." J. B. Green, S. McKnight, and I. H. Marshall (eds.), *Dictionary of Jesus and the Gospels.* Downers Grove: Intervarsity. 146–163.

Greenhut, Z. 1992. "The 'Caiaphas' Tomb in North Talpiyot, Jerusalem." *'Atiqot* 21: 63–72.

Greenhut, Z. 2006. "Where the High Priest Caiaphas Was Buried." H. Shanks (ed.), *Where Christianity was Born.* Washington: Biblical Archaeology Society. 146–155.

Grenfell, B. P., and Hunt, A. S. 1908. *Fragment of an Uncanonical Gospel From Oxyrhynchus*. Egypt Exploration Fund (Graeco-Roman Branch). London: Oxford University.

Haas, N. 1970. "Anthropological Observations on the Skeletal Remains from Giv'at ha-Mivtar." *Israel Exploration Journal* 20: 38–59.

Habermas, G. R. 2007. *The Secret of the Talpiot Tomb*. Nashville: Band H Publishing.

Hachlili, R. 2005. *Jewish Funerary Customs, Practices and Rites in the Second Temple Period*. Leiden and Boston: Brill.

Hachlili, R., and Killebrew, A. E. 1999. *Jericho. The Jewish Cemetery of the Second Temple Period*. Jerusalem: Israel Antiquities Authority.

Haupt, P. 1920. "Golgotha." *Proceedings of the American Philosophical Society* 59 (3): 237–244.

Heller, R. M., Heller, T. W., and Sasson, J. M. 2003. "Mold, 'tsara'at,' Leviticus, and the History of a Confusion." *Perspectives in Biology and Medicine* 46 (4): 588–591.

Hengel, M. 1977. *Crucifixion in the Ancient World and the Folly of the Message of the Cross*. Philadelphia: Fortress.

Hewitt, J. W. 1932. "The Use of Nails in the Crucifixion." *The Harvard Theological Review* 25 (1): 29–45.

Hoade, E. 1973. *Guide to the Holy Land*. Jerusalem: Franciscan Printing Press.

Horbury, W. 1994. "The 'Caiaphas' Ossuaries and Joseph Caiaphas." *Palestine Exploration Quarterly* 126: 32–48.

Horsley, R. A. 1984. "Popular Messianic Movements Around the Time of Jesus." *Catholic Biblical Quarterly* 46 (3): 471–495.

Horvath, T. 1969. "Why was Jesus Brought to Pilate?" *Novum Testamentum* 11 (3): 174–184.

Hulse, E. V. 1975. "The Nature of Biblical Leprosy and the Use of Alternative Medical Terms in Modern Translations of the Bible." *Palestine Exploration Quarterly* 107 (July): 87–105.

Hunt, E. D. 1984. *Holy Land Pilgrimage in the Later Roman Empire AD 312–460.* Oxford: Clarendon.

Ilan, T. 2002. *Lexicon of Jewish Names in Late Antiquity I. Palestine 330 BCE–200 CE.* Tübingen: Mohr Siebeck.

Israeli, Y. (ed.) 1998. *In the Light of the Menorah. Story of a Symbol.* Jerusalem: Israel Museum.

Jacobovici, S., and Pellegrino, C. 2007. *The Jesus Family Tomb.* San Francisco: HarperCollins.

Jacobson, D. M. 1990–1991. "The Plan of Herod's Temple." *Bulletin of the Anglo-Israel Archaeological Society* 10: 37–44.

Jacobson, D. M. 1997. "Search for the Holy Temple. Digging the Temple Mount." *Eretz* 52: 26–34.

Jacobson, D. M., and Gibson, S. 1997. "The Original Form of Barclay's Gate." *Palestine Exploration Quarterly* 130: 138–149.

Jeffrey, G. 1919. *A Brief Description of the Holy Sepulchre, Jerusalem, and Other Christian Churches in the Holy City.* Cambridge: Cambridge University.

Jeremias, J. 1966. *The Rediscovery of Bethesda, John 5:2.* New Testament Archaeology Monograph No. 1. Louisville: Southern Baptist Theological Seminary.

Jeremias, J. 1969. *Jerusalem in the Time of Jesus.* London: SCM Press.

Kane, J. P. 1978. "The Ossuary Inscriptions of Jerusalem." *Journal of Semitic Studies* 23 (2): 268–282.

Kauffmann, J. 2005. *The Nazareth Jesus Knew.* Nazareth: Nazareth Village.

Kaufman, A. S. 2004. *The Temple Mount. Where is the Holy of Holies?* Jerusalem: Har Year'eh.

Kee, H. C. 1992. "Early Christianity in the Galilee: Reassessing the Evidence from the Gospels." L. I. Levine (ed.), *The Galilee in Late Antiquity.* New York and Jerusalem: Harvard University. 3–22.

Kelso, J. L. 1969. *An Archaeologist Looks at the Gospels.* Waco: Word Books.

Kennard, J. S. 1955. "The Burial of Jesus." *Journal of Biblical Literature* 74 (4): 227–238.

Kenyon, K. M. 1967. *Jerusalem. Excavating 3000 Years of History.* New York and London: Thames and Hudson.

Kenyon, K. M. 1974. *Digging up Jerusalem.* London: Benn.

Kingsley, S. 2006. *God's Gold. The Quest for the Lost Temple Treasure of Jerusalem.* London: John Murray.

Kloner, A., 1996. "A Tomb with Inscribed Ossuaries in East Talpiyot, Jerusalem." *'Atiqot* 29: 15–22.

Kloner, A. 2000 a. *Survey of Jerusalem. The Southern Sector.* Jerusalem: Israel Antiquities Authority.

Kloner, A. 2000 b. "Hippodrome/Amphitheater in Jerusalem." A. Faust and E. Baruch (eds.), *New Studies on Jerusalem. Proceedings of the Sixth Conference.* Jerusalem: Bar Ilan University. 75–86.

Kloner, A. 2001. *Survey of Jerusalem. The Northeastern Sector.* Jerusalem: Israel Antiquities Authority.

Kloner, A. 2005. "Reconstruction of the Tomb in the Rotunda of the Holy Sepulchre According to Archaeological Finds and Jewish Burial Customs of the First Century CE." J. Pastor and M. Mor, *The Beginnings of Christianity. A Collection of Articles.* Jerusalem: Ben-Zvi. 269–278.

Kloner, A., and Zissu, B. 2007. *The Necropolis of Jerusalem in the Second Temple Period.* Leuven: Peeters.

Kochav, S. 1995. "The Search for a Protestant Holy Sepulchre: The Garden Tomb in Nineteenth-Century Jerusalem." *Journal of Ecclesiastical History* 46 (2): 278–301.

Kokkinos, N. 1980. *The Enigma of Jesus the Galilean.* 4th ed. 2007. Athens (Greek).

Kokkinos, N. 1989. "Crucifixion in A.D. 36: The Keystone for Dating the Birth of Jesus." J. Vardaman and E. M. Yamauchi (eds.), *Chronos, Kairos, Christos: Nativity and Chronological Studies Presented to Jack Finegan.* Winona Lake: Eisenbrauns. 133–163.

Kokkinos, N. 1998. *The Herodian Dynasty. Origins, Role in Society and Eclipse.* Sheffield: Sheffield Academic.

Kokkinos, N. 2002. "Herod's Horrid Death." *Biblical Archaeology Review* 28 (2): 28–35.

Kokkinos, N. 2007. "The Royal Court of the Herods." N. Kokkinos (ed.), *The World of the Herods.* Stuttgart: Franz Steiner Verlag. 279–303.

Kraeling, C. H. 1942. "The Episode of the Roman Standards at Jerusalem." *The Harvard Theological Review* 35 (4): 263–289.

Kraemer, D. 2000. *The Meanings of Death in Rabbinic Judaism.* London and New York: Routledge.

Küchler, M. 2007. *Jerusalem. Ein Handbuch und Studienreiseführer zur Heiligen Stadt.* Göttingen: Vandenhoeck and Ruprech.

Kuhn, H.-W. 1979. "Der Gekreuzigte von Giv'at ha-Mivtar. Theologia Crucis—Signum Crucis. Festschrift für Erich Dinkler zum 70." Geburtstag: 305–334.

Lechat, M. F. 2002. *The Palaeopidemiology of Leprosy: An Overview. The Past and Present of Leprosy. Archaeological, Historical, Palaeopathological and Clinical Approaches.* C. A. Roberts, M. E. Lewis, and K. Manchester (eds.) *BAR International Series* 1054: 157–162.

Legault, A. 1954 "An Application of the Form-Critique Method to the Anointings in Galilee (Lk 7: 36–50) and Bethany (Mt 26: 6–13; Mk 14: 3–9; Jn 12: 1–8)." *Catholica Biblical Quarterly* 16: 131–145.

Lémonon, J.-P. 1981. *Pilate et le Gouvernement de la Judée. Textes et Monuments.* Paris: Gabalda.

Levin, S. S. 1969. *Jesus Alias Christ.* New York: Philosophical Library.

Levine, L. I. 2002. *Jerusalem. Portrait of the City in the Second Temple Period (538 B.C.E.–70 C.E.).* Philadelphia: Jewish Publication Society.

Lewis, G. 1987. "A Lesson from Leviticus: Leprosy." *Man* 22 (4): 593–612.

Lewy, H. 1945. "A Note on the Fate of the Sacred Vessels of the Second Temple." *Kedem: Studies in Jerusalem Archaeology* II: 123–125 (Hebrew).

Lichtenberger, A. 2006. "Jesus and the Theater in Jerusalem." J. H. Charlesworth (ed.), *Jesus and Archaeology*. Grand Rapids and Cambridge: Eerdmans. 283–299.

Lieber, E. 2000. "Old Testament 'Leprosy,' Contagion and Sin." L. I. Conrad and D. Wujastyk (eds.), *Contagion: Perspectives from Pre-Modern Societies*. Aldershot: Ashgate. 99–136.

Lieberman, S. 1965. "Some Aspects of Afterlife in Early Rabbinic Literature." L. W. Schwartz (ed.), *Harry Austryn Wolfson Jubilee Volume*. Jerusalem: American Academy of Jewish Research. 495–532.

Macalister, A. 1903. "Leprosy." J. Hastings (ed.), *A Dictionary of the Bible, dealing with its Language, Literature, and Contents, including the Biblical Theology III*. New York: 95–99.

Magen, Y. 2002. *The Stone Vessel Industry in the Second Temple Period. Excavations at Hizma and the Jerusalem Temple Mount*. Jerusalem: Israel Exploration Society.

Magness, J. 1991. "The Walls of Jerusalem in the Early Islamic Period." *Biblical Archaeologist* 54: 208–217.

Magness, J. 2005. "Ossuaries and the Burials of Jesus and James." *Journal of Biblical Literature* 124 (1): 121–154.

Magness, J. 2006. "Jesus' Tomb—What Did It Look Like?" H. Shanks (ed.), *Where Christianity was Born*. Washington: Biblical Archaeology Society. 212–226.

Magness, J. 2007 a. "The Burial of Jesus in Light of Archaeology and the Gospels." *Eretz-Israel* (Teddy Kollek Volume) 28: 1–7.

Magness, J. 2007 b. "Why Ossuaries?" S. W. Crawford (ed.), *"Up to the Gates of Ekron." Essays on the Archaeology and History of the Eastern Mediterranean in Honor of Seymour Gitin*. Jerusalem: Israel Exploration Society. 228–239.

Maier, P. 1969. "The Episode of the Golden Roman Shields at Jerusalem." *The Harvard Theological Review* 62 (1): 109–121.

Maier, P. L. 2004. "Pilate in the Dock: For the Defense." *Bible Review* 20 (3): 27–30, 32.

Mantel, H, 2007. "Sanhedrin." *Encyclopaedia Judaica*. Second Edition. 18: 21–23. Detroit: Macmillan.

Mare, W. H. 1987. *The Archaeology of the Jerusalem Area*. Grand Rapids.

Mariotti, V., Dutour, O., Belcastro, M. G., Faccini, F., and Brasili, P. 2005. "Probable Early Presence of Leprosy in Europe in a Celtic Skeleton of the 4th–3rd Century BC (Casalecchio di Reno, Bologna, Italy)." *International Journal of Osteoarchaeology* 15: 311–325.

Mark, S. 2002. "Alexander the Great, Seafaring, and the Spread of Leprosy." *Journal of the History of Medicine and Allied Sciences* 57 (3): 285–311.

Masterman, E. W. G. 1920. *Hygiene and Disease in Palestine in Modern and Biblical Times*. London: Palestine Exploration Fund.

Mazar, B. 1975. *The Mountain of the Lord*. New York: Doubleday.

Mazar, E. 2000. *A Complete Guide to the Temple Mount Excavations*. Jerusalem: Shoham Academic.

McCane, B. R. 1990. " 'Let the Dead Bury Their Own Dead': Secondary Burial and Matt 8:21–22." *The Harvard Theological Review* 83 (1): 31–43.

McCasland, S. V. 1957. "Signs and Wonders." *Journal of Biblical Literature* 76 (2): 149–152.

McCown, C. C. 1932. "The Geography of Jesus' Last Journey to Jerusalem." *Journal of Biblical Literature* 51 (2): 107–129.

McCown, C. C. 1941. "Gospel Geography: Fiction, Fact, and Truth." *Journal of Biblical Literature* 60 (1): 1–25.

Meier, J. P. 1990. "Jesus in Josephus: A Modest Proposal." *Catholic Biblical Quarterly* 52 (1): 76–103.

Meyers, E. M. 1971. *Jewish Ossuaries: Reburial and Rebirth*. Rome: Biblical Institute.

Meyers, E. M. 2003. "Jesus and His World: Sepphoris and the Quest for the Historical Jesus." C. G. den Hertog, U. Hübner, and S. Münger (eds.), *Saxa Loquentur: Studien zur Archäologie Palästinas/Israels. Festschrit für Volkmar Fritz*. Münster: Vgarit-Verlag. 185–197.

Meyers, E. M., and Strange, J. F. 1981. *Archaeology, the Rabbis and Early Christianity.* Bungay: Abingdon.

Milikowsky, C. 2000. "Reflections on Hand-washing, Hand-purity and Holy Scripture in Rabbinic Literature." M. J. H. M. Poorthuis and J. Schwartz, (eds.), *Purity and Holiness: The Heritage of Leviticus.* Leiden: Brill. 149–162.

Millar, F. 1990. "Reflections on the Trial of Jesus." P. R. Davies and R. T. White (eds.), *A Tribute to Geza Vermes.* Sheffield: Sheffield University. 356–381.

Millar, F. 1993. *The Roman Near East 31 BC–AD 337.* Cambridge and London: Harvard University.

Møller-Christensen, V. 1976. "Skeletal Remains from Giv'at ha-Mivtar." *Israel Exploration Journal* 26 (1): 35–38.

Morison, F. 1930. *Who Moved the Stone?* London: Faber and Faber.

Murphy-O'Connor, J. 1995. "The Cenacle—Topographical Setting for Acts 2:44–45." R. Bauckham (ed.), *The Book of Acts in Its First Century Setting* 4: *The Book of Acts in Its Palestinian Setting.* Grand Rapids and Carlisle: Eerdmans. 303–321.

Naveh, J. 1970. "The Ossuary Inscriptions from Giv'at ha-Mivtar." *Israel Exploration Journal* 20: 33–37.

Negev, A., and Gibson, S. (eds.) 2001. *Archaeological Encyclopedia of the Holy Land.* New York and London: Continuum.

Nesbitt, C. F. 1961. "The Bethany Tradition in the Gospel Narratives." *Journal of Bible and Religion* 29 (2): 119–124.

Netzer, E. 2006. *The Architecture of Herod, the Great Builder.* Tübingen: Mohr Siebeck.

Notley, R. S. 2006. "Historical Geography of the Gospels." A. Rainey and R. S. Notley (eds.), *The Sacred Bridge. Carta's Atlas of the Biblical World: An Overview of the Ancient Levant.* Jerusalem: Carta. 349–369.

Ousterhout, R. 2003. "Architecture as Relic and the Construction of Sanctity: The Stones of the Holy Sepulchre." *The Journal of the Society of Architectural Historians* 62 (1): 4–23.

Parrot, A. 1957 a. *Golgotha and the Church of the Holy Sepulchre.* London: SCM.

Parrot, A. 1957 b. *The Temple of Jerusalem.* London: SCM.

Patterson, S. J. 2004. "Pilate in the Dock: For the Prosecution." *Bible Review* 20 (3): 30–32.

Peters, F. E. 1985. *Jerusalem. The Holy City in the Eyes of Chroniclers, Visitors, Pilgrims, and Prophets from the Days of Abraham to the Beginnings of Modern Times.* Princeton: Princeton University.

Pfann, S. J. 2006. "Mary Magdalene has left the Room: A Suggested New Reading of Ossuary CJO 701." *Near Eastern Archaeology* 69 (3–4): 118–124.

Pfann, S., Voss, R., and Rapuano, Y. 2007. "Surveys and Excavations at the Nazareth Village Farm (1997–2002): Final Report." *Bulletin of the Anglo-Israel Archaeological Society* 25: 11–71.

Pierre, M.-J., and Rousée, J.-M. 1981. "Sainte-Marie de la Probatique état et orientation des recherches." *Proche-Orient Chrétien* 31: 23–42.

Pixner, B. 1976. "An Essene Quarter on Mount Zion?" *Studia Hierosolymitana I: Studi archeologici in onore a Bellarmino Bagatti.* Jerusalem: Franciscan Printing Press. 245–284.

Pixner, B. 1979. "Noch einmal das Prätorium. Versuch einer neuen Lösung." *Zeitschrift des Deutschen Palästina-Vereins* 95: 56–86.

Pixner, B., 1989. "The History of the 'Essene Gate' Area." *Zeitschrift des Deutschen Palästina-Vereins* 105: 96–104.

Pixner, B. 1992 a. Archäologische Beobachtungen zum Jerusalemer Essener-Viertel und zur Urgemeinde. 89–113 in B. Mayer (ed.), *Christen und Christliches in Qumran?* Eichstätter Studien, Neue Folge, Bd. 32. Regensburg.

Pixner, B. 1992 b. "The Jerusalem Essenes, Barnabas and the Letter to the Hebrews." Z. J. Kapera (ed.), *Intertestamental Essays in Honour of Jósef Tadeusz Milik.* Cracow: Enigma. 167–178.

Pixner, B. 1997. "Jerusalem's Essene Gateway: Where the Community Lived in Jesus' Time." *Biblical Archaeology Review* 23 (3): 23–31, 64–66.

Pixner, B. 2006. "Mount Zion, Jesus and Archaeology." J. H. Charlesworth (ed.), *Jesus and Archaeology*. Grand Rapids: Eerdmans. 309–322.

Pixner, B, Chen, D., and Margalit, S. 1989. "The 'Gate of the Essenes' Re-excavated." *Zeitschrift des Deutschen Palästina-Vereins* 105: 85–95.

Poirier, J. C. 2003. "Purity beyond the Temple in the Second Temple Era." *Journal of Biblical Literature* 122 (2): 247–265.

Politis, K. D. 2001. "Qazone." A. Negev and S. Gibson (eds.), *Archaeological Encyclopedia of the Holy Land*. New York and London: Continuum. 419.

Pringle, D. 1993. *The Churches of the Crusader Kingdom of Jerusalem. A Corpus I.*, Cambridge: Cambridge University.

Rahmani, L. Y. 1967. "Jason's Tomb." *Israel Exploration Journal* 17: 61–100.

Rahmani, L. Y. 1994. *A Catalogue of Jewish Ossuaries in the Collections of the State of Israel*. Jerusalem: Israel Antiquities Authority.

Reed, J. L. 2007. *The Harper Collins Visual Guide to the New Testament: What Archaeology Reveals About the First Christians*. New York: HarperCollins.

Regev, E. 1996. "Ritual Baths of Jewish Groups and Sects in the Second Temple Period." *Cathedra* 79: 3–20 (Hebrew).

Rehman, H. U. 2005. "Did Jesus Christ Die of Pulmonary Embolism? A Rebuttal." *Journal of Thrombosis and Haemostasis* 3: 2131–2133.

Reich, R. 1980. "Mishnah, Sheqalim 8:2 and the Archaeological Evidence." A. Oppenheimer, U. Rappaport, and M. Stern (eds.), *Jerusalem in the Second Temple Period. Avraham Schalit Memorial Volume*. Jerusalem: Yad Ben-Zvi. 225–256.

Reich, R. 1988. "The Hot Bath-House (*balneum*), the Miqweh and the Jewish Community in the Second Temple Period." *Journal of Jewish Studies* 39: 102–107.

Reich, R. 1991. "Miqwa'ot (Jewish Ritual Baths) in the Second Temple Period of Mishna and Talmud." Unpublished Ph.D. Thesis, Hebrew University, Jerusalem (Hebrew).

Reich, R. 1992. "Ossuary Inscriptions from the 'Caiaphas' Tomb." *'Atiqot* 21: 72–77.

Reich, R. 1997. "Ritual Baths." E. M. Meyers (ed.), *The Oxford Encyclopedia of Archaeology in the Near East* IV. New York: 430–431.

Reich, R. 2000. "Miqwa'ot at Qumran and the Jerusalem Connection." L. H. Schiffman, E. Tov and J. C. VanderKam (eds.), *The Dead Sea Scrolls: Fifty Years After Their Discovery.* Jerusalem: Israel Exploration Society. 728–733.

Reich, R. 2006. "Caiaphas' Bone Box Discovered." H. Shanks (ed.), *Where Christianity was Born.* Washington: Biblical Archaeology Society. 156–163.

Reich, R., Avni, G., and Winter, T. 1999. *The Jerusalem Archaeological Park.* Jerusalem: Israel Antiquities Authority.

Reich, R., and Shukrun, E. 2004. "The Siloam Pool in the Wake of Recent Discoveries." *New Studies on Jerusalem* 10: 137–139 (Hebrew).

Reisner, R. 1989. "Josephus' 'Gate of the Essenes' in Modern Discussion." *Zeitschrift des Deutschen Palästina-Vereins* 105: 105–109.

Reisner, R., 1992 a. "Essener und Urkirche in Jerusalem." B. Mayer (ed.), *Christen und Christliches in Qumran?* Eichstätter Studien, Neue Folge, Bd. 32. Regensburg: 139–155.

Reisner, R., 1992 b. "Das Jerusalemer Essenerviertel Antwort auf einige Einwände." Z. J. Kapera (ed.), *Intertestamental Essays in Honour of Jósef Tadeusz Milik.* Cracow: Enigma. 179–186.

Reisner, R., 1992 c. "Jesus, the Primitive Community, and the Essene Quarter of Jerusalem." J. H. Charlesworth (ed.), *Jesus and the Dead Sea Scrolls.* New York: Doubleday. 198–234.

Ritmeyer, L. 1992. "Locating the Original Temple Mount." *Biblical Archaeology Review* 18 (2): 24–45.

Ritmeyer, L. 2006. *The Quest. Revealing the Temple Mount in Jerusalem.* Jerusalem: Carta.

Ritmeyer, L., and Ritmeyer, K. 2004. *Jerusalem in the Year 30 A.D.* Jerusalem: Carta.

Roitman, A. 2003. *Envisioning the Temple.* Jerusalem: Israel Museum.

Roloff, J. 2000. *Jesus.* München: Beck.

Rubin, R. 1999. *Image and Reality. Jerusalem in Maps and Views.* Jerusalem.

Safrai, S. 1976. "Home and Family." S. Safrai and M. Stern (eds.), *The Jewish People in the First Century.* Assen: Van Giorcum. 784–785.

Saliba, W. R., 2006. "Did Jesus Christ Die of Pulmonary Embolism?" *Journal of Thrombosis and Haemostasis* 4: 891–892.

Saller, S. J. 1957. *Excavations at Bethany.* Jerusalem: Franciscan Printing Press.

Samet, M. 1993. "Conversion in the First Centuries C.E." I. Gafni, A. Oppenheimer and M. Stern (eds.), *Jews and Judaism in the Second Temple, Mishna and Talmud Periods.* Jerusalem: Yad Ben-Zvi. 316–343 (Hebrew).

Sanders, E. P. 1985. *Jesus and Judaism.* Philadelphia: Fortress.

Sanders, E. P. 1993. *The Historical Figure of Jesus.* London: Penguin.

Sanders, J. N. 1954–1955. "Those Whom Jesus' (John 11.5)." *New Testament Studies* 1: 29–41.

Schick, C. 1887. *Beit el Makdas, oder Der alte Tempelplatz zu Jerusalem; wie er jetzt ist.* Jerusalem.

Schick, C. 1896. *Die Stiftshütte, der Tempel in Jerusalem und der Tempelplatz der Jetztzeit.* Berlin: Weidmann.

Schiffman, L. H. 1982. "Proselytism in the Writings of Josephus: Izates of Adiabene in Light of the Halakhah." U. Rappaport (ed.), *Josephus Flavius: Historian of Eretz-Israel in the Hellenistic-Roman Period.* Jerusalem: Yad Ben-Zvi. 247–265 (Hebrew).

Schneemelcher, W. 1991. *New Testament Apocrypha* I. Revised edition, translated by R. McL. Wilson. Cambridge: Clarke.

Schonfield, H. J. 1967. *The Passover Plot.* New York: Bantam.

Schonfield, H. J. 1974. *The Jesus Party.* New York: Macmillan.

Schwartz, D. R. 1992 a. *Studies in the Jewish Background of Christianity.* Tübingen.

Schwartz, D. R. 1992 b. "Pontius Pilate." D. N. Freedman et al. (eds.), *The Anchor Bible Dictionary*. Vol. 5. New York: Doubleday. 395–401.

Schwartz, D. R. 2006. " 'Stone House,' Birah, and Antonia During the Time of Jesus." J. H. Charlesworth (ed.), *Jesus and Archaeology*. Grand Rapids and Cambridge: 341–348.

Schwartz, J. A. 2005. "Temple and Temple Mount in the Book of Acts: Early Christian Activity, Topography, and Halakha." J. Pastor and M. Mor, (eds.), *The Beginnings of Christianity. A Collection of Articles*. Jerusalem: 279–295.

Setzer, C. 1997. "Excellent Women: Female Witnesses to the Resurrection." *Journal of Biblical Literature* 116 (2): 259–272.

Shanks, H., and Witherington, B. 2003. *The Brother of Jesus. The Dramatic Story and Meaning of the First Archaeological Link to Jesus and His Family*. London: HarperCollins.

Sherwin-White, A. N. 1963. *Roman Society and Roman Law in the New Testament*. Oxford: Oxford University.

Simons, J. 1952. *Jerusalem in the Old Testament. Researches and Theories*. Leiden: Brill.

Smith, D. E. 2004. "Dinner with Jesus and Paul: The Social Role of Meals in the Greco-Roman World." *Bible Review* 20 (4): 30–45.

Smith, G. A. 1907. *Jerusalem. The Topography, Economics and History from the Earliest Times to A.D. 70*. Vols. I and II. Jerusalem: Hoelder.

Spigelman, M. 2006. "The Jerusalem Shroud: A Second Temple Burial Answers Modern Medical Questions." *Bulletin of the Anglo-Israel Archaeological Society* 24: 127.

Spigelman, M., and Donoghue, H. D. 2002. "The Study of Ancient DNA Answers a Palaeopathological Question. The Past and Present of Leprosy. Archaeological, Historical, Palaeopathological and Clinical Approaches." C. A. Roberts, M. E. Lewis, and K. Manchester (eds.), *BAR International Series* 1054: 293–296.

Stegemann, H., 1998. *The Library of Qumran. On the Essenes, Qumran, John the Baptist, and Jesus*. Grand Rapids: Brill.

Stern, M. (ed.) 1980. *Greek and Latin Authors on Jews and Judaism*. Vol. II. Jerusalem: Israel Academy of Sciences and Humanities.

Strange J. F., and Shanks, H. 2006. "Where Jesus Stayed in Capernaum." H. Shanks (ed.), *Where Christianity was Born*. Washington: Biblical Archaeology Society. 67–78.

Sukenik, E. L. 1947. "The Earliest Records of Christianity." *American Journal of Archaeology* 51 (4): 351–365.

Tabor, J. D. 2006. *The Jesus Dynasty. The Hidden History of Jesus, His Royal Family, and the Birth of Christianity*. New York: Simon and Schuster.

Taylor, J. E. 1987. "The Cave at Bethany." *Revue Biblique* 94 (1): 120–123.

Taylor, J. E. 1989–1990. "Capernaum and its 'Jewish-Christians': a Re-examination of the Franciscan Excavations." *Bulletin of the Anglo-Israel Archaeological Society* 9: 9–28.

Taylor, J. E. 1990. "The Bethany Cave: A Jewish-Christian Cult Site?" *Revue Biblique* 97 (3): 453–465.

Taylor, J. E. 1993. *Christians and the Holy Places. The Myth of Jewish-Christian Origins*. Oxford: Clarendon.

Taylor, J. E. 1998. "Golgotha: A Reconsideration of the Evidence for the Sites of Jesus' Crucifixion and Burial." *New Testament Studies* 44: 180–203.

Taylor, J. E. 2006 a. "Pontius Pilate and the Imperial Cult in Roman Judaea." *New Testament Studies* 52: 555–582.

Taylor, J. E. 2006 b. "The Garden of Gethsemane." H. Shanks (ed.), *Where Christianity was Born*. Washington: Biblical Archaeology Society. 116–127.

Taylor, J. E. 2008. "The Nea Church. Were the Temple Treasures Hidden Here?" *Biblical Archaeology Review* 34 (1): 50–59, 82.

Theissen, G., and Merz, A. 1998. *The Historical Jesus: A Textbook*. London and Minneapolis: Fortress.

Thiede, C. P. 2004. *The Cosmopolitan World of Jesus. New Light from Archaeology*. London: SPCK.

Thiede, C. P., and D'Ancona, M. 2000. *The Quest for the True Cross*. London: Phoenix.

Thompson, P. 1988. *The Voice of the Past: Oral History*. Oxford: Oxford University.

Toynbee, J. M. C. 1996. *Death and Burial in the Roman World*. Baltimore, London: Johns Hopkins.

Tzaferis, V. 1970. Jewish Tombs at and near Giv'at ha-Mivtar, Jerusalem. *Israel Exploration Journal* 20: 18–32.

Tzaferis, V. 1993. "Nazareth." E. Stern (ed.), *The New Encyclopedia of Archaeological Excavations in the Holy Land*. Vol. 3. Jerusalem: Israel Exploration Society.

Tzaferis, V. 2006. "Crucifixion: The Archaeological Evidence." H. Shanks (ed.), *Where Christianity was Born*. Washington: Biblical Archaeology Society. 165–175.

Tsafrir, Y., Di Segni, L., and Green, J. (eds.). 1994. *Tabula Imperii Romani Iudaea Palaestina*. Jerusalem: Israel Academy of Sciences and Humanities..

Vermes, G. 1973. *Jesus the Jew*. Glasgow: Fontana/Collins.

Vermes, G. 1987. "The Jesus Notice of Josephus Re-examined." *Journal of Jewish Studies* 38: 1–10.

Vermes, G. 2001. *The Changing Faces of Jesus*. London: Penguin.

Vermes, G. 2003. *The Authentic Gospel of Jesus*. London: Penguin.

Vermes, G., and Millar, F. 1973. "Excursus I: The Census of Quirinius." E. Schürer, *The History of the Jewish People in the Age of Jesus Christ (175 BC—AD 135)*. Revised and edited by G. Vermes and F. Millar. Vol. I. Edinburgh: Clarke. 420–427.

Vincent, H., and Abel, F.-M. 1914. *Jérusalem. Recherches de Topographie, d' Archéologie et d'Histoire II:* Jérusalem Nouvelle. Paris: Gabalda.

von Wahlde, U. C. 2006. "Archaeology and John's Gospel." J. H. Charlesworth (ed.), *Jesus and Archaeology*. Grand Rapids and Cambridge: 523–586.

Waheeb, M. 2003. *The Discovery of Bethany Beyond the Jordan. Site of Jesus' Baptism.* Amman: private publisher.

Walaskay, P. W. 1975. "The Trial and Death of Jesus in the Gospel of Luke." *Journal of Biblical Literature* 94 (1): 81–93.

Walker, P. 1999. *The Weekend that Changed the World. The Mystery of Jerusalem's Empty Tomb.* London: John Knox.

Warren, C. 1876. *Underground Jerusalem. An Account of Some of the Principal Difficulties Encountered in its Exploration and the Results Obtained.* London: Bentley.

Warren, C. 1880. *The Temple of the Tomb.* London: Bentley.

Waywell, G. B., and Berlin, A. 2007. "Monumental Tombs. From Maussollos to the Maccabees." *Biblical Archaeology Review* 33 (3): 54–65.

Webb, R. L. 2006. "Jesus Heals a Leper: Mark 1.40–45 and Egerton Gospel 35–47." *Journal for the Study of the Historical Jesus* 4: 177.

Weksler-Bdolah, S. 2007. "The Fortifications of Jerusalem in the Byzantine Period." *ARAM* 19: 85–112.

Wightman, G. J. 1993. *The Walls of Jerusalem. From the Canaanites to the Mamluks.* Sydney: Meditarch.

Wilkinson, J. 1975. "The Way from Jerusalem to Jericho." *The Biblical Archaeologist* 38 (2): 10–24.

Wilkinson, J. 1977. *Jerusalem Pilgrims Before the Crusades.* Jerusalem: Ariel.

Wilkinson, J. 1978. *Jerusalem as Jesus knew it. Archaeology as Evidence.* London: Thames and Hudson.

Wilkinson, J. 1981. *Egeria's Travels to the Holy Land.* Jerusalem and Warminster: Ariel.

Wilson, C. W., and Warren, C. 1871. *The Recovery of Jerusalem. A Narrative of Exploration and Discovery in the City and the Holy Land.* London: Bentley.

Wilson, I. 1978. *The Turin Shroud.* London: Gollancz.

Wilson, I. 1984. *Jesus. The Evidence.* Frome and London: Guild.

Wilson, I. 1986. *The Evidence of the Shroud.* London: Michael O'Mara.

Wilson, I. 1991. *Holy Faces, Secret Places. The Quest for Jesus' True Likeness.* London: Doubleday.

Wilson, W. R. 1961. *The Trial of Jesus: A Judicial, Literary, and Historical Study.* Durham: Duke.

Winter, P. 1964. "The Trial of Jesus." *Commentary*, September: 35–41.

Winter, P. 1974. *On the Trial of Jesus.* Berlin, New York: de Gruyter.

Witherington, B. 1994. *Jesus the Sage: The Pilgrimage of Wisdom.* Minneapolis: Fortress.

Yadin, Y. 1973. "Epigraphy and Crucifixion." *Israel Exploration Journal* 23: 18–22.

Yadin, Y. 1975. "The Gate of the Essenes and the Temple Scroll." Y. Yadin (ed.), *Jerusalem Revealed: Archaeology in the Holy City 1968–1974.* Jerusalem: Israel Exploration Society. 90–91.

Yadin, Y., 1985. *The Temple Scroll.* London: Weidenfeld and Nicolson.

Zangenberg, J. 2006. "Between Jerusalem and the Galilee: Samaria in the Time of Jesus." J. H. Charlesworth (ed.), *Jesus and Archaeology.* Grand Rapids and Cambridge: Eerdmans. 393–432.

Zertal, A. 2005. *The Manasse Hill Country Survey. Vol. IV: From Nahal Bezeq to the Sartaba.* Tel Aviv (Hebrew).

Zias, J. 1989. "Lust and Leprosy: Confusion or Correlation?" *Bulletin of the American Schools of Oriental Research* 275: 27–31.

Zias, J. 1991 a. "Leprosy and Tuberculosis in the Byzantine Monasteries of the Judean Desert." D. J. Ortner and A. C. Aufderheide (eds.), *Current Synthesis and Future Options.* Washington: Smithsonian. 197–199.

Zias, J. 1991 b. "Current Archaeological Research in Israel: Death and Disease in Ancient Israel." *Biblical Archaeologist* 54 (3): 146–159.

Zias, J. 1992. "Human Skeletal Remains from the 'Caiaphas' Tomb." *'Atiqot* 21: 78–80.

Zias, J. 2002. "New Evidence for the History of Leprosy in the Ancient Near East: An Overview. C. A. Roberts, M. E. Lewis, and

K. Manchester (eds.), *The Past and Present of Leprosy. Archaeological, Historical, Palaeopathological and Clinical Approaches.*" *BAR* International Series 1054. Oxford. 259–268.

Zias, J., and Charlesworth, J. H. 1992. "Crucifixion: Archaeology, Jesus, and the Dead Sea Scrolls." J. H. Charlesworth (ed.), *Jesus and the Dead Sea Scrolls.* New York and London: Doubleday. 273–289.

Zias, J., and Sekeles 1985. "The Crucified Man from Giv'at ha-Mivtar: A Reappraisal." *Israel Exploration Journal* 35: 22–27.

Zissu, B. 1998. "'Qumran Type' Graves in Jerusalem: Archaeological Evidence of an Essene Community?" *Dead Sea Discoveries* 5 (2): 158–171.

Zugibe, F. T. 1989. "Two Questions About Crucifixion: Does the Victim Die of Asphyxiation? Would Nails in the Hands Hold the Weight of the Body?" *Bible Review* 5 (2): 34–43.

LIST OF ILLUSTRATIONS

MAPS

LINE DRAWINGS ARRANGED BY CHAPTER

CHAPTER TWO: RAISING A DEAD MAN

CHAPTER THREE: FESTIVITIES AT THE HOUSE OF GOD

CHAPTER FIVE: THE HEAVY HAND OF THE LAW: A TRIAL

CHAPTER SIX: THE SPLIT IN THE TREE: A CRUCIFIXION

CHAPTER SEVEN: THE BURIAL OF JESUS

CHAPTER EIGHT: WHO MOVED THE STONE?

EXCURSUS: THE TALPIOT TOMB AND THE "JAMES" OSSUARY

INSERT PHOTOGRAPHS

All photographs are by the author unless otherwise indicated. Page numbers following captions are text pages that discuss photo subject.

INSERT 1

The gate leading to the *Praetorium* the way it looks today (p. 96).

The crucified Jesus in a reconstruction of that event (photo: Jim Haberman) (p. 107).

The top of an ossuary from the Giv'at ha-Mivtar tomb showing the human bones inside (photo: Israel Antiquities Authority) (p. 111).

A typical iron nail from the first century CE (photo: James Tabor) (p. 112).

A reconstruction showing how the skeletal foot of the crucified man from the Giv'at ha-Mivtar tomb would have been fixed to the cross, with the original nail and heel bone next to it (photo: Joe Zias) (p. 112).

The nail and the heel bone of the crucified man from the Giv'at ha-Mivtar tomb at the time of the discovery (Photo: Israel Antiquities Authority) (p. 112).

INSERT 3

The rock surface at the top of Calvary in the Church of the Holy Sepulchre (p. 117).

The apse of the Constantinian church marking Golgotha in the Church of the Holy Sepulchre (photo: courtesy of the Israel Antiquities Authority) (p. 122).

A reconstruction showing a shrouded corpse in a first-century CE tomb (p. 136).

An ossuary decorated with carved rosettes from the Shroud Tomb (photo: Sandu Mendrea) (p. 142).

Remnants of shroud and human hair from the Shroud Tomb (p. 142).

Subterranean rock quarries discovered beneath the Church of the Holy Sepulchre (p. 153).

The façade of the Church of the Holy Sepulchre (p. 149).

The so-called Tomb of Joseph of Arimathea in the Church of the Holy Sepulchre (p. 154).

The Edicule / Tomb of Jesus with a shaft of light coming through the domed ceiling of the Rotunda in the Church of the Holy Sepulchre (p. 153).

The façade of a first-century CE rock-cut tomb at Akeldama with John Dominic Crossan (*right*) and the author (photo: James Tabor) (p. 156).

The façade of the Talpiot Tomb in a recent photograph (photo: Daniel Gibson) (p. 176).

INDEX OF SCRIPTURE

AND OTHER ANCIENT WRITINGS

INDEX

Page references followed by *fig* indicate an illustration.